Women's Work

EDITED BY

LAURIE F.
MAFFLY-KIPP

AND

KATHRYN LOFTON

Women's Work

An Anthology of African-American
Women's Historical Writings
from Antebellum America
to the Harlem Renaissance

OXFORD
UNIVERSITY PRESS

2010

OXFORD
UNIVERSITY PRESS

Oxford University Press, Inc., publishes works that further
Oxford University's objective of excellence
in research, scholarship, and education.

Oxford   New York
Auckland   Cape Town   Dar es Salaam   Hong Kong   Karachi
Kuala Lumpur   Madrid   Melbourne   Mexico City   Nairobi
New Delhi   Shanghai   Taipei   Toronto

With offices in
Argentina   Austria   Brazil   Chile   Czech Republic   France   Greece
Guatemala   Hungary   Italy   Japan   Poland   Portugal   Singapore
South Korea   Switzerland   Thailand   Turkey   Ukraine   Vietnam

Copyright © 2010 by Oxford University Press, Inc.

Published by Oxford University Press, Inc.
198 Madison Avenue, New York, New York 10016

www.oup.com

Oxford is a registered trademark of Oxford University Press.

Library of Congress Cataloging-in-Publication Data
Women's work : an anthology of African-American women's historical writings from antebellum America to the
Harlem Renaissance / edited by Laurie F. Maffly-Kipp and Kathryn Lofton.
p. cm.
ISBN 978-0-19-533198-1; 978-0-19-533199-8 (pbk)
1. African Americans—History—19th century—Sources.   2. African American women—History—
19th century—Sources.   3. African Americans—History—20th century—Sources.   4. African American
women—History—20th century—Sources.   5. African Americans—Historiography.   6. African American
historians.   7. Women historians—United States.   8. African American women authors.
9. African American women—Intellectual life—19th century.   10. African American women—Intellectual
life—20th century.   I. Maffly-Kipp, Laurie F., 1960–   II. Lofton, Kathryn.
E184.6.W66 2010
973—dc22 2010010246

9 8 7 6 5 4 3 2 1

Printed in the United States of America
on acid-free paper

ACKNOWLEDGMENTS

The labor of this book has been facilitated by many friends and colleagues. Support from the University Research Council at the University of North Carolina at Chapel Hill enabled some great working trips. David Wills at the African American Religion Documentary History Project at Amherst College provided space, sources, and support. Librarians at the University of North Carolina at Chapel Hill, Reed College, Indiana University Bloomington, and the University of Delaware provided documents. Conversations with colleagues Judith Weisenfeld and Bill Andrews enriched our thinking. Wesley Maffly-Kipp did some crucial last-minute proofreading. Our collaboration is testimony to the power of women's work when women work together.

TABLE OF CONTENTS

Introduction   3

1   Maria W. Stewart   14
    *"An Address Delivered Before the Afric-American
    Female Intelligence Society of America" (1832)*   15

2   Ann Plato   20
    "Education" (1841)   22
    "Death of the Christian" (1841)   24
    "Louisa Sebury" (1841)   25
    "The Natives of America" (1841)   27

3   Frances Ellen Watkins Harper   29
    "Liberty for Slaves" (1857)   31
    "Moses: A Story of the Nile" (1869)   33
    "Then and Now" (1895)   49

4   Frank A. Rollin   53
    *"The Life and Public Services of Martin R. Delany"
    (1883)*   55

5   Mary V. Cook   67
    *"Woman's Place in the Work of the Denomination"
    (1887)*   68

6   Josephine Heard   82
    "Welcome to Hon. Frederick Douglass" (1890)   83
    "Wilberforce" (1890)   85
    "They Are Coming?" (1890)   86
    *"Resting: In Memoriam of Mrs. Bishop Turner"
    (1890)*   88

7   Anna Julia Cooper   89
     "The Status of Woman in America" (1892)   91

8   S. Elizabeth Frazier   100
     "Some Afro-American Women of Mark"
     (1892)   101

9   Virginia W. Broughton   112
     "Woman's Work" (1894)   113

10   Gertrude Bustill Mossell   119
     "The Work of the Afro-American Woman"
     (1894)   121

11   Hardie Martin   132
     "How the Church Can Best Help the Condition
     of the Masses" (1896)   133

12   Victoria Earle Matthews   136
     "The Awakening of the Afro-American Woman"
     (1897)   137

13   Amelia Etta Hall Johnson   144
     "Some Parallels of History" (1899)   145

14   Katherine Davis Tillman   150
     "Heirs of Slavery. A Little Drama of Today"
     (1901)   151

15   Pauline Hopkins   156
     "Of One Blood: Or, the Hidden Self"
     (1902–1903)   158
     "Famous Women of the Negro Race: Educators"
     (1902)   164

16   Leila Amos Pendleton   186
     "A Narrative of the Negro" (1912)   187

17   Olivia Ward Bush-Banks   198
     "Unchained, 1863" (1914)   199
     "A Hero of San Juan Hill" (1914)   201

18   Drusilla Dunjee Houston   203
     "Wonderful Ethiopians of the Ancient Cushite Empire"
     (1926)   205

19   Hallie Quinn Brown   218
     "Harriet—The Moses" (1926)   219

Women's Work

IN 1887, UNION ARMY VETERAN and prominent Baptist pastor William J. Simmons published *Men of Mark: Eminent, Progressive and Rising*, a series of 117 sketches profiling representative race men. Weighing in at over one thousand pages, this survey included recognizable heroes like Frederick Douglass, Crispus Attucks, Henry Highland Garnet, and Alexander Crummell. But there were also many more chapters devoted to lesser known figures, including attorneys, carpenters, pastors, merchants, phrenologists, artists, and scholars. In his Preface, Simmons hoped his would be a suitable text "to be put into the hands of intelligent, aspiring young people everywhere, that they might see the means and manners of men's elevation, and by this be led to undertake the task of going through high schools and colleges."[1] Like William Cooper Nell's *The Colored Patriots of the American Revolution* (1855) and William Wells Brown's *The Black Man: His Antecedents, His Genius, and His Achievements* (1863), Simmons' *Men of Mark* related the stories of particular black men in order to serve the whole of the race. This was a usable history, supplying for young students not only a source of race pride, but also standard-bearers to which they might aspire.[2]

Simmons dedicated *Men of Mark* to the very people he excluded from his admiring survey, "the women of our race." Not just any women, but "especially to the devoted, self-sacrificing mothers who molded the lives of the subjects of these sketches, laboring and praying for their success," Simmons

[1] William J. Simmons, *Men of Mark: Eminent, Progressive and Rising* (Cleveland: W.W. Williams, 1887), 6.
[2] Steven Mailloux, "Thinking with Rhetorical Figures: Performing Racial and Disciplinary Identities in Late-Nineteenth-Century America," *American Literary History* 18:4 (2006), 700.

continued. "It is sent forth with the earnest hope that future mothers will be inspired to give special attention to the training of their children, and thereby fit them for honorable, happy and useful lives."[3] Some analogous collections, like Monroe Majors' *Noted Negro Women: Their Triumphs and Activities* (1893), included descriptions of notable black women. But Simmons chose instead to celebrate models of black manhood, assigning to women the conveyance of his message. For Simmons and other contemporaneous black historians, women could conduct eminence, but they were not eminent. Women educated, but they did not revolutionize. It was little wonder that Fannie Barrier Williams argued in 1900 that "the consciousness of being fully free has not yet come to the great masses of the colored women in this country."[4] In Reconstruction America, many black women served to promote the progress of men.

Despite the limits of their social circumstances, women spoke. They educated. They wrote. Simmons' dedication indicated how some historians understood black women's fostering role in history. But it missed just how much women were also, always, participating in the process of historical authorship. Whether in schoolrooms or kitchens, state houses or church pulpits, women have always been historians. Although few women, white or black, participated in the academic study of history until the mid-twentieth century, women functioned as primary translators and teachers, offering explanations, allegories, and scholastic narrations of the past.

To understand the histories written by women, it is necessary to appreciate the importance of historical narration within African America. "Almost as soon as blacks could write," Henry Louis Gates and Gene Andrew Jarrett have written, "they set out to redefine—against already received racial stereotypes—who and what a black person was, and how unlike the racist stereotype the black original could actually be."[5] From eighteenth-century ruminations on ancient Ethiopia to twentieth century celebrations of Black History Month, African Americans have sought to frame, explicate, and resolve their individual lives through the communal rehabilitations of history. The relating of history has provided African Americans with a

---

[3] Simmons, *Men of Mark*, 3.

[4] Fannie Barrier Williams, "The Club Movement among Colored Women of America," *The New Negro: Readings on Race, Representation, and African American Culture, 1892–1938*, eds. Henry Louis Gates and Gene Andrew Jarrett (Princeton: Princeton University Press, 2007), 54.

[5] Henry Louis Gates and Gene Andrew Jarrett, "Introduction," *The New Negro: Readings on Race, Representation, and African American Culture, 1892–1938*, eds. Henry Louis Gates and Gene Andrew Jarrett (Princeton: Princeton University Press, 2007), 3.

consistent and defiant counter to white claims that Africans had no past of any value.[6]

Even as they have been occasionally exiled from the encyclopedias and monographs of celebratory race memory, women have played a central role in the dissemination of this mystical historiography. In the United States, black women have labored to sustain the cogency of their race and their families through the promotion of Christian and historical education for themselves and for their families. Their narratives permeated their childrearing, Sunday school education programs, and public activism. Long before black women entered print culture in large numbers in the twentieth century, several orators, church women, and organizers found their voices, and committed them to print. These are the texts anthologized in *Women's Work*. "Persons of color who endeavor to inhabit and nurture cultural spaces outside of the traditions that define them as 'other' and 'outsider' face a dilemma," writes philosopher Christa Acampora, "they can cling to romantic notions of a cultural past from which they are geographically and historically separated, or they can strive to invent a culture anew."[7] In the texts that follow, readers will find romance and invention in abundance. Spanning from antebellum America to the Harlem Renaissance, this collection observes women of color as they borrow, remake, and retell the stories about their collective racial past.

Gathering together African-American women's historical writing fills a lacuna in the documentary record. As others have argued, the rise of the modern university accompanied a celebration of the singular, self-motivated intellect. Documentary scholarship throughout the twentieth century tended to highlight singular historical events and individual statements that mirrored this individuated aesthetic of modern achievement. Historians of African-American literature found themselves succumbing to these interpretive standards, with frequently majestic results. Due to the impressive documentary efforts of William Andrews, Herbert Aptheker, Henry Louis Gates, Jr., and Dorothy Porter, contemporary students and scholars have at their disposal a wide variety of slave narratives, political statements, and fictional works written by African Americans in the nineteenth century. These collections have formed the groundwork in the effort to reclaim African-American history. Relying upon modern presumptions about political engagement and

---

[6] Laurie F. Maffly-Kipp, *Setting Down the Sacred Past: African-American Race Histories* (Harvard University Press, 2010); Wilson Jeremiah Moses, *Afrotopia: The Roots of African American Popular History* (Cambridge University Press, 1998), 38.

[7] Christa Davis Acampora, "On Making and Remaking: An Introduction," *Unmaking Race, Remaking Soul: Transformative Aesthetics and the Practice of Freedom*, eds. Christa Davis Acampora and Angela L. Cotton (Albany: State University of New York Press, 2007), 2.

selfhood, they anthologized documents that reflected the new academic standards in the African-American past.

Yet gaps in this republished record are increasingly evident. Reviewing the last generation of documentary collections would likely lead the average reader to assume that African Americans had but two writing ambitions. Either they were informed by a Romantic literary aspiration that employed the narrative form to construct an individuated self, or they were motivated by the desire for racial uplift that resulted in political manifestos and sermons. While the reclamation of the literary record focuses on the "discovery" of the individual African-American intellectual genius, documents recounting African-American political labors tend to consolidate this polity into a body determined by phenotype and common oppression. In his 1971 overview of African-American historiography, *Black Historians*, Earl E. Thorpe may have provided the thesis for these documentary efforts when he suggested that "the central theme of black history is the quest of Afro-Americans for freedom, equality, and manhood."[8] For many twentieth-century documentary editors, the only way to understand African-American history was as the history of a racial struggle limited by the liberties of democratic politics and promoted by heroic conceptions of modern man.

Recent scholarship, however, has yielded new and useful insights about the experiences, perceptions, and practices of nineteenth-century African Americans. Ongoing studies of African-American literature have investigated the assortment of socially conscious fictions produced during and after slavery.[9] Meanwhile, work by Eddie Glaude, Wilson Moses, Albert Raboteau, and David Wills, among others, has insightfully demonstrated the crucial shaping power of history—especially history fueled by religious paradigms—for the development of black culture and politics in this period.[10]

---

[8] Earl E. Thorpe, *Black Historians* (New York: William Morrow and Company, 1971), 4.

[9] For more on African-American women's literature, see Joanne Braxton, *Black Women Writing Autobiography: A Tradition Within a Tradition* (Philadelphia: Temple University Press, 1989); Barbara Christian, *Black Women Novelists: The Development of a Tradition, 1892–1976* (Westport, CT: Greenwood Press, 1980); Ann duCille, *The Coupling Convention: Sex, Text, and Tradition in Black Women's Fiction* (New York: Oxford University Press, 1985); Karla F. C. Holloway, *Moorings and Metaphors: Figures of Culture and Gender in Black Women's Literature* (New Brunswick, NJ: Rutgers University Press, 1992); Marjorie Pryse and Hortense J. Spillers, *Conjuring: Black Women, Fiction, and Literary Tradition* (Bloomington: Indiana University Press, 1985). See also Casper LeRoy Jordan, *A Bibliographical Guide to African-American Women Writers* (Westport, CT: Greenwood Press, 1993).

[10] Eddie Glaude, *Exodus! Religion, Race and Nation in Early Nineteenth-Century Black America* (University of Chicago Press, 2000); Wilson Moses, *Afrotopia: The Roots of African American Popular History* (Cambridge: Cambridge University Press, 1998); Albert J. Raboteau, "African-Americans, Exodus, and the American Israel," in *Fire in the Bones: Reflections on African-American Religious History* (Boston: Beacon Press, 1995), 17–36; and David W. Wills, "Exodus Piety: African American Religion in an Age of Immigration," in Jonathan D. Sarna, ed., *Minority Faiths and the American Protestant Mainstream* (University of Illinois Press, 1998), 136–190.

This scholarship encourages investigations into denominational and sacred histories as much as heroic sermons and spiritual memoirs. To be sure, sermons and autobiographies reveal a great deal about the historical past. But equally abundant are works of history by African Americans that do not merely speak of the individual, or cohere to modern conceptions of history or self. Rather than providing clear political polemic or social argument, these works are laced with Christian imagery and the idiosyncratic ancient historiographies. They make prophetic claims about the future, but these claims are frequently more supernatural than material. The documents included in *Women's Work* are simultaneously fantastical and revolutionary, Christian and scholarly, intellectual and popular. They pull us from the rarified historical imagination of the university and into the quotidian educational spaces of lived religion and lay institutional engagement.

It is here that we find women writing, speaking, and mapping long stories of the black past. In periodical literature, in self-published books of essays, plays, and poetry, and in speeches delivered to audiences both in the United States and abroad, African-American women helped shape narratives of the collective past that encouraged commitment to, and faith in, the present and future of the race, their gender, and the nation as a whole. While many scholars have carefully traced other sorts of domestic and reform work performed by African-American women in the ninety-year period recorded here, we focus on their scholasticism, on the process of creating community through the pen and the voice, as a vital and overlooked form of work performed by black women. Monographs and anthologies about white women's intellectual activity suggest that women played a important role in the creation of national history.[11] Yet if European American women are only recently being noticed for these intellectual contributions, African-American women are still largely represented in the scholarship primarily as religious enthusiasts (such as Eliza Foote or Zilpha Elaw), artists (Edmonia Lewis), or political reformers (Sojourner Truth and Ida B. Wells-Barnett). New studies of black historicism in the early national and Reconstruction eras do not mention female contributions to that historiography.[12] But women were also, alongside

[11] Nina Baym, "Between Enlightenment and Victorian: Toward a Narrative of American Women Writers Writing History," *Critical Inquiry* 18:1 (Autumn 1991), 22–41; Mary Kelley, "Whether to Make Her Surname More or Adams: Writing Women's History," in *Learning to Stand & Speak: Women, Education, and Public Life in America's Republic* (Chapel Hill: University of North Carolina Press, 2006), 191–244.

[12] John Ernest, *Liberation Historiography: African-American Writers and the Challenge of History, 1794–1861* (Chapel Hill: University of North Carolina Press, 2004); Stephen Hall, *A Faithful Account of the Race: African American Historical Writing in Nineteenth-Century America* (Chapel Hill: University of North Carolina Press, 2009).

and in conversation with their black male counterparts, the creators of collective values and loyalties passed along in intellectual activity.

Most of these women did not receive notice for their work in their lifetimes. Nonetheless, their renderings of a racial past set the stage for much of the acclaimed black literature of the twentieth century.[13] Years before women were admitted to seminary Maria Stewart interpreted biblical prophecy to speak to the plight of black women in Boston in the 1830s in a style that presaged the declarations of later black clergy. She left public life after delivering only four public speeches. Hallie Quinn Brown, who published half a dozen historical volumes between 1880 and the 1920s, was one of the most prominent churchwomen, elocutionists, and educational fundraisers of her day. Even though the main library at Central State University in Ohio is named after her, her historical works have been largely forgotten by contemporary audiences. Tropes, themes, and signal figures of these documents may be discerned in later novels and poems of twentieth- and twenty-first century black literature.

The best known set of authors represented in this volume are those who wrote and spoke in the critical chronological pivot of the 1890s, when a flood of institutional developments and demographic factors fostered a moment of immense historical creativity.[14] Within a short set of years, the novels *Megda* (1891) and *Iola Leroy* (1892), as well as the short story *"Aunt Lindy"* (1893) were published.[15] The year 1893 also included the Congress of Representative Women, where Frances Harper, Fannie Barrier Williams, Anna Julia Cooper, Fanny Jackson Coppin, Sarah J. Early, and Hallie Q. Brown delivered addresses on the current dilemmas and future prospects of black women. The club movement among African-American women expanded greatly, and in 1895 the first Congress of Colored Women of the United States convened in Boston. These club women, as Anne Ruggles Gere and Sarah R. Robbins have demonstrated,

---

[13] Writing on the social efficacy of black women's writings, Jacqueline Royster has made three observations. First, that "the very act of writing...is a bold and courageous enterprise" for women without significant social status. Second, African-American women have consistently included "social, political, and economic problems" as "focal points" in their writing. Third, most writing by African-American women was in preparation for presentation in public arenas and, therefore, functions locatively. Jacqueline Jones Royster, *Traces of a Stream: Literacy and Social Change Among African American Women* (Pittsburgh: University of Pittsburgh Press, 2000), 104.

[14] Hazel Carby, *Reconstructing Womanhood: The Emergence of the Afro-American Women Novelist* (New York: Oxford University Press, 1987), 116. For more on religious activism by women in the same time period, see Evelyn Brooks Higginbotham, *Righteous Discontent: The Women's Movement in the Black Baptist Church, 1880–1920* (Cambridge: Harvard University Press, 2003).

[15] Duchess Harris, "Nineteenth Century Black Feminist Writing and Organizing as a Humanist Act," in *By These Hands: A Documentary History of African American Humanism*, ed. Anthony Pinn (New York: New York University Press, 2001), 59.

"used literacy to create gendered spaces of collaborative agency," encouraging book clubs, recommending reading lists, and promoting literary education across black America.[16] The subsequent organization of the National Federation of Afro-American Women, the National League of Colored Women, and the National Association of Colored Women provided networks for political activism, educational innovation, and intellectual community.[17] There were black women historians prior to 1890, but after that date, they began to have a recognizable audience.

What was remarkable about these women was their stunning, overlapping productivity, as they simultaneously engaged antilynching efforts, church missionary work, curriculum development, and writing. Few leading African-American women were any one thing exclusively: no one was *just* a novelist, or just a poet, or just an activist, Christian, or mother. Indeed, the fusion of multiplicity is partly what we seek to document in *Women's Work*. The texts mirror this variety, as none of them offer only one genre of expression, demonstrating instead the overlap between fiction and nonfiction, between history and romance. In these texts one sees the constructed nature of any decision about proper historical form. There is surprising historical truth found in poems, plays, and novels; there are surprising inaccuracies in textbooks, treatises, footnotes, and speeches. Such claims are commonplace in postmodern conversations about historicity; it is striking to witness them here, in these texts, in the voices of authors so confident in the malleability of form in service of historical knowledge.

This malleability was also imposed on many women by external circumstances. African-American women who wanted to write history had to overcome the double handicap of race and gender discrimination. At the turn of the twentieth century, as the first African-American male academics earned PhDs and gained access to previously all-white professional guilds, black women were largely excluded from occupational advancement on the basis of their sex. Even the earliest historical organizations founded by African-American men to advance race literature, such as the American Negro Academy (1897), did not accept female members and rarely published the work of female authors. And African-American Protestant churches, long the seedbed for the growth of Christian historical narration, excluded women

---

[16] Anne Ruggles Gere and Sarah R. Robbins, "Gendered Literacy in Black and White: Turn-of-the-Century African-American and European-American Club Women's Printed Texts," *Signs: Journal of Women in Culture and Society* 21:3 (1996), 674.

[17] Duchess Harris, "Nineteenth-Century Black Feminist Writing and Organizing as a Humanist Act," in *By These Hands: A Documentary History of African American Humanism*, ed. Anthony Pinn (New York: New York University Press, 2001), 59–60.

from their pulpits into the late twentieth century. Women had to find alternative venues for their work to those occupied by men, and they did so through the creative adaptation of the genres of fiction, poetry, plays, pageants, and speeches.[18]

Some constants can be discerned amidst this mélange. First, among the many sites in which these texts were produced (including denominations, clubs, and seminaries), the most hallowed was the home. African-American women writers of the late nineteenth and early twentieth century wrote many sentimental fictions that celebrated bourgeois domesticity.[19] Such excess of attention was, in part, an attempt to promote the presence of something that, in slavery, was absent. "A look back upon African-American literature shows that home is ubiquitous and nowhere at the same time," describes literary scholar Valerie Prince.[20] Indeed, for many of the women in this volume, the task of preserving the black home was central to their activism. Sometimes this created nostalgic renditions of the past, or simplified renditions of identity. "African American clubwomen followed the lead of white women once again in the twentieth century, writing histories that presented figures as upstanding matriarchs devoid of sexuality," writes historian Julie Des Jardins.[21] Sexuality was not the only thing female characters seemed devoid of in these narratives; all crevices or personal complexities were smoothed over in service to the promotion of a racial ideal. Any problems in these stories were those made by social situations. The women are drawn to be of impeccable character, and it is the world which corrupts. This was an intentional consistency, advised by leaders in the community. Fannie Barrier Williams, for example, argued that the job of the New Negro Woman was primarily to foster homemaking, to create, in her words, "shrines of all the domestic virtues." This was, she suggested, the only way to defend against cultural presumptions of the black woman's rootlessness.[22] Naming home, and profiling its careful preservation by women throughout the African-American past, was a central task for black women historians.

Other themes, too, appear repeatedly in the texts that follow. Particular emphasis was placed on the reclamation of ancient sources and genealogies.

[18] Mary Helen Washington, ed., *Invented Lives: Narratives of Black Women, 1860–1960* (Garden City, NY: Anchor-Doubleday, 1987), xviii.

[19] Martha H. Patterson, *Beyond the Gibson Girl: Reimagining the American New Woman, 1895–1915* (Urbana: University of Illinois Press, 2005), 62.

[20] Valerie Sweeney Prince, *Burnin' Down the House: Home in African American Literature* (New York: Columbia University Press, 2005), 2.

[21] Julie Des Jardins, *Women and the Historical Enterprise in America: Gender, Race, and the Politics of Memory, 1880–1945* (Chapel Hill: University of North Carolina Press, 2003), 126.

[22] Patterson, *Beyond the Gibson Girl*, 60.

Long before black nationalist histories of the Sixties and subsequent Afrocentric curricula, African Americans turned to ancient sources and civilizations to situate their respectable roots in triumphant civilizations. Black historians and activists in the nineteenth century attacked the "curse of Ham" and rewrote paradigms of "Western" civilization in order to demonstrate their dominant communal presence throughout the ages. Through the use of analogies and figures from classical literature and history, African-American women attempted to continue the promise of the ancient black past into the present, articulating a prideful sense of history and a stalwart Christian decorum. Included here are excerpts from textbooks, pedagogical polemics, popular poems, and sermons assessing ancient Ethiopia and African preslavery experiences. Looking backward to an African past from which they were ripped away, these authors sought to profile a continent, and a united people from that continent, in which young black Americans could take pride and emulate.[23] They were, as many of these texts invoke, once kings and queens.

Religion threads nearly all of these texts, either invisibly as the site of production or obviously in the narrative tropes, examples, and moral expressions. In African-American communities, religion was often divisive, as denominational competition was a contested aspect of collective African-American experience. But in these texts, unity of Christian disposition is favored over and above institutional discrimination. Their authors often seem to construct an alternative world, in which biblical chronology is more vivid and predictive than the American social context. On the whole, these authors actively explain their commentaries, teaching as they write, presuming little about the audience's knowledge of what they preach. Yet in matters of religion, much is presumed, including a basic familiarity with the Bible and knowledge of the basic chronology of Christian history. The postulated audience of these texts is presumptively Protestant. African-American women writers "defined their faith not only as a miraculous fire that invited prayerful thoughts and thoughtful souls to Zion but as a flame that invigorated earthly lives," writes literary historian Barbara McCaskill, "Their short fiction, poetry, memoirs, and speeches describe a Christianity that is relevant, immediate, politicized."[24] Within religious history, African-American women are often

---

[23] Not everyone agreed looking back was the right prescription for black progress, as explained by Henry Louis Gates, Jr., "The Trope of a New Negro and the Reconstruction of the Image of the Black," *Representations* 24 (Autumn 1988), 139.

[24] Barbara McCaskill, "'To Labor...and Fight on the Side of God': Spirit, Class, and Nineteenth-Century African American Women's Literature," in *Nineteenth Century American Women Writers: A Critical Reader*, ed. Karen L. Kilcup (Malden, MA: Wiley-Blackwell, 1998), 164.

memorialized as sages, radicals, or ecstatics. *Women's Work* contributes to an ongoing complication of this typology, adding to it the roles of theologian and church historian.[25]

Pervading these works is the importance of a united historical consciousness. Unity resounds in these texts, as their writers profile a people and a culture united in a variety of ways: in a history of enslavement, in gendered experience, in racial segregation, in American patriotism, and in religious devotion. Sometimes privileging African-American political unity or nationalism, but sometimes not, these voices cohere into a communal aspiration. Preserving black history was not just a textual venture for these women but also an activist one. The National Association of Colored Women (NACW), for example, became custodian of Douglass's Cedar Hill estate in 1916 when male executors of the Frederick Douglass Memorial Home Association (FDMHA) expressed to then NACW president Mary Talbert that they were no longer willing to raise funds to maintain the property.[26] Preservation occurred too through conversations about historical subjects at club meetings and the new black literary associations. Historical discussions at meetings of the Boston Literary and Historical Association "were the catalyst for the debate of intricate issues of historical representation, misrepresentation, and self-representation," writes literary historian Elizabeth McHenry.[27] "Questions of historical representation remained so important to the Boston Literary Association that its membership decided to strengthen the 'Historical' aspect of the organization to ensure that research would be conducted and publications written to augment their understanding of their own past."[28] Historical

---

[25] Other work seeking to recalibrate descriptions of African-American female religiosity include Anthea Butler, *Women in the Church of God in Christ: Making a Sanctified World* (Chapel Hill: University of North Carolina Press, 2007); Delores Carpenter, "Black Women in Religious Institutions: A Historical Summary from Slavery to the 1960s," *Journal of Religious Thought* 46 (Winter 1989–Spring 1990), 7–27; Richard J. Douglass-Chin, *Preacher Woman Sings the Blues: The Autobiographies of Nineteenth-Century African American Evangelists* (Columbia: University of Missouri Press, 2001); Cheryl Townsend Gilkes, "'Together and in Harness': Women's Traditions in the Sanctified Church," *Signs: Journal of Women in Culture and Society* 10:4 (Summer 1985), 678–699; R. Marie Griffith and Barbara Dianne Savage, eds., *Women and Religion in the African Diaspora: Knowledge, Power and Performance* (Baltimore: Johns Hopkins University Press, 2006); Sylvia M. Jacobs, "African-American Women Missionaries Confront the African Way of Life," in *Women in Africa and the African Diaspora*, eds. Rosalyn Terborg-Penn, Sharon Harley, and Andrea Benton Rushing (Washington, DC: Howard University Press, 1997), 89–100; Judith Weisenfeld and Richard Newman, eds., *This Far by Faith: Readings in African-American Women's Religious Biography* (New York: Routledge, 1996).

[26] Des Jardins, *Women and the Historical Enterprise in America*, 124.

[27] Elizabeth McHenry, *Forgotten Readers: Recovering the Lost History of African-American Literary Societies* (Durham, NC: Duke University Press, 2002), 174–175.

[28] McHenry, *Forgotten Readers*, 177.

investigation, education, and conversation offered an opportunity to construct a common vocabulary, as well as a common sense of progress.

"The passage from memory to history has required every social group to redefine its identity through the revitalization of its own history," wrote historian Pierre Nora. "The historian is one who prevents history from becoming *merely* history."[29] The women anthologized here labored in their texts to make history present, to make sure it never became mere history. Emerging in the century prior to the large-scale professionalization of historical studies within the American academy, they were, with a few exceptions, not certified by "experts" in the field. Relying on memory, limited libraries, and the Bible, they constructed tales to tell the stories that needed to be heard, not those stories that needed to be proven. As historian Bonnie G. Smith has noted with respect to the gendered character of history, "Professionalism is a relationship dependent on discredited voices and devalued narratives," on accounts that serve as a "low" foil to the "high" status of authorized renderings of the past.[30] In contrast to "professional history," the documents assembled here are histories with a particular political, cultural, and collective purpose: to assemble the diversity of African-American lives into a common narrative experience. With their unique domestic and social authority, black women offered a compelling portrait of the black historical past. By reading these anthologized texts, readers can trace the process by which the socially marginalized narrate their identities into the American mainstream. Through the discourse of history, African-American women educated their children, parishioners, and students to the tactics of endurance, survival, and ascendance in the republic.

[29] Pierre Nora, "Between Memory and History: *Les Lieux de Mémoire*," in *History and Memory in African-American Culture*, eds. Geneviève Fabre and Robert O'Meally (New York: Oxford University Press, 1994), 291, 294.

[30] Bonnie G. Smith, *The Gender of History: Men, Women, and Historical Practice* (Harvard University Press, 1998), 10.

ONE | Maria W. Stewart
(1803–1879)

BORN MARIA MILLER IN HARTFORD, Connecticut, and orphaned at the age of five, Maria W. Stewart might never have risen above the ranks of many indentured blacks in the nominally free north save for a string of bad luck, a solid knowledge of the Bible, and a fiery temperament. Little is known about her parents or her early childhood. Taken under the wing of a local clergy family at age five, Stewart was "bound out" as a servant, an occupation at which she would toil for the subsequent two decades. While she received no formal education, she did attend Sabbath school classes offered to blacks and learned enough to read the Bible, the text that formed the basis of her worldview.

In 1826 she married James W. Stewart, an entrepreneurial Boston shipping outfitter, and joined the ranks of the small black middle-class community in that city. She and her husband also became friends with David Walker, an ardent Methodist, antislavery advocate, and writer. Walker contributed to the first black newspaper, *Freedom's Journal*, but it was in his incendiary 1829 pamphlet, *Appeal to the Colored Citizens of the World*, that Walker called for revolt in the face of racial oppression and encouraged southern slaves to rise up against their masters. Copies of his work were smuggled into southern ports on ships and in sailors' clothes and distributed widely, likely with the help of the Stewart shipping business, among others.

Source: Maria W. Stewart, "An Address Delivered before the Afric-American Female Intelligence Society of America," *The Liberator* (28 April 1832).

Between late 1829 and 1830, however, Maria Stewart lost these two most important relationships through the deaths of both James Stewart and David Walker. Despite a protracted legal battle, white businessmen then robbed the widow of her husband's sizable estate, leaving her alone and destitute. But Stewart found her political and religious convictions and her public voice over the next few years: Between 1831 and 1833 she delivered a series of addresses in Boston that were published in the pages of *The Liberator*, the most widely circulated antislavery newspaper of the day. Taking up Walker's cause and clothing herself in the mantle of biblical prophecy, Stewart delivered scathing speeches that called upon African Americans to improve themselves morally, economically, and politically. As much as she hated the oppression of blacks by whites, she also despised the failings of the black community to attain Christian purity, and to argue more vehemently for their civil rights.

Stewart was the first known African-American woman to speak to mixed-race audiences of both men and women. More than a civil leader, she saw herself as a holy warrior for Christ. In her 1832 address to the Afric-American Female Intelligence Society of America, reprinted here, Stewart placed the African race in a sacred history and located herself as a prophet in a millennial battle. "I am speaking as one who expects to give account at the bar of God," she proclaimed. "I have enlisted in holy warfare, and Jesus is my captain." Stewart enjoined black women to recognize the role of the race in the divine plan, and called on them to rise up and live out their God-given destiny. She likened their work to that of ancient Israel, and compared the cause to the recent revolutionary efforts in France, Haiti, and Poland. Only through recognizing their place in history, Stewart suggested, would African Americans save themselves politically and spiritually, in this world and in the world to come.

An Address Delivered Before the Afric-American Female Intelligence Society of America (1832)

The frowns of the world shall never discourage me, nor its smiles flatter me; for with the help of God, I am resolved to withstand the fiery darts of the devil, and the assaults of wicked men. The righteous are as bold as a lion, but the wicked teeth when no man pursueth. I fear neither men nor devils; for the God in whom I trust is able to deliver me from the rage and malice of my enemies, and from them that rise up against me. The only motive that has prompted me to raise my voice in your behalf, my friends, is because I have discovered that religion is held in low repute among some of us; and purely to promote the cause of Christ, and the good of souls, in the hope that others more experienced, more able and talented than myself, might go forward and do likewise. I expect to render a strict, a solemn, and an awful account to God for the motives that have prompted me to exertion, and for those with which I shall address you this evening.

What I have to say, concerns the whole of us as Christians and as a people; and if you will be so kind as give me a hearing this once, you shall receive the incense of a grateful heart.

The day is coming, my friends, and I rejoice in that day, when the secrets of all hearts shall be manifested before saints and angels, men and devils. It will be a great day of joy and rejoicing to the humble followers of Christ, but a day of terror and dismay to hypocrites and unbelievers. Of that day and hour knoweth no man, no, not even the angels in heaven, but the Father only. The dead that are in Christ shall be raised first. Blessed is he that shall have a part in the first resurrection. Ah, me thinks I hear the finally impenitent crying, "Rocks and mountains! fall upon us, and hide us from the wrath of the Lamb; and from him that sitteth upon the throne!"

> High on a cloud our God shall come,
> Bright thrones prepare his way;
> Thunder and darkness, fire and storm,
> Lead on the dreadful day.

Christ shall descend in the clouds of heaven, surrounded by ten thousand of his saints and angels, and it shall be very tempestuous round about him; and before him shall be gathered all nations, and kindred, and tongues, and people; and every knee shall bow, and every tongue confess; they also that pierced him shall look upon him, and mourn. Then shall the King separate the righteous from the wicked, as a shepherd divideth the sheep from the goats, and shall place the righteous on his right hand, and the wicked upon his left. Then, says Christ, shall be weeping, and wailing, and gnashing of teeth, when ye shall see Abraham and the prophets, sitting in the kingdom of heaven, and ye yourselves thrust out. Then shall the righteous shine forth in the kingdom of their Father as the sun. He that hath ears to hear, let him hear. The poor despised followers of Christ will not then regret their sufferings here; they shall be carried by angels into Abraham's bosom, and shall be comforted; and the Lord God shall wipe away their tears. You will then be convinced before assembled multitudes, whether they strove to promote the cause of Christ, or whether they sought for gain or applause. "Strive to enter it at the strait gate; for many, I say unto you, shall seek to enter in, and shall not be able. For except your righteousness shall exceed the righteousness of the Scribes and Pharisees, ye shall in no wise enter into the kingdom of heaven."

Ah, methinks I see this people lying in wickedness; and as the Lord liveth, and as your souls live, were it not for the few righteous that are to be found among us, we should become as wisdom, and like unto Gomorrah. Christians have too long slumbered and slept; sinners stumbled into hell, and still are stumbling, for the want of Christian exertion; and the devil is going about like a roaring lion, seeking whom he may devour. And I make bold to say, that many who profess the name of Christ at the present day, live so widely different from what becometh the Gospel of our Lord Jesus Christ, that they cannot and they dare not reason to the world upon righteousness and judgment to come.

Be not offended because I tell you the truth; for I believe that God has fired my soul with a holy zeal for his cause. It was God alone who inspired my heart to publish the meditations thereof; and it was done with pure motives of love to your souls, in the hope that Christians might examine themselves, and sinners become picked in their hearts. It is the word of God, though men and devils may oppose it. It is the word of God; and little did I think that any of the professed followers of Christ would have frowned upon me, and discouraged and hindered its progress.

Ah, my friends, I am speaking as one who expects to give account at the bar of God; I am speaking as a dying mortal to dying mortals. I fear there are many who have named the name of Jesus at the present day, that strain at a gnat and swallow a camel; they neither enter into the kingdom of heaven themselves, nor suffer others to enter in. They would pull the motes out of their brother's eye, when they have a beam in their own eye. And were our blessed Lord and Saviour, Jesus Christ, upon the earth, I believe he would say of many that are called by his name, "O, ye hypocrites, ye generation of vipers, how can you escape the damnation of hell." I have enlisted in the holy warfare, and Jesus is my captain; and the Lord's battle I mean to fight, until my voice expire in death. I expect to by hated of all men, and persecuted even unto death, for righteousness and the truth's sake.

A few remarks upon moral subjects, and I close. I am a strong advocate for the cause of God, and for the cause of freedom. I am not your enemy, but a friend both to you and to your children. Suffer me, then, to express my sentiments but this once, however severe they may appear to be, and then hereafter let me sink into oblivion, and let my name die in forgetfulness.

Had the ministers of the gospel shunned the very appearance of evil; had they faithfully discharged their duty, whether we would have heard them or not; we should have been a very different people from what we now are; but they have kept the truth as it were, hid from our eyes, and have cried, "Peace!

Peace!" when there was no peace; they have plastered us up with untempered mortar, and have been as it were blind leaders of the blind.

It appears to me that there are no people under the heavens, so unkind and so unfeeling towards their own, as are the descendants of fallen Africa. I have been something of a traveller in my day; and the general cry among the people is, "Our own color are our greatest opposers;" and even the whites say that we are greater enemies towards each other, than they are towards us. Shall we be a hissing and a reproach among the nations of the earth any longer? Shall they laugh us to scorn for ever? We might become a highly respectable people; respectable we now consider ourselves, but we might become a highly distinguished and intelligent people. And how? In convincing the world, by our own efforts, however feeble, that nothing is wanting on our part but opportunity. Without these efforts, we shall never be a people, nor our descendants after us.

But God has said, that Ethiopia shall stretch forth her hands unto him. True, but God uses means to bring about his purposes; and unless the rising generation manifest a different temper and disposition towards each other from what we have manifested, the generation following will never be an enlightened people. We this day are considered as one of the most degraded races upon the face of the earth. It is useless for us any longer to sit with our hands folded, reproaching the whites; for that will never elevate us. All the nations of the earth have distinguished themselves, and have shown forth a noble and a gallant spirit. Look at the suffering Greeks! Their proud souls revolted at the idea of serving a tyrannical nation, who were no better than themselves, and perhaps not so good. They made a mighty effort and arose; their souls were knit together in the holy bonds of love and union; they were united, and came off victorious. Look at the French in the late revolution! no traitors among them, to expose their plans to the crowned heads of Europe! "Liberty or Death!" was their cry. And the Haytians, though they have not been acknowledged as a nation, yet their firmness of character, and independence of spirit have been greatly admired, and high applauded. Look at the Poles, a feel able people! They rose against three hundred thousand mighty men of Russia; and though they did not gain the conquest, yet they obtained the name of gallant Poles. And even the wild Indians of the forest are more united than ourselves. Insult one of them, and you insult a thousand. They also have contended for their rights and privileges, and are held in higher repute than we are.

And why is it, my friends, that we are despised above all the nations upon the earth? Is it merely because our skins are tinged with a sable hue? No, nor will I ever believe that it is. What then is it; Oh, it is because that we and our fathers have dealt treacherously one with another, and because many of us now possess that envious and malicious disposition, that we had rather die than see each other rise an inch above a beggar. No gentle methods are used to promote love and friendship among us, but much is done to destroy it. Shall we be a hissing and a reproach among the nations of the earth any longer? Shall they laugh us to scorn forever?

Ingratitude is one of the worst passions that reigns in the human breast; it is this that cuts the tender fibres of the soul; for it is impossible for us to love those who are ungrateful towards us. "Behold," says that wise man, Soloman, counting one by one, "a man have I found in a thousand, but a woman among all those have I not found."

I have sometimes thought, that God had almost departed from among us. And why? Because Christ has said, if we say we love the Father, and hate our brother, we are liars, and the truth is not in us; and certainly if we were the true followers of Christ, I think we could not show such a disposition towards each other as we do: for God is all love.

A lady of high distinction among us, observed to me, that I might never expect your homage. God forbid! I ask it not. But I beseech you to deal with gentleness and godly sincerity towards me; and there is not one of you, my dear friends, who has given me a cup of cold water in the name of the Lord, or soothed the sorrows of my wounded heart, but God will bless, not only you, but your children for it. Cruel indeed, are those that indulge such an opinion respecting me as that.

Finally, I have exerted myself both for your temporal and eternal welfare, as far as I am able; and my soul has been so discouraged within me, that I have almost been induced to exclaim, "Would to God that my tongue hereafter might cleave to the roof of my mouth, and become silent forever!" and then I have felt that the Christian has no time to be idle, and I must be active, knowing that the night of death cometh, in which no man can work; and my mind has become raised to such an extent, that I will willingly die for the cause that I have espoused; for I cannot die in a more glorious cause than in the defence of God and his laws.

O women, woman! upon you I call; for upon your exertions almost entirely depends whether the rising generation shall be any thing more than we have been or not. O woman, woman! your example is powerful, your influence great; it extends over your husbands and over your children, and throughout the circle of your acquaintance. Then let me exhort you to cultivate among yourselves a spirit of Christian love and unity, having charity one for another, without which all our goodness is as sounding brass, and as a tinkling cymbal. And O, my God, I beseech thee to grant that the nations of the earth may hiss at us no longer! O suffer them not to laugh us to scorn forever!

TWO

Ann Plato

(1820–?)

A NN PLATO WAS THE FIRST African American to publish a book of essays in English, a work that would stand as one of only a few clues about her life. Born in Hartford, Connecticut, to an African American mother and a Native American father, Plato spent much of her life working as a schoolteacher at the Zion Methodist Church School in that city. She was a member of the Colored Congregational Church on Talcott Street, a community served during this period by the Reverend James W. C. Pennington (1807–1870). In this setting, Plato was surrounded by a remarkable set of Christian intellectuals and activists. During the 1840s Pennington, a fugitive slave who had studied at Yale and the University of Heidelberg, transformed his church into a magnet of antislavery activity and a stop on the Underground Railroad. Notable African-American leaders came through town frequently and lectured at the church to large crowds. The congregation also saw its share of racial violence, including race riots in the mid-1830s in which church members were attacked as they left the building.

African-American authors of the day needed legitimation of their work, and so when Plato published her essays in 1841, she included a preface by Pennington, who assured the reader that Plato was a member of his church and "of pleasing piety and modest worth." Stressing her youth, he commented on the accuracy of her pious sentiments, and placed her in a lineage of black authors: "My authoress has followed the example of Philis Wheatly, and of Terence, and Capitain, and

Source: Ann Plato, "Education," "Death of the Christian," "Louisa Seabury," "Natives of America," from *Essays* (Hartford: Printed for the author, 1841), pp. 26–33, 70–72, 77–79, 110–112.

Francis Williams, her compatriots....She, like as Philis Wheatly was, is passionately fond of reading, and delights in searching the Holy Scriptures." If that buildup were not sufficient to convince readers of her talent, the minister enlarged the framework still further: "Egypt, Greece and Rome, successively, gave their own authors success....When Egypt was a school for the world, all the Egyptians were not teachers of the arts and sciences. The Romans were not all Ciceros, nor were the Greeks all Homers, or Platos. But as Greece had a Plato why may we not have a Platoess?" In Pennington's hands, Plato herself had become part of the epic story of African achievement.

Despite her own brushes with race consciousness, Plato herself was little inclined to write about racial uplift or attainment. Her essays are filled with history informed by traditional classical learning, and her allusions favor European history and historiography. For Plato, ancient and modern history confirmed and elucidated the moral truths of the Bible, but the Bible itself did not serve as a narrative framework. Her base of knowledge, while in keeping with standard Euro-American historical interpretation, was astonishingly broad. In her discussion of education, she cited Alexander, Aristotle, Milton, Walter Scott, Cicero, Adam Clarke, and Newton. In an essay on character she drew from Christopher Columbus, Demosthenes, Pompey, Benjamin Franklin, Robert Fulton, and Robert Bruce.

These four pieces highlight important aspects of Plato's Calvinist-inflected thought. In "Education," she emphasizes the importance of learning leavened by religious faith as a critical component of historical progress. Like other authors of the day, Plato talks about historical development in terms of nations and representative men, and she points out the distinctive role of books as the "silent teachers" who can speak to multiple generations. In "Death of the Christian" she stresses the singular capacity of Christian faith to overcome the "agonies of dissolving nature," to triumph over history and mortality. Her homage to the departed Louisa Sebury again emphasizes that intellect and other human virtues, particularly for young women, must always be tempered by Christian piety and humility. It might well be argued that the entire volume is geared towards the edification of young women, an education reminding them of their social obligations. Christianity, Plato asserts, provides women with liberation through education, a "gift" not provided by other religious traditions. "How does she prize the gift?" Plato presses. "Does she press to gain a stand at the temple of knowledge, or will she clothe her brow in vanity, and be satisfied with ignorance." In the last reprinted selection, "The Natives of America," Plato forthrightly broaches the topic of race by narrating the story of the near-extinction of Native Americans after the arrival of Columbus. Speaking from the perspective of a Native American girl,

Plato relates a history that speaks to the horrors of racial violence that might be read to presage the fate of African Americans as well. Her poem assigns to a young woman, the silent and solitary representative of her people, to preserve collective memory in the face of impending disaster.

—⬦⬦⬦—

Education (1841)

This appears to be the great source from which nations have become civilized, industrious, respectable and happy. A society or people are always considered as advancing, when they are found paying proper respect to education. The observer will find them erecting buildings for the establishment of schools, in various sections of their country, on different systems, where their children may at an early age commence learning, and having their habits fixed for higher attainments. Too much attention, then, can not be given to it by people, nation, society or individual. History tells us that the first settlers of our country soon made themselves conspicuous by establishing a character for the improvement, and diffusing of knowledge among them.

We hear of their inquiry, how shall our children be educated? and upon what terms or basis shall it be placed? We find their questions soon answered to that important part; and by attending to this in every stage of their advancement, with proper respect, we find them one of the most enlightened and happy nations on the globe.

It is, therefore, an unspeakable blessing to be born in those parts where wisdom and knowledge flourish; though it must be confessed there are even in these parts several poor, uninstructed persons who are but little above the late inhabitants of this country, who knew no modes of the civilized life, but wandered to and fro, over the parts of the then unknown world.

We are, some of us, very fond of knowledge, and apt to value ourselves upon any proficiency in the sciences; one science, however, there is, worth more than all the rest, and that is the science of living well—which shall remain "when tongues shall cease," and "knowledge shall vanish away."

It is owing to the preservation of books, that we are led to embrace their contents. Oral instructions can benefit but one age and one set of hearers; but these silent teachers address all ages and all nations. They may sleep for a while and be neglected; but whenever the desire of information springs up in the human breast, there they are with mild wisdom ready to instruct and please us.

No person can be considered as possessing a good education without religion. A good education is that which prepares us for our future sphere of action and makes us contented with that situation in life in which God, in his infinite mercy, has seen fit to place us, to be perfectly resigned to our lot in life, whatever it may be. Religion has been decreed as the passion of weak persons; but the Bible tells us "to seek first the kingdom of heaven, and His righteousness, and all other things shall be added unto us." This world is only a place to prepare for another and a better.

If it were not for education, how would our heathen be taught therefrom? While science and the arts boast so many illustrious names; there is another and more extended sphere of action where illustrious names and individual effort has been exerted with the happiest results, and their authors, by their deeds of charity, have won bright and imperishable crowns in the realms of bliss. Was it the united effort of nations, or of priestly synods that first sent the oracles of eternal truth to the inhospitable shores of Greenland—or placed the lamp of life in the hut of the Esquemaux—or carried a message of love to the burning climes of Africa—or that directed the deluded votaries of idolatry in that benighted land where the Ganges rolls its consecrated waters, to Calvary's Sacrifice, a sacrifice that sprinkled with blood the throne of justice, rendering it accessible to ruined, degraded man.

In proportion to the education of a nation, it is rich and powerful. To behold the wealth and power of Great Britain, and compare it with China; America with Mexico; how confused are the ideas of the latter, how narrow their conceptions, and are, as it were in an unknown world.

Education is a system which the bravest men have followed. What said Alexander about this? Said he: "I am more indebted to my tutor, Aristotle, than to my father Philip; for Philip gives me my living, but Aristotle teaches me how to live." It was Newton that threw aside the dimness of uncertainty which shrouded for so many centuries the science of astronomy; penetrated the arena of nature, and soared in his eagle-flight far, far beyond the wildest dreams of all former ages, defining with certainty the motions of those flaming worlds, and assigning laws to the fartherest star that lies on the confines of creation—that glimmers on the verge of immensity.

Knowledge is the very foundation of wealth, and of nations. Aristotle held unlimited control over the opinions of men for fifteen centuries, and governed the empire of mind where ever he was known. For knowledge, men brave every danger, they explore the sandy regions of Africa, and diminish the arena of contention and bloodshed. Where ever ignorance holds unlimited sway, the light of science, and the splendor of the gospel of truth is obscure and nearly obliterated by the gloom of monkish superstition, merged in the sable hues of idolatry and popish cruelty; no ray of glory shines on those degraded minds; "darkness covers the earth, and gross darkness the people."

Man is the noblest work in the universe of God. His excellence does not consist in the beautiful symmetry of his form, or in the exquisite structure of his complicated physical machinery; capable of intellectual and moral powers. What have been the conquests of men in the field of general science? What scholastic intrenchment is there which man would not have wished to carry—what height is there which he would not have wished to survey—what depth that he would not like to explore?—even the mountains and the earth—hidden minerals—and all that rest on the borders of creation he would like to overpower.

But shall these splendid conquests be subverted? Egypt, that once shot over the world brilliant rays of genius, is sunk in darkness. The dust of ages sleeps on the besom of Roman warriors, poets, and orators. The glory of Greece has departed, and leaves no Demosthenes to thunder with his eloquence, or Homer to soar and sing.

It is certainly true that many dull and unpromising scholars have become the most distinguished men; as Milton, Newton, Walter Scott, Adam Clarke. Newton stated of himself, that his superiority to common minds was not natural, but acquired by mental discipline. Hence, we perceive that the mind is capable of wonderful improvement. The mother of Sir William Jones said to him when a child: "If you wish to understand, read;" how true, that "education forms the mind."

How altogether important, then, is education; it is our guide in youth, and it will walk with us in the vale of our declining years. This knowledge we ought ever to pursue with all diligence. Our whole life is but one great school; from the cradle to the grave we are all learners; nor will our education be finished until we die.

A good education is another name for happiness. Shall we not devote time and toil to learn how to be happy? It is a science which the youngest child may begin, and the wisest man is never weary of. No one should be satisfied with present attainments; we should aim high, and bend all our energies to reach the point aimed at.

We ought not to fail to combine with our clear convictions of what is right, a firmness and moral courage sufficient to enable us to "forsake every false way," and our course will be like that of the just—"brighter and brighter unto the perfect day."

Death of the Christian (1841)

The Christian, and he alone, can triumph amidst the agonies of dissolving nature, in a well grounded hope of future felicity. There is a genuine dignity in the death of the real believer. It is not the vanity of an Augustus Cæsar, who called his subjects around him; and after reminding them that he had lived in glory, bid them applaud him after death.

It is not the heroic stupidity of an Andre, who ostentatiously desired the spectators of his catastrophe, to witness that he died as a brave man. It is not the thoughtless courage of a professed hero, in the heat of spirits, and amidst the confusion of battles, rushing almost headlong upon certain destruction. It is not the hardy insensibility of an Indian warrior, exulting in the midst of surrounding flames, provoking his tormentors, and singing a merry song of death. He meanly retreats from evils, which Christian heroism would qualify to overcome by his exertions, or to endure with patience.

The votaries of fame may acquire a sort of insensibility to death and its consequences. But he alone whose peace is made with God, can walk with composure through the gloomy valley of the shadow of death, and fear no evil. Behold Chesterfield, after a life of pleasure, endeavoring to act the philosopher in death! But, alas! it proved fatal.

The man of intellectual genius may cause his wit to flash, and blaze, and burn; and as Pollock says of Byron, "He stands on the Alps—stands on the Appenines, and talks with thunder, as with friend to friend, and weave his garland from the lightning's flash in sportive twist," and then die, and is gone; but where?

A cultivated mind, and an unsanctified heart, may become one of the most awful scourges of this world. Such was Byron, such was Rosseau, and such was Voltaire, and many others.

On the other hand, behold the amiable, the virtuous, the pious Addison, in his dying scene. How humble, and at the same time, how dignified he appears. His setting sun shone bright. The evening of his life was pleasant and serene. Observe him, ye admirers of fortitude; view him in that critical hour, which emphatically tries men's souls; and learn with what superior dignity of mind a Christian can die.

Louisa Sebury (1841)

Louisa Sebury was born at Hartford, Connecticut, March 12th, 1816. An ingenuous temper, a quickness of understanding, a benevolent spirit, a flexibility of nature, and a solemn sense of divine things, were observed in her tender age; and in the dangerous ascent of life, her feet were guided and preserved in the paths of rectitude and goodness; so that she was not only free from the stain of vice and vanity in her rising years, but looked to things superior to the world, and its vain and trifling amusements.

Her thirst for knowledge was great, although she had not the advantage which many have, who less improve it. But although not skilled in the depths of knowledge, yet she possessed Christian virtue, which often the profound historian does not.

In friendship, she was firm, affectionate, and confiding. She rendered every service in her power to those whom she loved. She regarded all with whom she associated with Christian kindness, and by a warm and generous sympathy, she made their sorrows her own.

Though she was agreeable in her person, she did not sacrifice her time to the decoration of dress. She was always neat in her apparel, but did not allow the toilet to interfere with other duties. Her feelings were the kindest, and the most social; and her manners were unaffected. For empty ceremony and ostentious fashion, she had neither time nor taste.

All her deportment was marked by true humility. And though her excellence could not shield her from enmity, and from the slanders of that envy which follows eminent goodness, and "like the shadow, proves the substance true," she avoided resentment, and consided herself thus called upon to exercise the Christian virtue of forgiveness.

She was often a subject of ill health. Her last sickness was occasioned from a violent cold which she had taken. This terminated her existence. Now the value of that religion which she had chosen was fully realized. She was enabled to endure, without murmuring, severe affliction.

As religion was the subject of her meditations in health, it was more forcibly impressed upon her mind during illness. She knew the duty of resignation to the will of her Maker, and of dependence on the merits of a Redeemer. These sentiments were often expressed by her, to persons who visited her dying bed.

"A life so blameless, a trust so firm in God, a mind so conversant with a future and better world, seemed to have divested death of terror. He came as a messenger to conduct her to that state of purity and bliss for which she had been preparing."

All future hopes of recovery, by her friends, were at length given over. To her it was not unwelcome news. Her parents mourned to think of the loss of so affectionate a daughter; great was her loss, seemingly, to her sisters; and society mourned the loss of a valuable friend.

Death to her was no unwelcome messenger. The close of her life was like the fading of a serene Sabbath into the holy quiet of its evening. The virtues which made her beloved, continued to flourish, and put forth new and fresh blossoms, until her life's end.

With so calm and peaceful a mind, so blessed and lively a hope, did this resigned friend of Christ wait for her Master's summons. It was on the 16th day of December, 1838, that her spirit departed. And methought I heard a voice saying, "Such shall hunger no more, neither thirst any more; for they have washed their robes, and made them white in the blood of the Lamb?"

The Natives of America (1841)

Tell me a story, father please,
And then I sat upon his knees.
Then answer'd he,—"what speech make known,
Or tell the words of native tone,
Of how my Indian fathers dwelt,
And, of sore oppression felt;
And how they mourned a land serene,
It was an ever mournful theme."
Yes, I replied,—I like to hear,
And bring my father's spirit near;
Of every pain they did forego,
Oh, please to tell me all you know.
In history often I do read,
Of pain which none but they did heed.

He thus began. "We were a happy race,
When we no tongue but ours did trace,
We were in ever peace,
We sold, we did release—
Our brethren, far remote, and far unknown,
And spake to them in silent, tender tone.
We all were then as in one band,
We join'd and took each others hand;
Our dress was suited to the clime,
Our food was such as roam'd that time,
Our houses were of sticks compos'd;
No matter,—for they us enclos'd.

But then discover'd was this land indeed
By European men; who then had need
Of this far country. Columbus came afar,

And thus before we could say Ah!
What meaneth this?—we fell in cruel hands.
Though some were kind, yet others then held bands
Of cruel oppression. Then too, foretold our chief,—
Beggars you will become—is my belief.
We sold, then some bought lands,
We altogether moved in foreign hands.

Wars ensued. They knew the handling of firearms.
Mothers spoke,—no fear this breast alarms,
They will not cruelly us oppress,
Or thus our lands possess.
Alas! it was a cruel day; we were crush'd:
Into the dark, dark woods we rush'd
To seek a refuge.

My daughter, we are now diminish'd, unknown,
Unfelt! Alas! no tender tone
To cheer us when the hunt is done;
Fathers sleep,—we're silent every one.

Oh! silent the horror, and fierce the fight,
When my brothers were shrouded in night;
Strangers did us invade—strangers destroy'd
The fields, which were by us enjoy'd.

Our country is cultur'd, and looks all sublime,
Our fathers are sleeping who lived in the time
That I tell. Oh! could I tell them my grief
In its flow, that in roaming, we find no relief.

I love my country; and shall, until death
Shall cease my breath.

Now daughter dear I've done,
Seal this upon thy memory; until the morrow's sun
Shall sink, to rise no more;
And if my years should score,
Remember this, though I tell no more."

THREE ❧ Frances Ellen Watkins Harper
(1825–1911)

F RANCES ELLEN WATKINS WAS BORN into the free black community of
Baltimore in 1825. After the death of her mother in Frances' early
childhood, her aunt and uncle, William and Henrietta Watkins, reared the
young girl. The family attended Sharp Street Church, a historic black
Methodist congregation often called the "Mother Church" of Baltimore
Methodism. Sharp Street stood at the center of abolitionist activism in the
1820s and 1830s. Deeply committed to civil rights, William Watkins ran a
school for free blacks and worked with the abolitionist movement. Under his
tutelage Frances gained a classical education and inherited the mantle of a
distinctive legacy of Christian piety, protest, and racial advocacy, features
that remained with her throughout her long career.

Although best known today for her fiction and poetry, Frances lectured
frequently on contemporaneous issues and wrote essays on behalf of a variety
of reform causes, including temperance, women's rights, and abolition. After
several years of teaching, Frances published her first and most successful
work, *Poems on Miscellaneous Subjects* (1854), which established her reputation
as one of the foremost female writers of the century. It also launched her
speaking career for the abolitionist cause and placed her in the company of
John Brown and other activists. In 1860 she married Fenton Harper, a wid-
ower with three children, and the couple had their only child, Mary, in 1862.

Sources: Frances Ellen Watkins Harper, *National Anti-Slavery Standard* (23 May 1857), 3; *Moses: A Story of the Nile*, 3rd ed. (Philadelphia: Merrihew & Son, 1870), 3–13, 18–21, 32–36, 38–43; "Then and Now," *Poems* (Philadelphia: George S. Ferguson Co., 1900), 75–79.

After Fenton's death in 1864 and the end of the Civil War, Frances renewed her public speaking career and took up the cause of education and uplift for the newly freed slaves.

Harper's prolific literary output was almost always put to the service of the race. It was also couched in familial and domestic terms. Like many women of her generation, Harper understood her commitment to women's rights as perfectly in keeping with her advocacy of women's domestic responsibilities. She saw it as the particular duty of African-American women to advocate for future generations. Her capacious learning gave her a long view of history, and in her writing she sought creative ways to combine the grand sweep of sacred and national destiny with the local and intimate aspects of ordinary lives. As she once commented in a letter to a friend: "I am standing with my race on the threshold of a new era and though some may be far past me in the learning of the schools, yet today, with my limited and fragmentary knowledge, I may help the race forward a little." Domestic activity was the best way for women to participate, she believed, and thus she dedicated herself to addressing women as a means of encouraging all African Americans: "I am going to have a private meeting with the women. I am going to talk with them about their daughters and about things connected with the welfare of the race. Now is the time for our women to begin to try to lift up their heads and plant the roots of progress under the hearthstone."[1]

The three selections chosen illustrate the sweep of her interests. "Liberty for Slaves" was delivered at a meeting of the New York Anti-Slavery Society in 1857, and in it Harper emphasizes both the anti-Christian and anti-American nature of slavery. As she points out, even Muslim countries offer freedom, thus challenging the hypocritical identification of the United States as a "land of liberty." Her epic poem "Moses: A Story of the Nile," retells the story of this central figure in black biblical interpretation. Harper, however, narrates from the perspective of family, and especially the women in his life, lending the preeminent story of political emancipation a domestic cast. The story focuses on sisterly love and maternal affiliation, and implies that nations are linked together by lineages of women and families. Note that Miriam, Moses' sister, plays a prominent role both here and in "Liberty for Slaves."

"Then and Now," published in 1900, glances retrospectively at American history since emancipation, and argues that the nation is finally pulling out of a dark night of enslavement and emerging into a brighter day. It reflects

---

[1] Cited in Hallie Quinn Brown, ed., *Homespun Heroines and other Women of Distinction* (Xenia, OH: Aidine Publishing, 1926), 102.

Harper's advocacy of both racial and gender progress in a Christian environment. In keeping with her domestic concerns, Harper depicts this new era as one in which black families will now stay together, and mothers and fathers can now protect their own children in their own homes. Here she also rehearses a litany of names, including abolitionists Benjamin Lundy, William Lloyd Garrison, and Frederick Douglass; John Albion Andrew, the Civil War governor of Massachusetts who facilitated the creation of black military units; President Abraham Lincoln; and women's advocates Lucretia Mott and Lucy Stone, the latter being the first woman in the United States to revert to her birth name after marriage. She concludes with a homage to nation and God:

> Now God be praised from sea to sea,
> Our flag floats o'er a country free.

Liberty for Slaves (1857)

Could we trace the record of every human heart, the aspirations of every immortal soul, perhaps we would find no man so imbruted and degraded that we could not trace the word liberty either written in living characters upon the soul or hidden away in some nook or corner of the heart. The law of liberty is the law of God, and is antecedent to all human legislation. It existed in the mind of Deity when He hung the first world upon its orbit and gave it liberty to gather light from the central sun.

Some people say, set the slaves free. Did you ever think, if the slaves were free, they would steal everything they could lay their hands on from now till the day of their death—that they would steal more than two thousand millions of dollars? (applause) Ask Maryland, with her tens of thousands of slaves, if she is not prepared for freedom, and hear her answer: "I help supply the coffee-gangs of the South." Ask Virginia, with her hundreds of thousands of slaves, if she is not weary with her merchandise of blood and anxious to shake the gory traffic from her hands, and hear her reply: "Though fertility has covered my soil, though a genial sky bends over my hills and vales, though I hold in my hand a wealth of water-power enough to turn the spindles to clothe the world, yet, with all these advantages, one of my chief staples has been the sons and daughters I send to the human market and human shambles." (applause) Ask the farther South, and all the cotton-growing States chime in, "We have need of fresh supplies to fill the ranks of those whose lives have gone out in unrequited toil on our distant plantations."

A hundred thousand new-born babes are annually added to the victims of slavery; twenty thousand lives are annually sacrificed on the plantations of the South. Such a sight should send a thrill of horror through the nerves of civilization and impel the heart of humanity to lofty deeds. So it might, if men had not found out a fearful alchemy by which this blood can be transformed into gold. Instead of listening to the cry of agony, they listen to the ring of dollars and stoop down to pick up the coin. (applause)

But a few months since a man escaped from bondage and found a temporary shelter almost beneath the shadow of Bunker Hill. Had that man stood upon the deck of an Austrian ship, beneath the shadow of the house of the Hapsburgs, he would have found protection. Had he been wrecked upon an island or colony of Great Britain, the waves of the tempest-lashed ocean would have washed him deliverance. Had he landed upon the territory of vine-encircled France and a Frenchman had reduced him to a thing and brought him here beneath the protection of our institutions and our laws, for such a nefarious deed that Frenchman would have lost his citizenship in France. Beneath the feebler light which glimmers from the Koran, the Bey of Tunis would have granted him freedom in his own dominions. Beside the ancient pyramids of Egypt he would have found liberty, for the soil laved by the glorious Nile is now consecrated to freedom. But from Boston harbour, made memorable by the infusion of three-penny taxed tea, Boston in its proximity to the plains of Lexington and Concord, Boston almost beneath the shadow of Bunker Hill and almost in sight of Plymouth Rock, he is thrust back from liberty and manhood and reconverted into a chattel. You have heard that, down South, they keep bloodhounds to hunt slaves. Ye bloodhounds, go back to your kennels; when you fail to catch the flying fugitive, when his stealthy tread is heard in the place where the bones of the revolutionary sires repose, the ready North is base enough to do your shameful service. (applause)

Slavery is mean, because it tramples on the feeble and weak. A man comes with his affidavits from the South and hurries me before a commissioner; upon that evidence *ex parte* and alone he hitches me to the car of slavery and trails my womanhood in the dust. I stand at the threshold of the Supreme Court and ask for justice, simple justice. Upon my tortured heart is thrown the mocking words, "You are a negro; you have no rights which white men are bound to respect"! (loud and long-continued applause) Had it been my lot to have lived beneath the Crescent instead of the Cross, had injustice and violence been heaped upon my head as a Mohammedan woman, as a member of a common faith, I might have demanded justice and been listened to by the Pasha, the Bey or the Vizier; but when I come here to ask for justice, men tell me, "We have no higher law than the Constitution." (applause)

But I will not dwell on the dark side of the picture. God is on the side of freedom, and any cause that has God on its side, I care not how much it may be trampled upon, how much it may be trailed in the dust, is sure to triumph. The message of Jesus Christ is on the side of freedom, "I come to preach deliverance to the captives, the opening of the prison doors to them that are bound." The truest and noblest hearts in the land are on the side of freedom. They may be hissed at by slavery's minions, their names cast out as evil, their characters branded with fanaticism, but O, *"To side with Truth is noble when we share her humble crust Ere the cause bring fame and profit and it's prosperous to be just."*

May I not, in conclusion, ask every honest, noble heart, every seeker after truth and justice, if they will not also be on the side of freedom. Will you not resolve that you will abate neither heart nor hope till you hear the death-knell of human bondage sounded, and over the black ocean of slavery shall be heard a song, more exulting than the song of Miriam when it floated o'er Egypt's dark sea, the requiem of Egypt's ruined hosts and the anthem of the deliverance of Israel's captive people? (great applause)

Moses: A Story of the Nile (1869)

THE PARTING. — CHAPTER I.

Moses.

Kind and gracious princess, more than friend,
I've come to thank thee for thy goodness,
And to breathe into thy generous ears
My last and sad farewell. I go to join
The fortunes of my race, and to put aside
All other bright advantages, save
The approval of my conscience and the meed
Of rightly doing.

Princess.

What means, my son, this strange election?
What wild chimera floats across thy mind?
What sudden impulse moves thy soul? Thou who

Hast only trod the court of kings, why seek
Instead the paths of labor? Thou, whose limbs
Have known no other garb than that which well
Befits our kingly state, why rather choose
The badge of servitude and toil?

Moses.

Let me tell thee, gracious princess; 'tis no
Sudden freak nor impulse wild that moves my mind.
I feel an earnest purpose binding all
My soul unto a strong resolve, which bids
Me put aside all other ends and aims,
Until the hour shall come when God—the God
Our fathers loved and worshipped—shall break our chains,
And lead our willing feet to freedom.

Princess.

Listen to me, Moses: thou art young,
And the warm blood of youth flushes thy veins
Like generous wine; thou wearest thy manhood
Like a crown; but what king e'er cast
His diadem in the dust, to be trampled
Down by every careless foot? Thou hast
Bright dreams and glowing hopes; could'st thou not live
Them out as well beneath the radiance
Of our throne as in the shadow of those
Bondage-darkened huts?

Moses.

Within those darkened huts my mother plies her tasks,
My father bends to unrequited toil;
And bitter tears moisten the bread my brethren eat.
And when I gaze upon their cruel wrongs
The very purple on my limbs seems drenched
With blood, the warm blood of my own kindred race;
And then thy richest viands pall upon my taste,
And discord jars in every tone of song.
I cannot live in pleasure while they faint
In pain.

Princess.

How like a dream the past floats back: it seems
But yesterday when I lay tossing upon
My couch of pain, a torpor creeping through
Each nerve, a fever coursing through my veins.
And there I lay, dreaming of lilies fair,
Of lotus flowers and past delights, and all
The bright, glad hopes, that give to early life
Its glow and flush; and thus day after day
Dragged its slow length along, until, one morn,
The breath of lilies, fainting on the air,
Floated into my room, and then I longed once more
To gaze upon the Nile, as on the face
Of a familiar friend, whose absence long
Had made a mournful void within the heart.
I summoned to my side my maids, and bade
Them place my sandals on my feet, and lead
Me to the Nile, where I might bathe my weary
Limbs within the cooling flood, and gather
Healing from the sacred stream.
I sought my favorite haunt, and, bathing, found
New tides of vigor coursing through my veins.
Refreshed, I sat me down to weave a crown of lotus leaves
And lilies fair, and while I sat in a sweet
Revery, dreaming of life and hope, I saw
A little wicker-basket hidden among
The flags and lilies of the Nile, and I called
My maidens and said, "Nillias and Osiria
Bring me that little ark which floats beside
The stream." They ran and brought me a precious burden.
'Twas an ark woven with rushes and daubed
With slime, and in it lay a sleeping child;
His little hand amid his clustering curls,
And a bright flush upon his glowing cheek.
He wakened with a smile, and reached out his hand
To meet the welcome of the mother's kiss,
When strange faces met his gaze, and he drew back
With a grieved, wondering look, while disappointment
Shook the quivering lip that missed the mother's

Wonted kiss, and the babe lifted his voice and wept.
Then my heart yearned towards him, and I resolved
That I would brave my father's wrath and save
The child; but while I stood gazing upon
His wondrous beauty, I saw beside me
A Hebrew girl, her eyes bent on me
With an eager, questioning look, and drawing
Near, she timidly said, "shall I call a nurse?"
I bade her go; she soon returned, and with her
Came a woman of the Hebrew race, whose
Sad, sweet, serious eyes seemed overflowing
With a strange and sudden joy. I placed the babe
Within her arms and said, "Nurse this child for me;"
And the babe nestled there like one at home,
While o'er the dimples of his face rippled
The brightest, sweetest smiles, and I was well
Content to leave him in her care; and well
Did she perform her part. When many days had
Passed she brought the child unto the palace;
And one morning, while I sat toying with
His curls and listening to the prattle of his
Untrained lips, my father, proud and stately,
Saw me bending o'er the child and said,
"Charmian, whose child is this? who of my lords
Calls himself father to this goodly child?
He surely must be a happy man."
     Then I said, "Father, he is mine. He is a
Hebrew child that I have saved from death." He
Suddenly recoiled, as if an adder
Had stung him, and said, "Charmian, take that
Child hence. How darest thou bring a member
Of that mean and servile race within my doors?
Nay, rather let me send for Nechos, whose
Ready sword shall rid me of his hateful presence."
Then kneeling at his feet, and catching
Hold of his royal robes, I said, "Not so,
Oh! honored father, he is mine; I snatched
Him from the hungry jaws of death, and foiled
The greedy crocodile of his prey; he has
Eaten bread within thy palace walls, and thy

Salt lies upon his fresh young lips; he has
A claim upon thy mercy."
  "Charmian," he said
"I have decreed that every man child of that
Hated race shall die. The oracles have said
The pyramids shall wane before their shadow,
And from them a star shall rise whose light shall
Spread over earth a baleful glow; and this is why
I root them from the land; their strength is weakness
To my throne. I shut them from the light lest they
Bring darkness to my kingdom. Now, Charmian,
Give me up the child, and let him die."
Then clasping the child closer to my heart,
I said, "the pathway to his life is through my own;
Around that life I throw my heart, a wall
Of living, loving clay." Dark as the thunder
Clouds of distant lands became my father's brow,
And his eyes flashed with the fierce lightnings
Of his wrath; but while I plead, with eager
Eyes upturned, I saw a sudden change come
Over him; his eyes beamed with unwonted
Tenderness, and he said, "Charmian, arise,
Thy prayer is granted; just then thy dead mother
Came to thine eyes, and the light of Asenath
Broke over thy face. Asenath was the light
Of my home; the star that faded out too
Suddenly from my dwelling, and left my life
To darkness, grief and pain, and for her sake,
Not thine, I'll spare the child." And thus I saved
Thee twice—once from the angry sword and once
From the devouring flood. Moses, thou art
Doubly mine; as such I claimed thee then, as such
I claim thee now. I've nursed no other child
Upon my knee, and pressed upon no other
Lips the sweetest kisses of my love, and now,
With rash and careless hand, thou dost thrust aside that love.
There was a painful silence, a silence
So hushed and still that you might have almost
Heard the hurried breathing of one and the quick
Throbbing of the other's heart: for Moses,

He was slow of speech, but she was eloquent
With words of tenderness and love, and had breathed
Her full heart into her lips; but there was
Firmness in the young man's choice, and he beat back
The opposition of her lips with the calm
Grandeur of his will, and again he essayed to speak.

Moses.

Gracious lady, thou remembrest well
The Hebrew nurse to whom thou gavest thy foundling.
That woman was my mother; from her lips I
Learned the grand traditions of our race that float,
With all their weird and solemn beauty, around
Our wrecked and blighted fortunes. How oft!
With kindling eye and glowing cheek, forgetful
Of the present pain, she would lead us through
The distant past: the past, hallowed by deeds
Of holy faith and lofty sacrifice.
How she would tell us of Abraham,
The father of our race, that he dwelt in Ur;
Of the Chaldees, and when the Chaldean king
Had called him to his sacrifice, that he
Had turned from his dumb idols to the living
God, and wandered out from kindred, home a race,
Led by his faith in God alone: and she would
Tell us,—(we were three,) my brother Aaron,
The Hebrew girl thou sentest to call a nurse,
And I, her last, her loved and precious child;
She would tell us that one day our father
Abraham heard a voice, bidding him offer
Up in sacrifice the only son of his
Beautiful and beloved Sarah; that the father's
Heart shrank not before the bitter test of faith,
But he resolved to give his son to God
As a burnt offering upon Moriah's mount;
That the uplifted knife glittered in the morning
Sun, when, sweeter than the music of a thousand
Harps, he heard a voice bidding him stay his hand,
And spare the child; and how his faith, like gold

Tried in the fiercest fire, shone brighter through
Its fearful test. And then she would tell us
Of a promise, handed down from sire to son,
That God, the God our fathers loved and worshiped,
Would break our chains, and bring to us a great
Deliverance; that we should dwell in peace
Beneath our vines and palms, our flocks and herds
Increase, and joyful children crowd our streets;
And then she would lift her eyes unto the far
Off hills and tell us of the patriarchs
Of our line, who sleep in distant graves within
That promised land; and now I feel the hour
Draws near which brings deliverance to our race.

Princess.

These are but the dreams of thy young fancy;
I cannot comprehend thy choice. I have heard
Of men who have waded through slaughter
to a throne; of proud ambitions, struggles
fierce and wild for some imagined good; of men
Who have even cut in twain the crimson threads
That lay between them and a throne; but I
Never heard of men resigning ease for toil,
The splendor of a palace for the squalor
of a hut, and casting down a diadem
to wear a servile badge.
    Sadly she gazed
Upon the fair young face lit with its lofty
faith and high resolves—the dark prophetic eyes
Which seemed to look beyond the present pain
Unto the future greatness of his race.
As she stood before him in the warm
Loveliness of her ripened womanhood,
Her languid eyes glowed with unwonted fire,
And the bright tropical blood sent its quick
Flushes o'er the olive of her cheek, on which
Still lay the lingering roses of her girlhood.
Grief, wonder, and surprise flickered like shadows
O'er her face as she stood slowly crushing

With unconscious hand the golden tassels
Of her crimson robe. She had known life only
By its brightness, and could not comprehend
The grandeur of the young man's choice; but she
Felt her admiration glow before the earnest
Faith that tore their lives apart and led him
To another destiny. She had hoped to see
The crown of Egypt on his brow, the sacred
Leopard skin adorn his shoulders, and his seat
The throne of the proud Pharaoh's; but now her
Dream had faded out and left a bitter pang
Of anguish in its stead. And thus they parted,
She to brood in silence o'er her pain, and he
To take his mission from the hands of God
And lead his captive race to freedom.
With silent lips but aching heart she bowed
Her queenly head and let him pass, and he
Went forth to share the fortune of his race,
Esteeming that as better far than pleasures
Bought by sin and gilded o'er with vice.
And he had chosen well, for on his brow
God poured the chrism of a holy work.
And thus anointed he has stood a bright
Ensample through the changing centuries of time.

Flight Into Midian.—Chapter III.

The love of Moses for his race soon found
A stern expression. Pharaoh was building
A pyramid; ambitious, cold and proud,
He scrupled not at means to gain his ends.
When he feared the growing power of Israel
He stained his hands in children's blood, and held
A carnival of death in Goshen; but now
He wished to hand his name and memory
Down unto the distant ages, and instead
Of lading that memory with the precious
Fragrance of the kindest deeds and words, he
Essayed to write it out in stone, as cold
And hard, and heartless as himself.

And Israel was
The fated race to whom the cruel tasks
Were given. Day after day a cry of wrong
And anguish, some dark deed of woe and crime,
Came to the ear of Moses, and he said,
"These reports are ever harrowing my soul;
I will go unto the fields where Pharaoh's
Officers exact their labors, and see
If these things be so—if they smite the feeble
At their tasks, and goad the aged on to toils
Beyond their strength—if neither age nor sex
Is spared the cruel smiting of their rods."
And Moses went to see his brethren.
        'Twas eventide,
And the laborers were wending their way
Unto their lowly huts. 'Twas a sad sight,—
The young girls walked without the bounding steps
Of youth, with faces prematurely old,
As if the rosy hopes and sunny promises
Of life had never flushed their cheeks with girlish
Joy; and there were men whose faces seemed to say,
We bear our lot in hopeless pain, we've bent unto
Our burdens until our shoulders fit them,
And as slaves we crouch beneath our servitude
And toil. But there were men whose souls were cast
In firmer moulds, men with dark secretive eyes,
Which seemed to say, to day we bide our time,
And hide our wrath in every nerve, and only
Wait a fitting hour to strike the hands that press
Us down. Then came the officers of Pharaoh;
They trod as lords, their faces flushed with pride
And insolence, watching the laborers
Sadly wending their way from toil to rest.
And Moses' heart swelled with a mighty pain; sadly
Musing, he sought a path that led him
From the busy haunts of men. But even there
The cruel wrong trod in his footsteps; he heard
A heavy groan, then harsh and bitter words,
And, looking back, he saw an officer

Of Pharaoh smiting with rough and cruel hand
An aged man. Then Moses' wrath o'erflowed
His lips, and every nerve did tremble
With a sense of wrong, and bounding forth he
Cried unto the smiter, "Stay thy hand; seest thou
That aged man? His head is whiter than our
Desert sands; his limbs refuse to do thy
Bidding because thy cruel tasks have drained
Away their strength." The Egyptian raised his eyes
With sudden wonder; who was this that dared dispute
His power? Only a Hebrew youth. His
Proud lip curved in scornful anger, and he
Waved a menace with his hand, saying, "back
To thy task base slave, nor dare resist the will
Of Pharaoh." Then Moses' wrath o'erleaped the bounds
Of prudence, and with a heavy blow he felled
The smiter to the earth, and Israel had
One tyrant less. Moses saw the mortal paleness
Chase the flushes from the Egyptian's face,
The whitening lips that breathed no more defiance,
And the relaxing tension of the well knit limbs;
And when he knew that he was dead, he hid
Him in the sand and left him to his rest.
    Another day Moses walked
Abroad, and saw two brethren striving
For mastery; and then his heart grew full
Of tender pity. They were brethren, sharers
Of a common wrong: should not their wrongs more
Closely bind their hearts, and union, not division,
Be their strength? And feeling thus, he said, "ye
Are brethren, wherefore do ye strive together?"
But they threw back his words in angry tones
And asked if he had come to judge them, and would
Mete to them the fate of the Egyptian?
Then Moses knew the sand had failed to keep
His secret, that his life no more was safe
In Goshen, and he fled unto the deserts
Of Arabia and became a shepherd
For the priest of Midian.

Chapter VI.

But Pharaoh was strangely blind, and turning.
From his first-born and his dead, with Egypt's wail
Scarce still upon his ear, he asked which way had
Israel gone? They told him that they journeyed
Towards the mighty sea, and were encamped
Near Baalzephn.
Then Pharaoh said, "the wilderness will hem them in,
The mighty sea will roll its barriers in front,
And with my chariots and my warlike men
I'll bring them back, or mete them out their graves."
    Then Pharaoh's officers arose
And gathered up the armies of the king,
And made his chariots ready for pursuit.
With proud escutcheons blazoned to the sun,
In his chariot of ivory, pearl and gold,
Pharaoh rolled out of Egypt; and with him
Rode his mighty men, their banners floating
On the breeze, their spears and armor glittering
In the morning light; and Israel saw,
With fainting hearts, their old oppressors on their
Track: then women wept in hopeless terror;
Children hid their faces in their mothers' robes,
And strong men bowed their heads in agony and dread;
And then a bitter, angry murmur rose,—
"Were there no graves in Egypt, that thou hast
Brought us here to die?"
Then Moses lifted up his face, aglow
With earnest faith in God, and bade their fainting hearts
Be strong and they should his salvation see.
"Stand still," said Moses to the fearful throng
Whose hearts were fainting in the wild, "Stand still."
Ah, that was Moses' word, but higher and greater
Came God's watchword for the hour, and not for that
Alone, but all the coming hours of time.
"Speak ye unto the people and bid them
Forward go; stretch thy hand across the waters
And smite them with thy rod." And Moses smote

The restless sea; the waves stood up in heaps,
Then lay as calm and still as lips that just
Had tasted death. The secret-loving sea
Laid bare her coral caves and iris-tinted
Floor; that wall of flood which lined the people's
Way was God's own wondrous masonry;
The signal pillar sent to guide them through the wild
Moved its dark shadow till it fronted Egypt's
Camp, but hung in fiery splendor, a light
To Israel's path. Madly rushed the hosts
Of Pharaoh upon the people's track, when
The solemn truth broke on them—that God
For Israel fought. With cheeks in terror
Blenching, and eyes astart with fear, "let
Us flee," they cried, "from Israel, for their God
Doth fight against us; he is battling on their side."
They had trusted in their chariots, but now
That hope was vain; God had loosened every
Axle and unfastened every wheel, and each
Face did gather blackness and each heart stood still
With fear, as the livid lightnings glittered
And the thunder roared and muttered on the air,
And they saw the dreadful ruin that shuddered
O'er their heads, for the waves began to tremble
And the wall of flood to bend. Then arose
A cry of terror, baffled hate and hopeless dread,
A gurgling sound of horror, as "the waves
Came madly dashing, wildly crashing, seeking
Out their place again," and the flower and pride
Of Egypt sank as lead within the sea
Till the waves threw back their corpses cold and stark
Upon the shore, and the song of Israel's
Triumph was the requiem of their foes.
Oh the grandeur of that triumph; up the cliffs
And down the valleys, o'er the dark and restless
Sea, rose the people's shout of triumph, going
Up in praise to God, and the very air
Seemed joyous, for the choral song of millions
Throbbed upon its viewless wings.

Then another song of triumph rose in accents
Soft and clear; "'twas the voice of Moses' sister
Rising in the tide of song. The warm blood
Of her childhood seemed dancing in her veins;
The roses of her girlhood were flushing
On her cheek, and her eyes flashed out the splendor
Of long departed days, for time itself seemed
Pausing, and she lived the past again; again
The Nile flowed by her; she was watching by the stream,
A little ark of rushes where her baby brother lay;
The tender tide of rapture swept o'er her soul again
She had felt when Pharaoh's daughter had claimed
Him as her own, and her mother wept for joy
Above her rescued son. Then again she saw
Him choosing "'twixt Israel's pain and sorrow
And Egypt's pomp and pride." But now he stood
Their leader triumphant on that shore, and loud
She struck the cymbals as she led the Hebrew women
In music, dance and song, as they shouted out
Triumphs in sweet and glad refrains.

Miriam's Song.

A wail in the palace, a wail in the hut,
    The midnight is shivering with dread,
And Egypt wakes up with a shriek and a sob
    To mourn for her first-born and dead.
In the morning glad voices greeted the light,
    As the Nile with its splendor was flushed;
At midnight silence had melted their tones,
    And their music forever is hushed.
In the morning the princes of palace and court
    To the heir of the kingdom bowed down;
'Tis midnight, pallid and stark in his shroud
    He dreams not of kingdom or crown.
As a monument blasted and blighted by God,
    Through the ages proud Pharaoh shall stand,
All seamed with the vengeance and scarred with the wrath
    That leaped from God's terrible hand.

Chapter VIII.

It was a weary thing to bear the burden
Of that restless and rebellious race. With
Sinai's thunders almost crashing in their ears,
They made a golden calf, and in the desert
Spread an idol's feast, and sung the merry songs
They had heard when Mizraim's sons bowed down before
Their vain and heathen gods; and thus for many years
Did Moses bear the evil manners of his race—
Their angry murmurs, fierce regrets and strange
Forgetfulness of God. Born slaves, they did not love
The freedom of the wild more than their pots of flesh.
And pleasant savory things once gathered
From the gardens of the Nile.
If slavery only laid its weight of chains
Upon the weary, aching limbs, e'en then
It were a curse; but when it frets through nerve
And flesh and eats into the weary soul,
Oh then it is a thing for every human
Heart to loathe, and this was Israel's fate;
For when the chains were shaken from their limbs,
They failed to strike the impress from their souls.
While he who'd basked beneath the radiance
Of a throne, ne'er turned regretful eyes upon
The past, nor sighed to grasp again the pleasures
Once resigned; but the saddest trial was
To see the light and joy fade from their faces
When the faithless spies spread through their camp
Their ill report; and when the people wept
In hopeless unbelief and turned their faces
Egyptward, and asked a captain from their bands
To lead them back where they might bind anew
Their broken chains, when God arose and shut
The gates of promise on their lives, and left
Their bones to bleach beneath Arabia's desert sands.
But though they slumbered in the wild, they died
With broader freedom on their lips, and for their
Little ones did God reserve the heritage
So rudely thrust aside.

The Death of Moses.—Chapter IX.

His work was done; his blessing lay
Like precious ointment on his people's head,
And God's great peace was resting on his soul.
His life had been a lengthened sacrifice,
A thing of deep devotion to his race,
Since first he turned his eyes on Egypt's gild
And glow, and clasped their fortunes in his hand
And held them with a firm and constant grasp.
But now his work was done; his charge was laid
In Joshua's hand, and men of younger blood
Were destined to possess the land and pass
Through Jordan to the other side. He too
Had hoped to enter there—to tread the soil
Made sacred by the memories of his
Kindred dead, and rest till life's calm close beneath
The sheltering vines and stately palms of that
Fair land; that hope had colored all his life's
Young dreams and sent its mellowed flushes o'er
His later years; but God's decree was otherwise.
And so he bowed his meekened soul in calm
Submission to the word, which bade him climb
To Nebo's highest peak, and view the pleasant land
From Jordan's swells unto the calmer ripples
Of the tideless sea, then die with all its
Loveliness in sight.
As he passed from Moab's grassy vale to climb
The rugged mount, the people stood in mournful groups,
Some, with quivering lips and tearful eyes,
Reaching out unconscious hands, as if to stay
His steps and keep him ever at their side, while
Others gazed with reverent awe upon
The calm and solemn beauty on his aged brow,
The look of loving trust and lofty faith
Still beaming from an eye that neither care
Nor time had dimmed. As he passed upward, tender
Blessings, earnest prayers and sad farewells rose
On each wave of air, then died in one sweet
Murmur of regretful love; and Moses stood

Alone on Nebo's mount.

    Alone! not one
Of all that mighty throng who had trod with him
In triumph through the parted flood was there.
Aaron had died in Hor, with son and brother
By his side; and Miriam too was gone.
But kindred hands had made her grave, and Kadesh
Held her dust. But he was all alone; nor wife
Nor child was there to clasp in death his hand,
And bind around their bleeding hearts the precious
Parting words. And yet he was not all alone,
For God's great presence flowed around his path
And stayed him in that solemn hour.

    He stood upon the highest peak of Nebo,
And saw the Jordan chafing through its gorges,
Its banks made bright by scarlet blooms
And purple blossoms. The placid lakes
And emerald meadows, the snowy crest
Of distant mountains, the ancient rocks
That dripped with honey, the hills all bathed
In light and beauty; the shady groves
And peaceful vistas, the vines opprest
With purple riches, the fig trees fruit-crowned
Green and golden, the pomegranates with crimson
Blushes, the olives with their darker clusters,
Rose before him like a vision, full of beauty
And delight. Gazed he on the lovely landscape
Till it faded from his view, and the wing
Of death's sweet angel hovered o'er the mountain's
Crest, and he heard his garments rustle through
The watches of the night.

    Then another, fairer, vision
Broke upon his longing gaze; 'twas the land
Of crystal fountains, love and beauty, joy
And light, for the pearly gates flew open,
And his ransomed soul went in. And when morning
O'er the mountain fringed each crag and peak with light,
Cold and lifeless lay the leader. God had touched
His eyes with slumber, giving his beloved sleep.

Oh never on that mountain
Was seen a lovelier sight
Than the troupe of fair young angels
That gathered 'round the dead.
With gentle hands they bore him,
That bright and shining train,
From Nebo's lonely mountain
To sleep in Moab's vale.
But they sung no mornful dirges,
No solemn requiems said,
And the soft wave of their pinions
Made music as they trod.
But no one heard them passing,
None saw their chosen grave;
It was the angels secret
Where Moses should be laid.
And when the grave was finished,
They trod with golden sandals
Above the sacred spot,
And the brightest, fairest flowers
Sprang up beneath their tread.
Nor broken turf, nor hillock
Did e'er reveal that grave,
And truthful lips have never said
We know where he is laid.

Then and Now (1895)

"Build me a nation," said the Lord.
The distant nations heard the word,
Build me a nation true and strong,
Bar out the old world's hate and wrong;
For men had traced with blood and tears
The trail of weary wasting years,
And torn and bleeding martyrs trod
Through fire and torture up to God.

While in the hollow of his hand
God hid the secret of our land,

Men warred against their fiercest foes,
And kingdoms fell and empires rose,
Till, weary of the old world strife,
Men sought for broader, freer life,
And plunged into the ocean's foam
To find another, better home.

And, like a vision fair and bright
The new world broke upon their sight.
Men grasped the prize, grew proud and strong,
And cursed the land with crime and wrong.
The Indian stood despoiled of lands,
The Negro bound with servile bands,
Oppressed through weary years of toil,
His blood and tears bedewed the soil.

Then God arose in dreadful wrath,
And judgment streamed around his path;
His hand the captive's fetters broke,
His lightnings shattered every yoke.
As Israel through the Red sea trod,
Led by the mighty hand of God,
They passed to freedom through a flood,
Whose every wave and surge was blood.

And slavery, with its crime and shame,
Went down in wrath and blood and flame
The land was billowed-o'er with graves
Where men had lived and died as slaves.
Four and thirty years—what change since then!
Beings once chattles now are men;
Over the gloom of slavery's night,
Has flashed the dawn of freedom's light.

To-day no mother with anguish wild
Kneels and implores that her darling child
Shall not be torn from her bleeding heart,
With its quivering tendrils rent apart.
The father may soothe his child to sleep,

And watch his slumbers calm and deep.
No tyrant's tread will disturb his rest
Where freedom dwells as a welcome guest.

His walls may be bare of pictured grace,
His fireside the lowliest place;
But the wife and children sheltered there
Are his to defend and guard with care.
Where haughty tyrants once bore rule
Are ballot-box and public school.
The old slave-pen of former days
Gives place to fanes of prayer and praise.

To-night we would bring our meed of praise
To noble friends of darker days;
The men and women crowned with light,
The true and tried in our gloomy night.
To Lundy, whose heart was early stirred
To speak for freedom an earnest word;
To Garrison, valiant, true and strong,
Whose face was as flint against our wrong.

And Phillips, the peerless, grand and brave,
A tower of strength to the outcast slave.
Earth has no marble too pure and white
To enrol his name in golden light.
Our Douglass, too, with his massive brain,
Who plead our cause with his broken chain,
And helped to hurl from his bloody seat
The curse that writhed and died at his feet.

And Governor Andrew, who, looking back,
Saw none he despised, though poor and black;
And Harriet Beecher, whose glowing pen
Corroded the chains of fettered men.
To-night with greenest laurels we'll crown
North Elba's grave where sleeps John Brown,
Who made the gallows an altar high,
And showed how a brave old man could die.

And Lincoln, our martyred President,
Who returned to his God with chains he had rent.
And Sumner, amid death's icy chill,
Leaving to Hoar his Civil Rights Bill.
And let us remember old underground,
With all her passengers northward bound,
The train that ran till it ceased to pay,
With all her dividends given away.

Nor let it be said that we have forgot
The women who stood with Lucretia Mott;
Nor her who to the world was known
By the simple name of Lucy Stone.
A tribute unto a host of others
Who knew that men though black were brothers,
Who battled against our nation's sin,
Whose graves are thick whose ranks are thin.
Oh, people chastened in the fire,
To nobler, grander things aspire.

FOUR

⚭ Frank A. Rollin
(*1847–1901*)

FRANCES ANNE ROLLIN WAS BORN free in Charleston, South Carolina, to Margaretta and William Rollin, refugees from the Dominican Republic. William, a successful lumber merchant, brought up his five daughters in wealth and privilege, sending Frances to the Institute for Colored Youth, a Quaker school in Philadelphia, during the Civil War. Upon her return to Charleston, she taught at a school supported by the American Missionary Association (AMA). During that time, she was refused first-class accommodations on a steamer during a summer trip to Beaufort, South Carolina, an incident that inspired her to lodge a discrimination complaint with the Freedman's Bureau. During the proceedings for this early civil rights victory, Rollins met Major Martin R. Delany, who was, from 1865 to 1868, the head of the Freedman's Bureau in the Hilton Head Island region of South Carolina. Delany admired Rollin's pluck, and when she told him of her literary aspirations, he suggested that she write his biography. After gathering documents from Delany, as well as a promise from him for eventual financial remuneration, Rollins traveled to Boston in 1867 to complete the project.

Rollin could not have picked a more inspiring moment to work in cosmopolitan Boston. Although Delany was never able to procure funds to support Rollin's writing, she found work as a seamstress and secretary, filling her off hours with reading, researching, and socializing amid the large

Source: Frank A. Rollin, *The Life and Public Services of Martin R. Delany* (Boston: Lee and Shepard, 1883), 7–11, 43–46, 292–294, 298–301.

group of black intellectuals and white reformers who comprised Boston's elite intellectual community. "Writing as hard as ever," she recounted in her diary entry on January 3, 1868, "I know not with what success I shall meet, but I feel there is a strength in the endeavor which will be of service to me hereafter."[1] Rollin attended a liberal church, volunteered with aid societies, and participated in a séance or two as she immersed herself in the diversity, racial and religious, of her temporary home. The same year she arrived, a collection of freethinkers formed the Free Religious Association as an alternative to Christians seeking nondenominational outposts of spiritual conversation and moral debate. According to Rollin's diary, she attended association talks by abolitionists Amos Bronson Alcott, Ralph Waldo Emerson, Octavius Brooks Frothingham, James Freeman Clark, and Thomas Higginson, men who lectured on the nature of the soul, the meaning of the divine spirit, and the imperative of liberty in civilized society. Along with this all-star cast of religious thinkers, Rollin also befriended liberal lions William Wells Brown, William Cooper Nell, Wendell Phillips, and William Lloyd Garrison.

This cosmopolitan context infuses the optimism of Rollin's biographical reconstruction. Rollin's portrait is an ardent rejoinder to the popular image of black officials which was at that time "that of an ignorant, graft-ridden, erstwhile slave, a tool of sleazy carpetbaggers who was drunk on his own self-importance and intent on legislating the amalgamation of whites and blacks in every sphere of life from the public schoolroom to the private bedroom."[2] *Life and Public Services of Martin R. Delany* honors Delany as the exemplar of black manhood, as a self-made success modeling the highest values of human decency. In the selections excerpted below, Rollin emphasizes the war's clarifying aspect, suggesting that people were tested and purified by the experience. Note in particular her suggestion that the achievements of Delany could be interpreted as "indicative of the capability and progress of the race whose proud representative he is." Republicanism and Christianity are collaborating elements of this new battle-scarred society, encouraging individual discipline and social equality. Yet despite her ease with a presumptive Christendom, Rollin also emphasizes the multiple voluntary organizations and institutional networks of which Delany was a loyal member. She even selects as a telling incident one in which Delany likens himself to a

---

[1] Dorothy Sterling, *We Are Your Sisters: Black Women in the Nineteenth Century* (W.W. Norton & Co., 1985), 455.
[2] William L. Andrews, "Introduction," in *Two Biographies by African-American Women* (New York: Oxford University Press, 1991), xl.

Millerite, a member of an antebellum new religious movement. Only through the free expression of ideas and practice of religion might American society, and its black citizens, experience true enlightenment. Delany, Rollin argued, relied upon his "own identity" as "the blackest of the black." He never pretended to be anything other than what he was.

Published under a pseudonym in the summer of 1868, *Life and Public Services of Martin R. Delany* was reprinted in 1883. Upon appearing, it was touted as the first full-length biography written by an African American. Never again would Rollin achieve such literary heights. She returned to South Carolina to provide secretarial assistance for William J. Whipper, a northern-born lawyer and legislator whom she eventually married. After enduring ten years of his gambling and drinking, she took their three children to Washington, D.C., in 1881, where she worked as a clerk and court stenographer, eventually sending all of her children to Howard University. She died of consumption in Beaufort, South Carolina, on October 17, 1901.

The Life and Public Services of Martin R. Delany (1883)

INTRODUCTION

At the close of every revolution in a country, there is observed an effort for the gradual and general expulsion of all that is effete, or tends to retard progress; and as the nation comes forth from its purification with its existence renewed and invigorated, a better and higher civilization is promised.

Before entering upon such an effort, it is usual to compute the aid rendered in the past struggle for national existence, and the present status of the auxiliaries in connection with it. In this manner, as the sullen roar of battle ceases, as the war cloud fades out from our sky, we are enabled to look more soberly upon the stupendous revolution, its causes and teachings, and to consider the men and new measures developed through its agency, the material with which the country is to be reconstructed.

In reviewing the history of the late civil war, it will be found, as in former revolutions, that those who were able to master its magnitude were men who, prior to the occasion, were almost wholly unknown, or claimed but a local reputation. Measures which before were deemed impracticable and inexpedient, in the progress of the war were considered best adapted to meet the exigencies of the time. A race before persecuted, slandered, and brutalized, ostracized, socially and politically, have scattered the false theories of their enemies, and proved in every way their claim and identity to American citizenship in its every particular. While the war between sections has erased slavery from the statutes of the country, it has in nowise obliterated the inconsistent prejudice against color. Among the white Americans, since the rebellion, from the highest officer to the lowest subaltern, there is a recognized precedence for them, in view of their patriotism and valor in the hour of peril and treachery. They recognized their duty when Southerners had ignored it: for this we honor them; and none would gainsay an atom of the praise bestowed: the country had always honored and protected them at home and abroad, and in enhancing her prestige, they have added to their own as American citizens. But in the same dark hour of strife and treachery, there went forth from the despised and dusky sons of the republic a host, who, though faring differently, contributed no meagre offering to the cause of the Union. In the foremost rank of battle they stood, stimulated alone by their sublime faith in the future of their country, instead of being deterred by the disheartening experiences of the past. From their first hour in the rebellion to the last, theirs was a fierce, unequal contest; they were found enlisting, fighting, and even dying under circumstances from which the bravest Saxon would have been justified in shrinking. For them there was "death in the front and destruction in the rear"—torture and death as prisoners in the rebel lines, and the perils of the mob in many of the loyal cities awaiting them when seen in the United States uniform. Despite all opposition, they have traced their history in characters as indestructible as they are brilliant, to the confusion of their enemies. On every field, negro heroism and valor have been proved by them in a manner which has established for their race a grandeur of character in American annals, that, when read by the unprejudiced eyes of futurity, will gleam with increased splendor amid their unfavorable surroundings; while in song and story their deeds of prowess will live forever, reflecting the glories of Port Hudson, the criminal field of Olustee, and the holy memories which cluster about Fort Wagner.

Of an army of more than a quarter of a million men, less than a decade received promotion for their services. Lieutenant Stephen A. Swails, of Elmira, New York, a member of the Fifty-fourth Massachusetts Volunteers, had the honor of being first, for having signally distinguished himself both at Wagner and Olustee. Later followed the promotion of Lieutenants Dufree, Shorter, James T. Trotter, and Charles Mitchell, from the Fifty-fifth Massachusetts Volunteers; Lieutenants Peter Voglesang (Quartermaster), and Frank Welch, from the Fifty-fourth Massachusetts Volunteers. Dr. Alexander Augusta, of Canada, had been previously appointed surgeon, with the rank of major. Besides these, several complimentary promotions were given prior to the muster out of these two regiments. None of the officers above named have been retained in the service; one alone remains, who, during the rebellion, had attained the highest commission bestowed on any of the race by the government—that of Major of Infantry. Him whom the government had chosen for this position we have made the subject of this work. His great grasp of mind and fine executive ability eminently befitted him for the sphere, and the success which attends his measures renders him a distinct and conspicuous character at his post. His career throughout life has been very remarkable. Prior to his present appointment his name was familiar with every advance movement relative to the colored people: once it fell upon the ear of the terror-stricken Virginians, in connection with John Brown, of Ossowatomie; and scarcely had it been forgotten when it was borne back to us from the Statistical congress at London, encircled with the genius of Lord Brougham. To no more advantageous surroundings than were enjoyed by the masses he owes his successes; hence his achievements may be safely argued as indicative of the capability and progress of the race whose proud representative he is. The isolated and degraded position assigned the colored people precluding the possibility of gaining distinction, whenever one of their number lifts himself by the strength of his own character beyond the prescribed limits, ethnologists apologize for this violation of their established rules, charging it to some few drops of Saxon blood commingling with the African. But in the case of the individual of whom we write, he stands proudly before the country the blackest of the black, presenting in himself a giant's powers warped in chains, and evidencing in his splendid career the fallacy of the old partisan theory of Negro inferiority and degradation.

In this history will be noticed certain strong characteristics peculiarly his own, which are traceable more to the circumstances of his birth than his race. Aiming to render a faithful biography of this remarkable man, we narrate minutely his singularly active and eventful life, which, in view of the narrow limits apportioned to him, will bear favorable comparison with the great Americans of our time.

Charleston, S.C., October 19th, 1868.

CHAPTER IV

Moral Efforts

IN 1834 Major Delany was actively engaged in the organization of several associations for the relief of the poor of the city, and for the moral elevation of his people. Among them was the first total abstinence society ever formed among the colored people; and another known as the Philanthropic Society, which, while formed ostensibly for benevolent purposes, relative to the indigent of the city, was really the foundation of one of the great links connecting the slaves with their immediate friends in the North,—known as the "Underground Railroad,"—which, for long years, had baffled the slaveholders. Of its executive board he was for many years secretary.

The work contributed by this association constituted it the invaluable aid of the anti-slavery cause. Its efficiency may be judged from the fact that, while in its infancy, it is recorded that, within one year, not less than two hundred and sixty-nine persons were aided in escaping to Canada and elsewhere.

His sphere in life gave character to him, identifying him with a people and a time at once wonderful and perilous; wonderful that amid all the indignities and outrages heaped upon them, unrebuked by church or state, they did not degenerate into infidels and law-breakers, instead of being the Christian and truly law-abiding element of the republic—perilous, for the emissaries of the south instituted the fiendish spirit of mobbism, selecting either the dwellings or the business-places of the prominent colored men of the city. On one occasion, while this spirit was rife, they made an attack on the house of Mr. John B. Vashon. Major Delany, then quite a young man, but true to his principles of justice and humanity, and in view of future outrages, together with men of more mature age, called on Judge Pentland and other prominent citizens, to notify them that, though they were law abiding people, they did not intend to remain and be murdered in their houses without a most determined resistance to their assailants, as there was little or no assistance to their protection rendered by the authorities.

This resulted in his being chosen one of the special police from among the blacks and whites appointed in conjunction with the military called out by the intrepid mayor of Pittsburg, Dr. Jonas R. McClintock. Many were the occasions on which he stood among the foremost defenders against those mobs which at that time were more frequent than desirable.

The general grievances of the colored people of the North, occasioned solely on account of caste were a disgrace to the civilization of the age, and incompatible with the elements of our professed republicanism, which induced them to call an assemblage year after year, delegating their best talent to these, for the purpose of placing before the people the true condition of the colored people of the North, and also to devise methods of assisting the slaves of the South.

These conventions were held at an early date. As far back as 1829 we find a National Convention Meeting in Philadelphia, and where for many subsequent years they assembled; and enrolled on their list of members we find the honored names of Robert Douglass (the father of the artist), Hinton, Grice, Bowers, Burr, and Forten, together with Peck, Vashon, Shadd, and others whose names would give dignity and character to any convention.

Through a series of years these continued lifting up their voices against the existing political outrages to which they were subjected. To the last of these (about 1836) Major Delany, together with the Rev. Lewis Woodson, his former preceptor, who, being senior colleague, was chosen to represent other status of the community at large. On arriving at Philadelphia they found the Convention had been transferred to New York; and on their arrival at that point they were notified that it had been indefinitely postponed, chilling the hopes, doubtless, our young delegate with his maiden speech trembling on his lips, the "tremendous applause" ringing in his ears, and other fancies legitimately belonging to the role of a young man for the first time taking his place as a representative among the elders.

About three years after, he attended the Anti-slavery Convention at Pittsburgh. At this convention were many learned divines and a president of one of the universities of Western Pennsylvania. Here he brought upon himself the censure of some of his friends for saying in the course of his argument (concerning Jewish slavery as compared with that which existed in America), that *"Onesimus was a blood-kin brother to Philemon."* This extraordinary and then entirely new ground was so unexpected and original, that while many approached, congratulating him on his able arguments, they expressed their regrets that he ventured to use such weapons, as he rendered himself liable to severe criticism from the whites. He replied that, in the course of events soon to greet them, this would become an established fact. He was not incorrect, only "imprudent" as the time had not arrived to proclaim such bold opinions. His fault, in most cases, is in expressing the thoughts that shape themselves in his healthy, active brain far in advance of the time allotted by a conservative element for receiving it. He plans long before the workmen are ready or willing to execute. Says that friend of humanity, Wendell Phillips, "What world wide benefactors these imprudent men are—the Lovejoys, the Browns the Garrisons, the saints, the martyrs! How 'prudently' most men creep into nameless graves, while now and then one or two forget themselves into immortality."

A few years before this Delany began the study of medicine under the late Dr. Andrew N. McDowell, but for some cause did not continue to completion, as he entered practically upon dentistry. The knowledge acquired in surgery he made use of whenever immediate necessity required it. On one occasion, in 1839, he went down the Mississippi to New Orleans, thence to Texas. While at Alexandria he met with the chief of adventurers, General Felix Houston, whose attention was attracted by witnessing him dressing the wound of a man stabbed by an intoxicated comrade. General Houston offered him a good position and protection if he would join him.

He declined the offer, and continued his tour, spending several months among the slaveholding Indians of Mississippi, Louisiana, Arkansas, and Texas, viewing the "peculiar institution" as it existed in all its varied phases—its pride and gloom,—not loving freedom less, but hating slavery more, if possible.

He watched closely the scenes through which he had passed, and the experience gained among the slaves of the south-west was carefully garnered up for future usefulness. His present post of duty on the Sea Island of South Carolina, where he executes the duties of his office with zeal and ability, while his busy brain constantly devises some new measure for the advancement and elevation of the newly recognized people, attests this fact.

CHAPTER XXXVI

Conclusion

The order for mustering out the remaining volunteer officers was long anticipated, and anxiously looked for by these officers, and by none more than by Major Delany, who, as sub-assistant commissioner of the Bureau district of Hilton Head would be affected by this. At last it was received, as will be seen by the following document. While upon this subject, a humorous anecdote, bearing on this subject, may be related.

While awaiting the order, about the middle of December, he visited the headquarters of the assistant commissioner at Charleston.

On entering the department of the adjutant general, a group of officers surrounded the desk of the acting adjutant, who, at the time, was reading out the names of the officers mustered out by special orders, which had just been received from the war department that morning, erasing them from the roster suspended on the wall before him, among which was his own name.

"How is this, major?" asked the chief clerk; "I do not see your name among them. Do you report regularly?"

"I do; my report for this month was sent on now more than ten days," he replied.

"How is it that you are not among these named in the special order just received?" inquired the acting assistant adjutant general, with much interest.

"I suppose," said the major, very quaintly, "that I am in the position of the old black man, a devoted Second Adventurer, during the Millerite excitement, who, disposing of his earthly effects, betook himself to a cellar, with simply food and fuel sufficient to sustain him comfortably, the season being winter. While waiting, a snow storm came on, the drift completely embanking that side of the street, burying everything beneath it.

"Thus isolated, and enveloped in darkness for several days, except the light of his little fire, without the sound of a footstep or voice above, the old man believed that the final consummation of all things had taken place, and he was actually left in his tomb.

"Presently the scavengers reached his cellar door, when, first hearing footsteps, succeeded by scraping and prying, then light ushering in through the cracks as the snow was removed. Suddenly bursting up the cellar door, the old man exclaimed, 'Is de end come?' Being answered in the negative, 'O!' said he, 'I thought de end was come, an' all you white folks was gone up, an' forgot dis old black saint.' "Now," concluded the major turning to the assistant adjutant general, "I suppose de end is come, an' all you white folks is *gone up*, an' forgot dis black saint," amidst a roar of laughter among the officers.

A few days after this an order came from Washington, retaining Brevet Major General Scott in the service, as assistant commissioner, on the staff of Major General Canby, commanding the Second Military District, by whose advice and generous indorsement the retention of Major Delany was recommended to General Canby, and by which he has been retained in the service.

Thus, in addition to the established duties of his office, he is now the disbursing officer of soldiers' claims for the sub-district of Hilton Head.

This is another testimony, as exhibited by different commanders, of the ability and usefulness of this officer in retaining him. But while fully appreciating these repeated recognitions of his service to the government by these high officials, giving it the full value of its civil and political worth, construing it to a desire of recognizing the true status of the colored race as American citizens by the continuance of their only representative, as an incumbent and military officer in this prominent and honorable position of the government, Major Delany says, "By this change or modification in its jurisdiction the Bureau loses nothing, but otherwise its status and prestige is thereby enhanced.

"Previous to this an important difficulty presented itself. A large force of volunteer officers must be kept up in a time of peace—which is contrary to the jurisprudence of all highly civilized nations,—for the volunteer officers must be mustered out, and thus leave an important arm of the war department without the necessary administrative government.

"To impose the duties of the Bureau on the officers of the regular army, would be to entail duties which they could not care to have upon them, and, therefore, for the most part, neglect. To employ civilians, would bring them directly under the military men, wholly ignorant of the details, import, and meaning of military orders and duties. To employ those who have been commissioned officers in the service, competent for the duties, would involve an expense equal, at least, to that already incurred by the volunteer officers now on duty.

"The only course left the government in carrying out the well-regulated custom of reducing the army to a true peace basis, by doing away with an independent volunteer force in time of peace, was to place the bureau under the regular army.

"This virtually places Major General O. O. Howard on the staff of General Grant; Brevet Major General R.K. Scott, and all other assistant commissioners, *de facto* on the staffs of the major generals commanding the military districts; brings the entire volunteer officers, retained in the service, under and subject to, without being in, the regular army; and cements a perfect harmony between these two branches of the government which nothing can detract.

"In this stride of statesmanship, will it be presumed that the American army, or the military branch of the government, has no statesmen as competent counsellors of the executive?"

> Headquarters Second Military District,
> Charleston, S.C., December 4, 1867.
> *General Orders. No. 140.*

The following general orders from the headquarters of the army are republished for the information and guidance of all concerned.

> Headquarters of the Army, Adjt. Gen. Office,
> Washington, November 26, 1867.
> *General Orders. No. 101.*

The following orders have been received from the War Department, and will be duly executed:—

Extract.

Par. III. All volunteer officers now retained in service will be mustered out, to take effect January 1, 1868, except the commissioner and the disbursing officers of the Bureau of Refugees, Freedmen, and Abandoned Lands.

> By command of General Grant
> E. D. Townsman.
> *Asst. Adjt. Gen*

By command of Brevet Major General ED. R.S. Canby.
Official. Louis v. Caziarc
Aid-de-Camp, Act'g Asst. Adjt. Gen.
Headquarters Second Military District,
Charleston, S.C., December 6, 1867
General Orders. No. 145.

The following arrangement of the troops in this district will be carried into effect with as little delay as possible.

Extract

In addition to duties with which they are charged by existing orders, commanding officers of posts are designated as sub-assistant commissioners of the Bureau of Refugees, Freedmen, and Abandoned Lands, for the districts embraced within the territorial limits of their commands, and will exercise all the functions of officers of that bureau, except so far as relates to the administration and control of the funds or property of the bureau.

Extract

All officers and agents of the bureau, who may be on duty within the territorial limits of any post, will report to its commander, and will be governed by his instructions in all that relates to the protection of persons and property, under the laws of the United States, the regulations of the bureau, and the orders of the district commander. In all that relates to the details of administration, they will report as heretofore to the assistant commissioner for the state in which they are stationed. The assistant commissioners for the States of North and South Carolina, respectively, will furnish the commanders of posts with the names and stations of the officers and agents of the bureau on duty within the limits of their respective commands, and with a statement of any special duties they may have been charged with in relation to the protection of person and property. They will also, by conference or correspondence with the post commander, determine what officers or agents of the bureau can be relieved or discharged, and report the same to district headquarters.

By command of Brevet Major General Ed. R.S. Canby
Official.
Louis V. Caziarco,
Aid-de-Camp, Act'g Asst. Adjt.Gen.
Headquarters Asst. Comr. Bureau Refugees, Freedmen, and Abandoned Lands, District of S.C.
Charleston, S.C., December 19, 1867.

Major M.R. Delany, *Asst. Sub-Asst.Comr.*

Major: In accordance with the provisions of general orders No. 145, C. S., Second Military District, I am directed by the assistant commissioner to inform you that your designation and limits of your district are as follows:—

You will hereafter be designated as Assistant Sub-Assistant Commissioner for Hilton Head, Savage, Bull, Dawfuskie, Pinckney, and Long Pine Islands, and will report to Brevet Brigadier General H.B. Glitz, port of Charleston, and sub-assistant commissioner, subject to existing orders and instructions.

> I am, major, very respectfully,
> Your most obedient servant,
> Edward L. Deane
> *Brevet Major, A.D.C., & A.A.A. Gen.*
> Headquarters Asst. Cour. Bureau Refugees,
> Freedmen, and Abandoned Lands, Dist. of S.C., Charleston, S.C.,
> February 8, 1868.
> Major M.R. DELANY *Acting Sub-Assistant*
> *Commissioner, Hilton Head, S.C.*

Major: The following copy of indorsement from War Department, Adjutant General's Office, dated January 28, 1868, is respectfully furnished for your information.

Respectfully returned to Major General O. O. Howard, Commissioner. Major M.R. Delany, 104th United States Colored Troops, having been reported in your letter of November 30, 1867, as on duty in the Bureau of Refugees, Freedmen, and Abandoned Lands, as a disbursing officer, was retained in service under the provisions of General Order 101, November 26, 1867, from this office.

> (Signed) Thomas M. Vincent,
> *Asst. Adjt. Gen.*
> Very respectfully, your obedient servant,
> H. Neide,
> *Brevet Major, 1st Lieut. 44th Infantry,*
> *Act'g Asst. Adjt. Gen.*

With this last order we will bring this volume to a close. We have endeavored to narrate the career of an individual of our time, living and still working in our midst, the extent of whose labors, and the great ability demonstrated in their execution, cannot be thoroughly understood or felt, without first having known the great struggle and anxiety entailed in its accomplishment.

This we have attempted to give, but found it no easy task; therefore we have simply narrated the events of his singularly active life, allowing the reader to deduce his own comments.

At this writing, Major Delany is still in the service of the government, as sub-assistant commissioner of the Freedmen's Bureau, while many of the volunteer officers have been mustered out, under order of the department at Washington.

In his retention, is shown the recognition and the thorough appreciation of the indefatigable zeal and great ability displayed by the black officer, especially as in conjunction with his former duties others, in which greater responsibilities are entailed, are assigned to him. His efficient labors in the department reader him a distinct character from his surroundings, while his administrative qualities attract the attention of friends and foes alike, as unprecedented in the history of his race in this country. While comments may vary, they unite in saying, "There is still a latent amount of greatness within the man, which has not yet been called forth."

To his lofty aspirations, and great originality of thoughts, together with his real earnestness in everything he undertakes, and his iron will to pursue to completion, we trace the secret of his success in this field.

Illustrating in his career entire personal sacrifice for the accomplishment of a grand purpose, no character has been produced by our civilization in comparison with which this remarkable man would be deemed inferior. Men have died for the freedom and elevation of the race, and thereby have contributed more to advance the cause than would their living efforts, while others have lived for it, and under circumstances where death would have been easier. Such describes Martin Delany. Nature marked him for combat and victory, and not for martyrdom. His life-long service, from which neither poverty nor dangers could deter him, his great vitality and energy under all and every circumstance, which have never abated, proclaim this truth. His life furnishes a rare enthusiasm for race not expected in the present state of American society, occasioned by his constant researches into anything relative to their history. No living man is better able to write the history of the race, to whom it has been a constant study, than he; as it is considered by the most earnest laborers in the same sphere that few, if any among them, have so entirely consecrated themselves to the idea of race as his career shows. His religion, his writings, every step in life, is based upon this idea. His creed begins and ends with it—that the colored race can only obtain their true status as men, by relying on their own identity; that they must prove, by merit, all that white men claim; then color would cease to be an objection to their progress—that the blacks must take pride in being black, and show their claims to superior qualities, before the whites would be willing to concede them equality. This he claims as the foundation of his manhood. Upon this point Mr. Frederick Douglass once wittily remarked, "Delany stands so straight that he leans a little backward."

Such is the personal history of an individual of the race, whose great strength of character, amid the multitudinous agencies adverse to his progress, has triumphantly demonstrated negro capability for greatness in every sphere wherein he has acted.

The late revolution has resulted in bringing the race to which he belongs into prominence. They have begun their onward march towards that higher civilization promised at the close of the war. Let no unhallowed voice be lifted to stay their progress; then, with all barriers removed, the glorious destiny promised to them can be achieved. And then our country, continuing to recognize merit alone in her children, as shown in the appointment of the black major of Carolina, will add renewed strength to her greatness. Be girt with loyal hearts and strong arms, the mission of our revolution shall embrace centuries in its March, securing the future stability of our country, and proclaiming with truthfulness the grandeur of republican institutions to the civilization of Christendom.

FIVE ❦ **Mary V. Cook**
(1868–1945)

BORN IN BOWLING GREEN, KENTUCKY, Mary V. Cook became an educator, journalist, and committed Baptist who used her pen to advocate for women's importance within her denomination. At an early age Cook distinguished herself as a brilliant scholar, and was noticed by Dr. William J. Simmons, then president of the State University at Louisville (later renamed Simmons College of Kentucky), a black-owned school founded to educate freed men and women. Given scholarships by the American Baptist Woman's Home Society of Boston, Cook graduated as valedictorian in 1883 and immediately took a position teaching at the school.[1]

From there Cook's professional star rose quickly. Alongside her teaching of Latin and Mathematics, Cook lectured for the Baptist Women's Home Mission Society, wrote for a variety of publications (sometimes under the pen name Grace Ermine), and advocated for racial equality. I. Garland Penn, historian of black journalism, praised her approach to women's rights, saying that "she is not a loud clamorer for 'Rights', but, nevertheless, she quietly and tenaciously demands all that is due her."[2] Equally committed to the cause of education for African-American children, Cook became the editor of the educational department of *Our Women and Children*, one of the most influential black periodicals of the late nineteenth century.

Source: *Journal and Lectures of the Second Anniversary of the American National Baptist Convention* (n.p., 1887), 45–56.
[1] I. Garland Penn, *The Afro-American Press and Its Editors* (Springfield, MA: Willey & Co., 1891), 370.
[2] Ibid., 373.

Cook's endeavors demonstrated the evangelical zeal of the Baptist cause. Married to Charles H. Parrish, Sr., a fellow graduate of the State University and a prominent Baptist minister in Louisville, Cook labored on behalf of the church across the United States. Parrish and Cook were the royal family of African-American Kentucky Baptists by the 1890s, with both playing formative roles in the growth of the newly created National Baptist Convention. Parrish later returned to Simmons College as its president, overseeing the work of that Kentucky Baptist school into the twentieth century.

Cook was a favorite on the convention circuit as well. As one observer remarked, "when she has appeared on the public platform, she has never failed to carry her audience by the force of her terse style and convincing argument."[3] In the instance reprinted here, her subject was women's role in the church. "Woman's Place in the Work of the Denomination" was delivered before the American National Baptist Convention in Mobile, Alabama, in August 1887, and in it Cook demonstrated an acceptable "feminine" modesty expected of a woman in her position. She also exhibited a precocious and even audacious facility with religious history and the role of women in its unfolding. She examined a long history of women's treatment around the world, judging past societies by how well they had treated women as a chief marker of their Christian civility. She invoked the Bible as a record of womanly virtues, and implored Baptist women to spread those virtues to other women around the world: "As the vitalizing principles of the Baptists expand and permeate the religious principles of the world women will become free." She argued that human freedom and equality would come about through the institutional work of women in the denomination, through journalism, education, and advocacy. Cook surveyed the sweep of women's influence from Eve through the Bible, into the Baptist faith, and up to the present: "Under her influence nations rise or fall."

<hr>

Woman's Place in the Work of the Denomination (1887)

How pleasant it is to wander over, and enjoy this beautiful world God has made. Its green meadows, its beautiful fields, its dense forests with wild flowers and rippling streams, its wide expanse of water and lofty mountains all delight us. But while charmed with its beauty, our joy is greater if we can comprehend that it "was without form and void" and

[3] G. F. Richings, *Evidence of Progress Among Colored People*, 8th ed. (Philadelphia: Geo. S. Ferguson Co., 1902), 226.

contrast its present beauty with the roughness of its former state. So in viewing the wonders of divine grace, we need to note its results in connection with what might have been, and before attempting to describe woman's work in the denomination and the great blessings God has bestowed upon her, we will first consider her condition when His gospel found her, that we may better appreciate the grace which wrought the change. Among all nations woman was degraded. Besides being bartered or sold as a thing of merchandise, there were barbarous laws and customs among the Phoenicians, Armenians, Carthaginians, Medes and Persians, and all too revolting and indecent to be mentioned. Greece, whose land abounded in scholars, heroes, and sages where the sun of intellect illumined the world, looked upon her as an object "without a soul." Gibbon says; "the Romans married without love, or loved without delicacy or respect."

In China, Japan and Africa the condition is the same except where christianity has emancipated her. And wherever the religion of the true Messiah has spread its snowy white pinions and lighted up the deep dark recesses of man's heart, woman has been loved adored respected. I will not affirm that all virtue and joy were unknown: There are some fertile spots in the most arid deserts; there is light in the darkest places amid all this wickedness and infidelity. God has preserved the spark of faith, purity, and love. Though we live in the Nineteenth century, and have it in its beauty and strength, our own beloved America is not free from the curse. Modern Athens is not totally unlike ancient Athens.

The leaven of infidelity is infesting this land. Immoralities, indecencies and crimes as revolting as ever withered and blighted a nation are of usual occurrence. They fearlessly maintain their hold and flaunt their wicked banners in the face of the government which is either too corrupt to care, or to timid to oppose. Who is to wipe these iniquities from our land if it be not christian women? A reform in these things can not be effected by the ballot, by political station, or by mere supremacy of civil law. It must come by woman's unswerving devotion to a pure and undefiled christianity, for to that alone, woman owes her influence, her power and all she is. To establish this truth we will recount history as its light comes to us from the pages of the Bible. Fortunately the records of the past present an array of heroic and saintly women whose virtues have made the world more tolerable, and chief among these are the wives, mothers and daughters of the Holy Scriptures.

In the formation of the world when the beasts of the field, the fowls of the air, the fish of the sea and the beautiful garden of Paradise were made for the happiness of man, and when man himself was made in the image of his Creator, God plucked Eve from the side of Adam "without childhood or growth" to be "a helpmeet for him." When Adam first looked upon her he was enraptured with the perfectness of her form, the splendor of her beauty, the purity of her countenance and in this excess of joy he exclaimed: "bone of my bone, flesh of my flesh, therefore shall a man leave his father and mother and shall cleave unto his wife." They knew naught but divine happiness. Their hearts were filled with pure love unsullied by sin, but alas! in a short time the scene was changed—Eve was tempted—partook of the forbidden fruit and gave to Adam and he did eat. In this fallen state they were driven from the garden, yet she proved still a helpmeet for her husband, sharing his sorrow as she had shared his joy. Many have been the reproaches uttered against her—few have been her defenders. Dr. Pendleton says: "Eve acting under a mistake and a delusion was by no means excusable, but Adam was far more inexcusable than she for he acted intelligently as well as voluntarily. He knew what he was doing." There is much to admire in the character of Sarah, wife of Abraham, her reverence for her husband; her devotion to her son; her faithfulness to duty; her willingness in its performance. She was beautiful, chaste, modest and industrious—all these she sacrificed for the good and welfare of those around her. It was in this family God preserved the seed of righteousness. Also we find Miriam cheering on the hosts of Israel with her timbrel in her hands as she uttered the songs of praise "Sing, sing ye to the Lord, for he has triumphed gloriously, the horse and his rider hath he thrown into the sea." God's thought and appreciation of woman's work appears when he appoints Deborah to be a warrior, judge and prophet. Her work was distinct from her husband's who, it seems took no part whatever in the work of God while Deborah was inspired by the Eternal expressly to do His will and to testify to her countrymen that He recognizes in His followers neither male nor female, heeding neither the "weakness" of one, nor the strength of the other, but strictly calling those who are perfect at heart and willing to do his bidding. She was a woman of much meekness and humility, but of great force of character. Her song of praise, when Israel overcame the enemy, has only been excelled by the Psalms of David: "and Israel had rest forty years." Mention might also be made of Huldah, wife of Shallum, who dwelt in Jerusalem in a college, to whom went Hilkiah, the priest, and Ahikam, and Achbor and Shapham and Asaiah to enquire concerning the words of the book that was found in the house of the Lord. It was a woman whom God had chosen as a medium between Him and His people who would faithfully report all that he desired. Huldah's dwelling in college shows that she was anxious to become familiar with the law—to better prepare herself for the work of Him Who had called her. Woman's faith and devotion are beautifully illustrated by the touching scene between Ruth and Naomi, when Naomi besought Ruth to return to the home of her birth, thinking that the pleasure of childhood days had endeared it to her, and when Ruth with that pathos of devotion, and fairness said: "Entreat me not to leave thee, or to return from following after thee: For whither thou goest, I will go; and where thou lodgest, I will lodge; thy people shall be my people and thy God my God; where thou diest I will die, and there will I be buried; the Lord do so to me and more too if aught but death part thee and me." We cannot forget the maternal tenderness of Hagar, the well kept promise of Hannah, the filial devotion of Jephthah's daughter, nor the queenly patriotism of Esther. But no woman bore such recognition as Mary the mother of Jesus, who was chosen to bear a prominent part in human regeneration. After the fall of our first parents, God promised that a virgin should bear a son who should be the Redeemer of the human race. The memory of this promise was preserved through all nations, and each was desirous of the honor. The story of the birth of Romulus and Remus coincides with the miraculous birth of Jesus Christ. Silvia became their mother by the God Mars, even as Christ was the son of the Holy Ghost. An effort was made to take the life of these boys by throwing the cradle which contained them into the river Arnio, whence it was carried into the Tiber. The cradle was stranded at the foot of Palatine and the infants were carried by a she-wolf into her den where they were tenderly cared for. This escape is likened to the flight into Egypt, and while this story has become a myth, the birth of Christ becomes more and more a reality. There are others who claim this mysterious birth. The most revered goddess of the Chinese sprung from the contact of a flower. Buddha was claimed to have been borne by a virgin named Maha-Mahai, but none realized the power of the words spoken by the angel, "*Hail full of grace, the Lord is with thee! Blessed are thou among women*, save Mary." History and tradition tell us she excelled all her young companions in her intelligence and skill. Denis, the Areopagite says: "She was a dazzling beauty." St. Epiphanius, writing in the fourth century, from traditions and manuscripts says: "In stature she was above the medium, her hair was blonde; her face oval; her eyes bright and slightly olive in color; her eyebrows perfectly arched, her nose equaline and of irreproachable perfection and her lips were ruby red. The ardent sun of her country had slightly bronzed her complexion; her hands were long, her fingers were slender" as a virgin she honored one of the most beautiful virtues of woman; as a mother she nourished a Redeemer. She gave the world an example of non-excelled maternal devotion; of the most magnificent grief which history affords. The life of Christ furnishes many examples of woman's work, love and devotion. They took part in the Savior's work, followed Him on His journeys, believed on Him and loved Him. They were "last at the cross and first at the grave." Christ did certainly atone for the sins of man, but His mission to woman was a great deal more; for He has not only saved her soul, but actually brought out and cultivated her intellect for the good of His cause. He was her friend, her counselor and her Savior. She bathed His feet with her tears and wiped them with the hairs of her head. He found comfort in the home of Mary and Martha when burdened, or tired from a day's journey. At the well of Samaria He converses with a woman which was unlawful for a man of respect to do, but He not only talked with her but permitted her to do good for mankind and the advancement of His cause. Filled with enthusiasm she leaves her water pot and hastens to proclaim her loyalty to One Who had won her heart and spoken to her of "living water." She testified that she had seen the true Messiah and invites others to see Him for themselves. To Mary Magdalene was the commission given to bear the joyful intelligence that Jesus had risen. It was the women more than men whose faith ventured to show Jesus those personal kindnesses which our Lord ever appreciated. In the lives and acts of the Apostles women are discovered praying, prophesying and spreading the gospel. Prominent for good works and alms deeds which she did was Dorcas. Like the Savior she went about doing good, but in the midst of this usefulness she died and so great was the grief of the widows unto whom she had ministered that the Lord again restored her to them. Paul placed much value on the work of Phebe and commends her to the churches as "our sister." Phebe was a deaconess of the church of Cenchrea and was, no doubt a great helper of Paul's "in the gospel." In the letter she carries to Rome, mention is made of quite a number of women who had been co-workers with the apostle. One of the first on the list was Priscilla, the wife of Aquilla who had with her husband laid down her neck for him. She possessed high qualities and did active work in the cause which she espoused. Lydia was the first European convert—after she received the word into her heart; at once opens her house and offers a home to the apostle who had been instrumental in her conversion. At Thessalonica we find "the chief women not a few" among the workers of the church. The church today wants more Priscillas, Phebes, Chloes, Elizabeths, Marys, Annas, Tryphenas, Tryphosas, Julias and Joannas to labor in the gospel, to give of their substance; to follow Jesus; to be willing to sacrifice their substance; to follow Jesus; to be willing to sacrifice their lives for the love they bear their Lord. It is not christianity which disparages the intellect of woman and scorns her ability for doing good, for its records are filled with her marvelous successes. Emancipate woman from the chains that now restrain her and who can estimate the part she will play in the work of denomination? In the Baptist denomination women have more freedom than in any other denomination on the face of the earth. I am not unmindful of the kindness you noble brethren have exhibited in not barring us from your platforms and deliberations. All honor I say to such men. Every woman in the world ought to be a Baptist, for in this blessed denomination men are even freer than elsewhere. Free men cannot conscientiously shut the doors against those whom custom has limited in privileges and benefits. As the vitalizing principles of the Baptists expand and permeate the religious principles of the world women will become free. As the Bible is an iconoclastic weapon—it is bound to break down images of error that have been raised. As no one studies it so closely as the Baptists their women shall take the lead. History gives a host of women who have achieved and now enjoy distinction as writers, linguists, poets, physicians, lecturers, editors, teachers and missionaries. Visit the temples of the living God and there you will find them kneeling at His shrine as ready now as in centuries past, to attest their faith by their suffering and if need be by the sacrifice of life. As they by their numbers, who followed Christ up Calvary's rugged road, caused the cowardice of man to blush, so in the crowds of worshippers who do Him honor to-day put to shame the indifference and the coldness of man's allegiance to God. But to the limited subject,

WHAT IS DENOMINATIONAL WORK?

I deem it to be the most honorable, the most exalted and the most enviable. It strengthens the link between the church militant and the church triumphant—between man and his Creator. All Woman who are truly christians are candidates in this broad field of labor. It calls for valiant hearted women who will enlist for life. None whose soul is not overflowing with love for Christ and whose chief aim is not to save souls need apply. Success need not necessarily depend on learning, genius, taste, style, elegant language, nor a rapid use of the tongue, but it is the earnestness of the soul, the simplicity of the Word accompanied by the Spirit of the living God. The Maker of all has wisely distributed these talents and whatever characterizes the individual He has commanded to "to occupy till I come" and to use well the talent entrusted to your care. It often happens that some humble woman bent on her staff full of fervor yet unlettered, does more by her upright living, her words of counsel, her ardent prayers "that go up to God as a sweet smelling savor" than many who pick their words and try to appear learned. This denominational work demands active labor in and for the churches. It does not demand that every woman shall be a Deborah, a Huldah, a Dorcas, or a Phoebe—It simply asks that every woman be a woman—a christian woman who is willing to consecrate all for the cause of Christ. A story is told of a woman who when she was unable to express intelligently and satisfactorily what the Lord had done for her and when the anxious crowd was about to turn away disappointed she exclaimed: "I cannot talk for Him, but I can die for Him." "Whosoever will lose his life for my sake, the same shall save it." To serve the church we must die daily to selfishness, pride, vanity, a lying tongue, a deceitful heart and walk worthy of the calling in Christ Jesus. We are to pray without ceasing—to be fervent in season and out of season—"to present our bodies a living sacrifice, holy and acceptable before God which is our reasonable service." We are to speak as the spirit shall give utterance, that He may work in us to will and to do His good pleasure. I know Paul said "Let the woman keep silence in the churches" but because he addressed this to a few Grecian and Asiatic woman who were wholly given up to idolatry and the fashion of the day is no reason why it should be quoted to the pious women of the present. A woman may suffer martyrdom, she may lift her voice in song, she may sacrifice modesty to collect money from the church, for her work in this particular is considered essential and it matters not how prominent a place she occupies in fairs, festivals, sociables, tea parties, concerts and tableaux, but to take part in the business meeting of the church is wholly out of place because Paul said so. We are apt to quote Paul and shut our eyes and ears to the recognition and privilege Christ, his Master, gave, us, and not only did the Apostle appreciate the labors of women, and show towards them the greatest care and tenderest affection, but we find him in some places greatly dependent upon them, for co-operation in the foundation of the churches. But a change is coming; it has already commenced, and God is shaking up the church—He is going to bring it up to something better and that, too, greatly through the work of the women. Already the harvest is great. Can ye not discern the signs of the time? Do you not see how wickedness and crime are flooding our country—how tares are growing up in the midst of the wheat? See the foothold the Catholics are getting in our christian land. They are taking our children putting clothes on their backs, food in their mouths and educating them that they must swell their number and represent their claim. See how nations, every where, are opening to the reception of the gospel. Listen to the cry of Africa's heathen sons—note the rush of other denominations to offer their faith, their belief, to satisfy the hunger of their souls and quench the thirst of their spirits. Can ye not discern the signs? It is quite time christian soldiers were taking the field for Christ. The doctrines of our denomination must be so thoroughly diffused that a man though he be a fool need not err. A good pastor should have a good wife. He should find in her rest from care; comfort when distressed; his depressed spirits must be lifted by her consoling words; she must be his wisdom; his courage; his strength; his hope; his endurance. She is to beautify his home and make it a place of peace and cheerfulness—she is to be an example worthy of pattern for the neighborhood in which she lives—she is to take the lead in all worthy causes. Women are to look after the spiritual interest of the church as well as the men. Let them be punctual at services and make the prayer meeting interesting. Woman's power of song, her heartfelt prayer, her ability to go into the highways and hedges and compel singers to come in, have marked her as proficient in revivals. A praying mother exerts more influence over the minds of the youth than all else. The recollections of such seasons when the tender plants were garnered in can never be effaced. The voice of that sainted mother still lingers upon them, and memory can never relinquish the priceless treasure she holds. Some of our best men owe their conversion and all that they are to the influence of a sainted mother, a devoted sister or some dear female friend. For money raising woman has no equals.

Our churches are largely supported by her financial efforts, but she should discountenance many of the plans to which she and her daughters are subjected—they are gates of vice that lead to destruction—this begging money from any and every body only invites and encourages insults and it must be stopped. Our churches must have some system in money raising and thereby save the girls. Many a girl with good intent got her start downward by this very act of soliciting money. A woman's place is to assist the pastor, work in the Sabbath school, visit the sick, to care for the sick and lift up the fallen. She has a conspicuous place in

THE NEWSPAPER WORK OF THE DENOMINATION

which is a powerful weapon for breaking down vice, establishing virtue, spreading the gospel and disseminating a general knowledge of the work of the denomination. Here she can command the attention of thousands. She can thunder from the editor's chair and make the people hear. It has a wider circulation and as has been said "penetrates the most remote corners of the country." In this field we need strong intellectual women. We need women of courage, who dare defend the faith and make the truth felt. As an editor a woman can better reach the mothers, daughters and sisters. Let her be a regular correspondent. Let the articles be strong and vigorous, let them show thought, learning and an earnestness for the cause represented. If she cannot be a regular correspondent she should write occasionally such articles as will give the people something to think and talk about. She should make them so plain and attractive that children will read them with eagerness and let some be especially to them; make them feel that some one else is interested in them besides mother and father and endeavor to impress them with upright living. Assist the editor in getting subscribers and see that a Baptist paper is in every home. See that the Baptist family reads your denominational paper.

The field of juvenile literature is open. I said recently before the National Press Convention, held in Louisville Ky. there are now published 24 secular papers and magazines in the United States for the children with a circulation of 775,934. The largest of which is the "Youth's Companion" with a circulation of 385,251. Of the religious journals there are 47 with 678,346 circulation. Sunday School Journal (Methodist) claim 81,090: "The Sunday School Times" 77,500 and "Our Young People" 47,000. Of this number, 71 secular and religious papers, there is not one so far as I know, edited especially for colored children. There is a little paper whose name does not appear on the list that is written for the colored youth, being edited and controlled by Miss J. P. Moore of Louisiana. It is known as "Hope" and though of humble pretentions, in its silent way it is sowing seed from which shall spring an abundant harvest.

The educational work of the denomination belongs principally to woman. Three centuries ago women were almost universally uneducated and a half century ago found American women shut out from all places of learning. Ignorance seemed a bliss while wisdom a foolish idea. A young girl in Italy and a young widow in France almost simultaneously conceived the idea of educating young girls. It was the beginning of an institution that was destined to reform the world and this they comprehended, for they said "This regeneration of this corrupt world must be accomplished by children, for children will reform the families, families will reform the provinces and the provinces will reform the world." Mademoiselle de Sainte-Beuve, foundress of the "Ursilines" of France, purchased a house at the Faubourg St. Jacques where she had two hundred pupils. It was her delight to watch them in their sport and as she looked upon them with maternal gaze she charmingly said "They sprung not from her loins, but from her heart." At her death her portrait represented her before a window, her eyes fixed with intent devotion upon a garden full of beehives, with the legend "Mother of Bees." Mary Lyons, in our own century, opened the way, and established Mount Holly Seminary, the first institution established for girls. This is what woman has done, and may not our women do ever more for the denomination with the surrounding advantages? May they not found more "Spelman" and "Hartshorn" seminaries, more "Vassars?" The women have been promoted from mere kitchen drudgery, household duties, and gossiping from house to house—they can teach not as subordinates merely, but as principals, as professors. Woman has not only the art of inspiring the affections in her pupils, but also in keeping them interested in the tasks to be performed. I think the duty of our women is to impressibly teach the Scriptures and the doctrines of our denomination to the young under their care. I think we talk and preach baptism, "The Lord's Supper," and the "Final Perseverance of the Saints," too little. Not one-half of the members of our churches can give a doctrinal reason why they are Baptists. We are too fearful of feelings, when we have the Bible that makes the Baptist churches on our side. They should instill in the child's mind love toward God, his Creator, his Benefactor, his Saviour, and respect for all mankind.

As an author, woman has shown rare talents. The profession of mind affords the strongest evidence that God created her for society. As the fragrance which is in the bud will, when the bud expands, escape from its confinement and diffuse itself through the surrounding atmosphere, so if forms of beauty and sublimity are in the mind, they will exhibit themselves, and operate on other minds. The genius of woman was long hidden. Greece had a Sappho and a Carina; Israel had a Miriam. Antiquity turned a deaf ear to the cultivation of woman's talent. The home of Cicero and Virgil neglected her intellect, but the revolution of ages and the progress of the present century have wrought a new change of affairs, and now woman has the pen, and participates in the discussion of the times. It was when Christianity and infidelity were wrestling in Europe, that Hannah More came from retirement to take part in the contest. It was when slavery was at its highest, that Phillis Wheatly, Francis Ellen Harper, and Harriet Beecher Stowe, gave vent to their fullness of their souls in beautiful lines of poetry and prose. The human voice is fast receding, the written voice predominates. Since this is true, let the women see that the best and purest literature comes from them. Let them feel that they are called upon to consecrate all to truth and piety. Lecturers address the people through the sense of hearing; writing through the sense of sight. Many persons will pay goodly sums to hear a good talk on some subject, rather than spend the time investigating books. As public lecturers women have been successful, and have secured good audiences. Rev. Mr. Higginson says: "Among the Spanish Arabs women were public lecturers and secretaries of kings, while Christian Europe was sunk in darkness. In Italy, from the fifteenth to the nineteenth century, it was not esteemed unfeminine for women to give lectures in public to crowded and admiring audiences. They were freely admitted members of learned societies, and were consulted by men of prominent scientific attainments as their equals in scholarship."

All good causes owe their success to the push of woman. The temperance cause had its origin in her, and to-day finds noble advocates in the persons of Frances E. Harper and Frances E. Willard. Indeed, the place of woman is broad, and of the vocations of life none are so grand, so inspiring, as that of being a missionary. Long before the organization of any general missionary society of our denomination in this country, Christian women were actively engaged in prosecuting the work of home missions. Little bands of women organized in the churches to help the pastors in the poor churches, by sending clothing and other supplies needed. When the Foreign Mission Enterprise was begun, it found in these women ready and powerful allies—they sent up contributions annually for both Home and Foreign work. The first missionary society ever organized in the country was by the women in 1800. It was composed of fourteen women. From this many branches sprang. The women of to-day are realizing that in the homes among the degraded there is a great work to be done. It belongs to woman's tender nature, sympathy, and love, to uplift the fallen. A home can not be raised above the mother, nor the race above the type of womanhood, and no women are more ready to respond to the call than the women of the Baptist Church. They feel the necessity of meeting the responsibility with organized forces in the field. Many have been effected, and great has been the result.

This work is not exclusively confined to the churches, but to orphans, asylums, hospitals, prisons, alms-houses, on the street, in the home, up the alley, and in all places where human souls are found, have woman, with her love for Christ and fallen humanity, found her way, amid the jeers and scorn of those who were too foolish to care for any other save self and household.

Woman sways a mighty influence. It began with Eve in the Garden of Eden, and is felt even now. It has not been exaggerated nor exhausted. She exalts man to the skies, or casts him beneath the brutes. She makes him strong or she makes him weak. Under her influence nations rise or fall. In the dark days of Rome, when woman received her most cruel treatment from the hand of her lord, Cato said: "Even then the Romans governed the world, but the women governed the Romans."

Bad women sometimes have great power with men. It was Phryne who inspired the chisel of Praxiteles. Cotytto had her altars at Athens and Corinth under the title of "Popular Venus." Aspasia decided peace or war, directing the counsel of Pericles. Demosthenes, the great orator, cast himself at the feet of Lais, and history gives scores of instances where women governed the passions of men for good or evil. It was Delilah who, by her words, persuaded Sampson to tell wherein his strength lay, and which Milton has so beautifully portrayed in these words:

> *"Of what I suffer, she was not the prime cause, but I myself,*
> *Who vanquished with a peal of words (Oh, weakness)!*
> *Gave up my forte of silence to a woman."*

It came to pass when Solomon was old, that his wives turned away his heart after other gods, and his heart was not perfect with the Lord his God, as was the heart of his father, David. There was none like unto Ahab, who did sell himself to work wickedness in the sight of God, whom Jezebel, his wife, stirred up. There are good women like Volumna, the mother of Coriolanus, who saved Rome by her influence over her son. The women of this country inspired the fathers and sons on to battle, and in all the affairs of life woman has encouraged or discouraged men; he is moved by her faintest smile, her lightest whisper. The Duke of Halifax says: "She has more strength in her looks than we have in our laws, and more power by hers than we have in our arguments." Though woman is a mixture of good and evil, be it said to her credit, that history has never recorded a single instance where she denied her Saviour. Her influence is entwined with every religion, and diffuses itself through every circle where there is mind to act upon. It gives tone to religion and morals and forms the character of man. Every woman is the center around which others move. She may send forth healthy, purifying streams, which will enlighten the heart and nourish the seeds of virtue; or cast a dim shadow, which will enshroud those upon whom it falls in moral darkness. Woman should consecrate her beauty, her wit, her learning, and her all, to the cause of Christ. She should put aside selfishness, for a selfish person is not only hideous, but fiendish, and destructive. She should not rest at ease, heedless of the perishing souls who need her prayers, her songs of praise, her words of counsel, her interpretations of the Scriptures for their salvation. Many a conversion has been attributed to some soul-stirring song; indeed, there is no music so penetrating, so effective as that produced by the human voice. Much good has been accomplished by a well written tract commending some word of God, which has certainly not returned unto Him void, but has prospered in the thing whereunto God sent it. Often a short article, setting forth some digestible truth, is like seed sown in good ground, which will bring forth a hundred fold, or like bread cast upon the water, that may be seen and gathered after many days hence.

Perhaps the most important place of woman in the denomination is to teach the children at home, and wherever she can reach them, to love God, to reverence His holy name, and to love the Baptist Church. The moral training of the youth is the highest kind, and it is of vast importance that the first opportunity be seized for installing into the minds of children the sentiment of morality and religion, and the principles of the Baptist doctrine. The future of the denomination depends on the rising generation, and too much care can not be taken in the development of their characters. It requires constant, anxious watching to realize the embryo. Though the seed be long buried in dust, it shall not deceive your hopes—"the precious gain shall never be lost, for grace insures the crop."

The only foundation for all Christian graces is humility. Practice, as far as possible, Christ's meekness, his benevolence, his forgiveness of injuries, and his zeal for doing good. Woman is the hope of the Church, the hope of the world. God is slowly but surely working out the great problem of woman's place and position in life. Virtue will never reign supreme, and vice will never be wiped from the land, until woman's work of head, heart, and hand is recognized and accepted. No great institution has flourished without her support, neither has man succeeded without her, but the two must be unified. The work is not confined within the narrow limits of the church walls, not to the prayers sent forth or the songs sung. It extends far beyond this. Her work is in every cause, place, and institution where Christianity is required. The platform is broad, and upon it she must stand. Although the responsibilities to be met are great, the position is to be maintained. China, with her degraded million, India, with her ignorance and idolatry, dark and benighted Africa, yea, the world, with its sin and wickedness, all have just and imperative claims on woman, such as she can and must meet.

Dear women, the cry comes to us from afar to bring the light of love, and to lead into the paths of peace and righteousness. From your ranks, as mother, wife, daughter, sister, friend, little as you have hitherto thought of it, are to come the women of all professions, from the humble Christian to the expounder of His word; from the obedient citizen to the ruler of the land. This may be objectionable to many, but no profession should be recognized that fails to recognize Christ, and all the Christians have a legal right where He is, for "with Him there is neither Jew nor Greek, there is neither bond nor free, there is neither male nor female, for ye are all one in Christ Jesus." There is no necessity for a woman to step over the bounds of propriety, or to lay aside modesty, to further the work, and she will not, if God be her guide. If, indeed, the King of all the Universe chooses a woman to kill a man who had opposed Israel for twenty years, it is all right, and who dare question God's right, if he raise up a woman who shall become a judge, and a leader of his people? God, at one time, used a dumb brute to do His service, and that alone is sufficient to convince any one that He can use whom He will, and glorify himself by whatever means he pleases to employ. Should woman be silent in this busy, restless world of missions and vast church enterprises? No! A long, loud No! Give place for her, brethren. Be ready to accept her praying heart, her nimble fingers, her willing hands, her swift feet, her quick eye, her charming voice, the superintendent's chair, the Sunday School teacher's place, the Bible student, the prayer circle, the sick bed, the house of mourning, the foreign mission field, all these are her place.

Dear brethren, point them out, direct my sisters, and help them to work for Christ. My dear sisters, wherever you are, and wherever this paper may be mentioned, remember that there is no department of your life that you can not bend your influence to the benefit of our blessed denomination. Let us take sharpness out of our tongues and put in our pens; take the beauty from our face and put it into our lives; let us love ourselves less and God more; work less for self-aggrandizement, and more for the Church of Christ.

> "Do not then stand idly waiting,
> For some greater work to do,
> Fortune is a lazy goddess—
> She will never come to you.

> "Go, and toil in any vineyard,
> Do not fear to do and dare;
> If you want a field of labor,
> You can find it anywhere."

SIX ‖ Josephine Heard
       (1861–1921)

"WILL YOU ACCEPT A BUNCH of 'Morning Glories,' freshly plucked and with the Dew Drops still upon them?" Josephine Heard asked her readers in 1890. The poems, she explained, came "from a heart that desires to encourage and inspire the youth of the Race to pure and noble motives." *Morning Glories* sought to inspire black children through powerful images of home, hope, Sabbath bells, mockingbirds and Easter morning. Including elegies for several prominent church leaders, *Morning Glories* collected over seventy poems and included an introduction by African Methodist Episcopal Bishop Benjamin Tucker Tanner. The poems "may here and there come short," noted Tanner, "but for brightness of imagination, for readiness of expression, and now and then for delicateness of touch, they are genuinely poetical" and may "redeem the good name of the Race."

Born Josephine Delphine Henderson in Salisbury, North Carolina, Heard's parents sent her to Scotia Seminary in Concord and the Bethany Institute in New York. She then worked as a teacher in Mayesville, South Carolina, where she met and married William Henry Heard in 1882. William had been born a slave, but worked to become a teacher, a railway postal clerk, and, in the year he married Josephine, a minister in the A.M.E. Church. During his first post in Philadelphia Josephine compiled and

Source: Josephine Heard, "Welcome to Honorable F. Douglass," "Wilberforce," "The Black Sampson," "They Are Coming," and "Resting: In Memoriam of Mrs. Bishop Turner," from *Morning Glories* (Philadelphia, 1890), 12–13, 77–79, 88–89, 89–91, 100.

published her only poetry collection. She moved frequently for the rest of her life, assisting her husband's work in West Africa and the American South until her death in Philadelphia.

In poems like "Welcome to Hon. Frederick Douglass," Heard draws strong visual pictures for her readers, creating a pantheon of heroic leaders from the past to inspire present dignity. Founded in 1856 by Daniel Payne (1811–1893) and other church leaders, Wilberforce University was honored by Heard as a place that offers "the rarest, richest gifts to youth." "They come!" Heard exclaims, announcing the arrival of a new generation of doctors, lawyers, and preachers who will attend universities and, as she says in "They Are Coming," "who with honor yet shall shine." The pulse of the poems is pressing and urgent, marking a historical moment that, for Heard, anticipated a brighter day ahead: "You will hear the humming / Of the thousands that are falling into line." Yet more quotidian images of birth and motherhood suggest that the future of the race lies in the cultivating nurturance supplied by women, like Eliza Turner, wife of Bishop Henry McNeal Turner, who died in 1889, and who Heard memorialized as joyously standing at "the Lord Christ's feet." Steeped in Christian imagery and transformative opportunity, the poems of Josephine Heard presage the era of the 'New Negro,' when men and women alike would break all fetters to obtain their rights.

~∞~

Welcome to Hon. Frederick Douglass (1890)

Mt. Zion Church, March 5th 1888

> OUR hearts are filled with pride to-day—
> We hail thee, Noble Sire,
> Stern prejudice is swept away
> By Freedom's cleansing fire.
>
> And o'er this Southland you may roam,
> With ne'er a cause to fear—
> We bid thee WELCOME to our home,
> Welcome, and right good cheer'!
>
> From rugged Blue Ridge mountain peak,
> To ocean's white crest wave:
> Even infant lips thy praises speak,
> And boast thy deeds so brave.

The bondsman's fetters long since broke
And tossed aside by thee,
Thou hurledst off the *cursed* yoke,
And panted to be free.

We see thee in thy cradle-bed,
Thy mother's pride and joy;
When from oppression's hand you fled,
When but a strippling boy.

Thou, Moses of the negro race,
This day we hail with pride;
The day that brings us face to face,
And Douglass by our side.

But foul incendiary's cruel hand,
Thy Territory did invade;
By ruthless and destructive brand,
Thy lonely walls were lowly laid.

When night had hushed the birds to sleep,
Out of his covert see him creep;
The crackling flame and lurid glare,
Burst out upon the midnight air.
And what had seemed so strong and fair,
Now lay a mass of ruins there;
Triumphantly look'd all our foes,
And gloated o'er our many woes.

But men of iron nerve and will,
Looked up to God, with courage still:
Believing He their cries would heed,
And prove a friend in time of need.

The tiny seeds of kindness sown,
Into a mighty tree has grown,
And youth and maiden side by side,
Sit 'neath its spreading branches wide.

And though the seed be sown in Payne,
The trite old saying we maintain:
That whosoe'er in Payne we sow,
By faith's tears watered it shall grow.
Our trust untarnished by alloy,
We sow in tears but reap in joy;
And may thy praises never cease,
And all thy paths be those of peace.

Wilberforce (1890)

Read at the 25th Anniversary of Wilberforce, Ohio, June, 1887

A quarter century ago,
A March morning, bleak and wild,
The joyful news spread to and fro:
To Afro Methodist is born a child;
Begotten in the time of strife,
And born in adverse circumstances,
All trembled for the young child's life,
It seemed to have so poor a chance.
But, nursed by every care,
It stronger grew, until at last
Our hearts no longer feel a fear,
The danger is forever past.
The feeble childhood's days are flown,
How swiftly speed the years away;
We hail thee now a woman grown
In regal robes and Queen's array.

Thou dark-browed beauty of the west,
Thy matchless grace is widely known;
Rich jewels sparkle on thy breast,
Thy head supports a royal crown.
And through thy veins pure Africa's blood
Flows fearlessly along its course;
Thy cheeks are mantled by the flood;
We hail thee, lovely *Wilberforce!*

Thy palace gates are open wide—
All are invited to the feast;
From frigid North or Southern side,
From every point, from West to East.
Thou holdest in thine outstretched hand
The richest, rarest gifts to youth;
From snow-capped peak to ocean strand,
Thou offerest all the words of truth.

They come! their burning thirst, quench,
For wisdom, honor, knowledge, power;
From hidden depths rich jewels wrench—
Successful effort crowns each hour.

"They Are Coming" (1890)

THEY are coming, coming slowly—
They are coming, surely, surely—
In each avenue you hear the steady tread.
From the depths of foul oppression,
Comes a swarthy-hued procession,
And victory perches on their banners' head.

They are coming, coming slowly—
They are coming; yes, the lowly,
No longer writhing in their servile bands.
From the rice fields and plantation
Comes a factor of the nation,
And threatening, like Banquo's ghost, it stands.

They are coming, coming proudly—
They are crying, crying loudly:
O, for justice from the rulers of the land!
And that justice will be given,
For the mighty God of heaven
Holds the balance of power in his hand.

Prayers have risen, risen, risen
From the cotton fields and prison;

Though the overseer stood with lash in hand,
Groaned the overburdened heart;
Not a tear-drop dared to start—
But the Slaves' petition reach'd the glory-land.

They are coming, they are coming,
From away in tangled swamp,
Where the slimy reptile hid its poisonous head;
Through the long night and the day,
They have heard the bloodhounds' bey,
While the morass furnished them an humble
     bed.

They are coming, rising, rising,
And their progress is surprising,
By their brawny muscles earning daily bread;
Though their wages be a pittance,
Still each week a small remittance,
Builds a shelter for the weary toiling head.

They are coming, they are coming—
Listen! You will hear the humming
Of the thousands that are falling into line:
There are Doctors, Lawyers, Preachers;
There are Sculptors, Poets, Teachers—
Men and women, who with honor yet shall shine.

They are coming, coming boldly,
Though the Nation greets them coldly;
They are coming from the hillside and the plain.
With their scars they tell the story
Of the canebrakes wet and gory,
Where their brothers' bones lie bleaching with the slain.

They are coming, coming singing,
Their thanksgiving hymn is ringing.
For the clouds are slowly breaking now away,
And there comes a brighter dawning—
It is liberty's fair morning,
They are coming surely, coming, clear the way.

Yes, they come, their stepping's steady,
And their power is felt already—
God has heard the lowly cry of the oppressed:
And beneath his mighty frown,
Every wrong shall crumble down,
When the *right* shall triumph and the world be blest!

Resting: In Memoriam of Mrs. Bishop Turner (1890)

WE mourn to-day o'er our sister dead,
But sweet seemed the rest to the weary head;
The hands were calmly laid to rest,
O'er the pulseless bosom and painless breast.
The lips are silent and closely sealed,
The love of the Saviour, her smile revealed;
The weary feet that so often trod
Rough ways that led to the throne of God,
They tire no more, but forever are still;
They've reached the summit of Zion's hill!

Thrice had she come to the river before—
The boatman tarried to take her o'er,
But the voice of loved ones raised in prayer,
Prevailed with the Master her life to spare;
Then through life's day she gladly gleaned,
For the dear Saviour on whom she leaned—
A cup of cold water, or binding a wound,
Samaritan-like she was always found.

Her labors are ended, her trials are o'er,
Her soul has flown to the golden shore,
Where saints are rejoicing in white robes dressed,
And star-decked crowns on their brows are pressed.
Yes, she has passed on to the glory-land,
And bearing the sheaves she has gleaned in her hand;
The conflict is ended, her victory complete,
She casts her crown now at the Lord Christ's feet.

SEVEN § Anna Julia Cooper
(1858?–1964)

A NNA JULIA COOPER WAS BORN in North Carolina to Hannah Stanley Haywood and her mother's white owner. Freed at a young age, Anna was given a scholarship to attend the inaugural class of St. Augustine's Normal School in Raleigh, a newly established training school for free blacks sponsored by the Episcopal Church. After graduation she joined the school's faculty, and soon married fellow instructor and divinity student George Cooper. In 1879, after two years of marriage, her husband died. Cooper subsequently attended Oberlin College, where she received an M.A. in mathematics. She then taught at Wilberforce Academy and again at St. Augustine's before moving to Washington, D.C., in 1887. There she was a math and science instructor at the renowned Washington Colored High School. She became principal in 1902, and was increasingly recognized as the most accomplished African-American female scholar of her era.

While she advanced her career as a professional educator, Cooper also threw herself into the black women's club movement that emerged in urban communities in the 1890s. Women's clubs advocated a variety of social, moral, and educational reforms to improve the condition of African Americans, and Cooper found herself at the center of debates about temperance, lynching, unemployment, and women's roles. She helped to organize the Colored Women's League of Washington, D.C., and participated actively in the founding meeting of the National Conference of Colored Women. She also spoke at major international conferences, including the International Women's Congress in Chicago (1893)

Source: Anna Julia Cooper, *Voice from the South* (1892), pp. 127–148. (Xenia, Ohio: The Aldine Printing House, 1892).

and the Pan-African Conference in London (1900). A fierce and eloquent advocate for the civil rights of blacks and women, Cooper helped to build numerous institutions that worked for those causes.

The subject of history also fascinated Cooper, and she spent much of her life researching and writing to understand better the plight of African Americans. One of the few women active in the Bethel Literary and Historical Association in Washington, D.C., she was also the first woman invited to join the American Negro Academy, an organization populated by the foremost male African-American intellectuals of the day, such as Alexander Crummell, Carter Woodson, and her near-contemporary, W. E. B. DuBois. Later in her life Cooper would complete a doctorate in history at the Sorbonne after writing a thesis about late eighteenth-century revolutions in France and Haiti. She was the first black woman to earn a PhD at that institution, and only the fourth African-American woman in the world to earn a doctorate.

The piece reprinted here comes from her collection of essays, *A Voice from the South* (1892), which represents Cooper's best-known intellectual achievement and showcases her wide range of interests. Although the collection deals broadly with the condition of African Americans in the day, Cooper casts a broad historical net to understand where the race has come from and where it is going. In this piece she focuses on the historical role of women, and black women in particular. She divides American history into four different eras, exploring the integral parts played by women in the founding era (Queen Isabella, pioneer women) and the building era (educational and reform leaders such as Mary Lyon and Lucretia Mott). The current era is an era of acquisitiveness, she explains in her most pointedly critical section. She distances women from the historical development of capitalism, placing them instead at the heart of its solution. Women can mitigate the effects of materialist acquisitiveness through their "heart-power" and moral force.

But it is the *coming* era that occupies Cooper's imagination. In that future, she writes, women, especially black women, will serve not simply as help-meets. They will lead, employing their moral abilities and instincts to ensure national righteousness. Like many nineteenth-century Protestants, Cooper believed in women's innate spiritual capacities, exemplified by groups like the Women's Christian Temperance Union, an organization of women combating the primarily "male" problem of alcohol on behalf of society. Yet her analysis of gender and race was remarkably progressive. Her essay outlines the multiple deficits faced by African-American women, who had been silenced or sidelined by white men on account of their race and black men on account of their gender. Rather than seeing this invisibility as a deficiency, Cooper argues that as spectators, black women have had the distance and time to reflect on society's problems and to "hear the voices of God." African-American women possess a unique vantage from which to inform and influence the future of the society.

⸺∞⸺

The Status of Woman in America (1892)

JUST four hundred years ago an obscure dreamer and castle builder, prosaically poor and ridiculously insistent on the reality of his dreams, was enabled through the devotion of a noble woman to give to civilization a magnificent continent.

What the lofty purpose of Spain's pure-minded queen had brought to the birth, the untiring devotion of pioneer women nourished and developed. The dangers of wild beasts and of wilder men, the mysteries of unknown wastes and unexplored forests, the horrors of pestilence and famine, of exposure and loneliness, during all those years of discovery and settlement, were braved without a murmur by women who had been most delicately constituted and most tenderly nurtured.

And when the times of physical hardship and danger were past, when the work of clearing and opening up was over and the struggle for accumulation began, again woman's inspiration and help were needed and still was she loyally at hand. A Mary Lyon, demanding and making possible equal advantages of education for women as for men, and, in the face of discouragement and incredulity, bequeathing to women the opportunities of Holyoke.

A Dorothea Dix, insisting on the humane and rational treatment of the insane and bringing about a reform in the lunatic asylums of the country, making a great step forward in the tender regard for the weak by the strong throughout the world.

A Helen Hunt Jackson, convicting the nation of a century of dishonor in regard to the Indian.

A Lucretia Mott, gentle Quaker spirit, with sweet insistence, preaching the abolition of slavery and the institution, in its stead, of the brotherhood of man; her life and words breathing out in tender melody the injunction

> "Have love. Not love alone for one
> But man as man thy brother call;
> And scatter, like the circling sun,
> Thy charities *on all*."

And at the most trying time of what we have called the Accumulative Period, when internecine war, originated through man's love of gain and his determination to subordinate national interests and black men's rights alike to considerations of personal profit and loss, was drenching our country with its own best blood, who shall recount the name and fame of the women on both sides the senseless strife,—those uncomplaining souls with a great heart ache of their own, rigid features and pallid cheek their ever effective flag of truce, on the battle field, in the camp, in the hospital, binding up wounds, recording dying whispers for absent loved ones, with tearful eyes pointing to man's last refuge, giving the last earthly hand clasp and performing the last friendly office for strangers whom a great common sorrow had made kin, while they knew that somewhere—somewhere a husband, a brother, a father, a son, was being tended by stranger hands—or mayhap those familiar eyes were even then being closed forever by just such another ministering angel of mercy and love.

But why mention names? Time would fail to tell of the noble army of women who shine like beacon lights in the otherwise sordid wilderness of this accumulative period—prison reformers and tenement cleansers, quiet unnoted workers in hospitals and homes, among imbeciles, among outcasts— the sweetening, purifying antidotes for the poisons of man's acquisitiveness,— mollifying and soothing with the tenderness of compassion and love the wounds and bruises caused by his overreaching and avarice.

The desire for quick returns and large profits tempts capital ofttimes into unsanitary, well nigh inhuman investments,—tenement tinder boxes, sti- fling, stunting, sickening alleys and pestiferous slums; regular rents, no waiting, large percentages,—rich coffers coined out of the life-blood of human bodies and souls. Men and women herded together like cattle, breathing in malaria and typhus from an atmosphere seething with moral as well as physical impurity, revelling in vice as their native habitat and then, to drown the whisperings of their higher consciousness and effectually to hush the yearnings and accusations within, flying to narcotics and opiates— rum, tobacco, opium, binding hand and foot, body and soul, till the proper image of God is transformed into a fit associate for demons,—a besotted, enervated, idiotic wreck, or else a monster of wickedness terrible and destructive.

These are some of the legitimate products of the unmitigated tendencies of the wealth-producing period. But, thank Heaven, side by side with the cold, mathematical, selfishly calculating, so-called practical and unsenti- mental instinct of the business man, there comes the sympathetic warmth and sunshine of good women, like the sweet and sweetening breezes of spring, cleansing, purifying, soothing, inspiring, lifting the drunkard from the gutter, the outcast from the pit. Who can estimate the influence of these "daughters of the king," these lend-a-hand forces, in counteracting the selfishness of an acquisitive age?

To-day America counts her millionaires by the thousand; questions of tariff and questions of currency are the most vital ones agitating the public mind. In this period, when material prosperity and well earned ease and luxury are assured facts from a national standpoint, woman's work and woman's influence are needed as never before; needed to bring a heart power into this money getting, dollar-worshipping civilization; needed to bring a moral force into the utilitarian motives and interests of the time; needed to stand for God and Home and Native Land *versus gain and greed and grasping selfishness.*

There can be no doubt that this fourth centenary of America's discovery which we celebrate at Chicago, strikes the keynote of another important transition in the history of this nation; and the prominence of woman in the management of its celebration is a fitting tribute to the part she is destined to play among the forces of the future. This is the first congressional recognition of woman in this country, and this Board of Lady Managers constitute the first women legally appointed by any government to act in a national capacity. This of itself marks the dawn of a new day.

Now the periods of discovery, of settlement, of developing resources and accumulating wealth have passed in rapid succession. Wealth in the nation as in the individual brings leisure, repose, reflection. The struggle with nature is over, the struggle with ideas begins. We stand then, it seems to me, in this last decade of the nineteenth century, just in the portals of a new and untried movement on a higher plain and in a grander strain than any the past has called forth. It does not require a prophet's eye to divine its trend and image its possibilities from the forces we see already at work around us; nor is it hard to guess what must be the status of woman's work under the new regime.

In the pioneer days her role was that of a camp-follower, an additional something to fight for and be burdened with, only repaying the anxiety and labor she called forth by her own incomparable gifts of sympathy and appreciative love; unable herself ordinarily to contend with the bear and the Indian, or to take active part in clearing the wilderness and constructing the home.

In the second or wealth producing period her work is abreast of man's, complementing and supplementing, counteracting excessive tendencies, and mollifying over rigorous proclivities.

In the era now about to dawn, her sentiments must strike the keynote and give the dominant tone. And this because of the nature of her contribution to the world.

Her kingdom is not over physical forces. Not by might, nor by power can she prevail. Her position must ever be inferior where strength of muscle creates leadership. If she follows the instincts of her nature, however, she must always stand for the conservation of those deeper moral forces which make for the happiness of homes and the righteousness of the country. In a reign of moral ideas she is easily queen.

There is to my mind no grander and surer prophecy of the new era and of woman's place in it, than the work already begun in the waning years of the nineteenth century by the W. C. T. U. in America, an organization which has even now reached not only national but international importance, and seems destined to permeate and purify the whole civilized world. It is the living embodiment of woman's activities and woman's ideas, and its extent and strength rightly prefigure her increasing power as a moral factor.

The colored woman of to-day occupies, one may say, a unique position in this country. In a period of itself transitional and unsettled, her status seems one of the least ascertainable and definitive of all the forces which make for our civilization. She is confronted by both a woman question and a race problem, and is as yet an unknown or an unacknowledged factor in both. While the women of the white race can with calm assurance enter upon the work they feel by nature appointed to do, while their men give loyal support and appreciative countenance to their efforts, recognizing in most avenues of usefulness the propriety and the need of woman's distinctive co-operation, the colored woman too often finds herself hampered and shamed by a less liberal sentiment and a more conservative attitude on the part of those for whose opinion she cares most. That this is not universally true I am glad to admit. There are to be found both intensely conservative white men and exceedingly liberal colored men. But as far as my experience goes the average man of our race is less frequently ready to admit the actual need among the sturdier forces of the world for woman's help or influence. That great social and economic questions await her interference, that she could throw any light on problems of national import, that her intermeddling could improve the management of school systems, or elevate the tone of public institutions, or humanize and sanctify the far reaching influence of prisons and reformatories and improve the treatment of lunatics and imbeciles,—that she has a word worth hearing on mooted questions in political economy, that she could contribute a suggestion on the relations of labor and capital, or offer a thought on honest money and honorable trade, I fear the majority of "Americans of the colored variety" are not yet prepared to concede. It may be that they do not yet see these questions in their right perspective, being absorbed in the immediate needs of their own political complications. A good deal depends on where we put the emphasis in this world; and our men are not perhaps to blame if they see everything colored by the light of those agitations in the midst of which they live and move and have their being. The part they have had to play in American history during the last twenty-five or thirty years has tended rather to exaggerate the importance of mere political advantage, as well as to set a fictitious valuation on those able to secure such advantage. It is the astute politician, the manager who can gain preferment for himself and his favorites, the demagogue known to stand in with the powers at the White House and consulted on the bestowal of government plums, whom we set in high places and denominate great. It is they who receive the hosannas of the multitude and are regarded as leaders of the people. The thinker and the doer, the man who solves the problem by enriching his country with an invention worth thousands or by a thought inestimable and precious is given neither bread nor a stone. He is too often left to die in obscurity and neglect even if spared in his life the bitterness of fanatical jealousies and detraction.

And yet politics, and surely American politics, is hardly a school for great minds. Sharpening rather than deepening, it develops the faculty of taking advantage of present emergencies rather than the insight to distinguish between the true and the false, the lasting and the ephemeral advantage. Highly cultivated selfishness rather than consecrated benevolence is its passport to success. Its votaries are never seers. At best they are but manipulators—often only jugglers. It is conducive neither to profound statesmanship nor to the higher type of manhood. Altruism is its *mauvais succes* and naturally enough it is indifferent to any factor which cannot be worked into its own immediate aims and purposes. As woman's influence as a political element is as yet nil in most of the commonwealths of our republic, it is not surprising that with those who place the emphasis on mere political capital she may yet seem almost a nonentity so far as it concerns the solution of great national or even racial perplexities.

There are those, however, who value the calm elevation of the thoughtful spectator who stands aloof from the heated scramble; and, above the turmoil and din of corruption and selfishness, can listen to the teachings of eternal truth and righteousness. There are even those who feel that the black man's unjust and unlawful exclusion temporarily from participation in the elective franchise in certain states is after all but a lesson "in the desert" fitted to develop in him insight and discrimination against the day of his own appointed time. One needs occasionally to stand aside from the hum and rush of human interests and passions to hear the voices of God. And it not unfrequently happens that the All-loving gives a great push to certain souls to thrust them out, as it were, from the distracting current for awhile to promote their discipline and growth, or to enrich them by communion and reflection. And similarly it may be woman's privilege from her peculiar coigne of vantage as a quiet observer, to whisper just the needed suggestion or the almost forgotten truth. The colored woman, then, should not be ignored because her bark is resting in the silent waters of the sheltered cove. She is watching the movements of the contestants none the less and is all the better qualified, perhaps, to weigh and judge and advise because not herself in the excitement of the race. Her voice, too, has always been heard in clear, unfaltering tones, ringing the changes on those deeper interests which make for permanent good. She is always sound and orthodox on questions affecting the well-being of her race. You do not find the colored woman selling her birthright for a mess of pottage. Nay, even after reason has retired from the contest, she has been known to cling blindly with the instinct of a turtle dove to those principles and policies which to her mind promise hope and safety for children yet unborn. It is notorious that ignorant black women in the South have actually left their husbands' homes and repudiated their support for what was understood by the wife to be race disloyalty, or "voting away," as she expresses it, the privileges of herself and little ones.

It is largely our women in the South to-day who keep the black men solid in the Republican party. The latter as they increase in intelligence and power of discrimination would be more apt to divide on local issues at any rate. They begin to see that the Grand Old Party regards the Negro's cause as an outgrown issue, and on Southern soil at least finds a too intimate acquaintanceship with him a somewhat unsavory recommendation. Then, too, their political wits have been sharpened to appreciate the fact that it is good policy to cultivate one's neighbors and not depend too much on a distant friend to fight one's home battles. But the black woman can never forget—however lukewarm the party may to-day appear—that it was a Republican president who struck the manacles from her own wrists and gave the possibilities of manhood to her helpless little ones; and to her mind a Democratic Negro is a traitor and a time-server. Talk as much as you like of venality and manipulation in the South, there are not many men, I can tell you, who would dare face a wife quivering in every fiber with the consciousness that her husband is a coward who could be paid to desert her deepest and dearest interests.

Not unfelt, then, if unproclaimed has been the work and influence of the colored women of America. Our list of chieftains in the service, though not long, is not inferior in strength and excellence, I dare believe, to any similar list which this country can produce.

Among the pioneers, Frances Watkins Harper could sing with prophetic exaltation in the darkest days, when as yet there was not a rift in the clouds overhanging her people:

> "Yes, Ethiopia shall stretch
> Her bleeding hands abroad;
> Her cry of agony shall reach the burning throne of God.
> Redeemed from dust and freed from chains
> Her sons shall lift their eyes,
> From cloud-capt hills and verdant plains
> Shall shouts of triumph rise."

Among preachers of righteousness, an unanswerable silencer of cavilers and objectors, was Sojourner Truth, that unique and rugged genius who seemed carved out without hand or chisel from the solid mountain mass; and in pleasing contrast, Amanda Smith, sweetest of natural singers and pleaders in dulcet tones for the things of God and of His Christ.

Sarah Woodson Early and Martha Briggs, planting and watering in the school room, and giving off front their matchless and irresistible personality an impetus and inspiration which can never die so long as there lives and breathes a remote descendant of their disciples and friends.

Charlotte Fortin Grimke, the gentle spirit whose verses and life link her so beautifully with America's great Quaker poet and loving reformer.

Hallie Quinn Brown, charming reader, earnest effective lecturer and devoted worker of unflagging zeal and unquestioned power.

Fannie Jackson Coppin, the teacher and organizer, pre-eminent among women of whatever country or race in constructive and executive force.

These women represent all shades of belief and as many departments of activity; but they have one thing in common—their sympathy with the oppressed race in America and the consecration of their several talents in whatever line to the work of its deliverance and development.

Fifty years ago woman's activity according to orthodox definitions was on a pretty clearly cut "sphere," including primarily the kitchen and the nursery, and rescued from the barrenness of prison bars by the womanly mania for adorning every discoverable bit of china or canvass with forlorn looking cranes balanced idiotically on one foot. The woman of to-day finds herself in the presence of responsibilities which ramify through the profoundest and most varied interests of her country and race. Not one of the issues of this plodding, toiling, sinning, repenting, falling, aspiring humanity can afford to shut her out, or can deny the reality of her influence. No plan for reno-vating society, no scheme for purifying politics, no reform in church or in state, no moral, social, or economic question, no movement upward or down-ward in the human plane is lost on her. A man once said when told his house was afire: "Go tell my wife; I never meddle with household affairs." But no woman can possibly put herself or her sex outside any of the interests that affect humanity. All departments in the new era are to be hers, in the sense that her interests are in all and through all; and it is incumbent on her to keep intelligently and sympathetically *en rapport* with all the great move-ments of her time, that she may know on which side to throw the weight of her influence. She stands now at the gateway of this new era of American civ-ilization. In her hands must be moulded the strength, the wit, the statesman-ship, the morality, all the psychic force, the social and economic intercourse of that era. To be alive at such an epoch is a privilege, to be a woman then is sublime.

In this last decade of our century, changes of such moment are in progress, such new and alluring vistas are opening out before us, such original and rad-ical suggestions for the adjustment of labor and capital, of government and the governed, of the family, the church and the state, that to be a possible factor though an infinitesimal in such a movement is pregnant with hope and weighty with responsibility. To be a woman in such an age carries with it a privilege and an opportunity never implied before. But to be a woman of the Negro race in America, and to be able to grasp the deep significance of the possibilities of the crisis, is to have a heritage, it seems to me, unique in the ages. In the first place, the race is young and full of the elasticity and hopefulness of youth. All its achievements are before it. It does not look on the masterly triumphs of nineteenth century civilization with that *blasé*, world-weary look which charac-terizes the old washed out and worn out races which have already, so to speak, seen their best days.

Said a European writer recently: "Except the Sclavonic, the Negro is the only original and distinctive genius which has yet to come to growth—and the feeling is to cherish and develop it."

Everything to this race is new and strange and inspiring. There is a quick-ening of its pulses and a glowing of its self-consciousness. Aha, I can rival that! I can aspire to that! I can honor my name and vindicate my race! Something like this, it strikes me, is the enthusiasm which stirs the genius of young Africa in America; and the memory of past oppression and the fact of present attempted repression only serve to gather momentum for its irre-pressible powers. Then again, a race in such a stage of growth is peculiarly sensitive to impressions. Not the photographer's sensitized plate is more delicately impressionable to outer influences than is this high strung people here on the threshold of a career.

What a responsibility then to have the sole management of the primal lights and shadows! Such is the colored woman's office. She must stamp weal or woe on the coming history of this people. May she see her opportunity and vindicate her high prerogative.

EIGHT | S. Elizabeth Frazier
| (1864–1924)

SUSAN ELIZABETH FRAZIER WAS BORN in New York to Louis M. and Helen Eldridge Frazier. She attended the public schools and graduated from Hunter College in 1888. After working as a substitute teacher, she applied to work full-time in the New York City public schools only to be deferred multiple times. She then lodged a discrimination complaint against the school authorities only to be told that race was not a factor in their assessment of candidates. Several months later, she received a teaching position which she held for more than thirty years. This appointment caused some controversy, as she was the first woman of color teaching at an integrated school in New York. In addition to her educational career, she was the president of the Woman's Auxiliary to the Old Fifteenth National Guard, president of the Woman's Loyal Union, and an active member of St. Phillip's Protestant Episcopal Church, where she was a teacher in the Sunday school and served as president of the Church Missionary Society.

In addition to her teaching and reform work, Frazier contributed to *Woman's Era*, the first newspaper aimed specifically toward African-American women. Josephine St. Pierre Ruffin, editor of the monthly *Woman's Era*, recommended to women that they expand their horizons beyond the home. "We as women," Ruffin remarked, "have been too unobtrusive, too little known." Frazier was possibly also a member of the National Federation of Afro-American Women and the National Association of Colored Women, both of which used *Woman's*

Source: "Some Afro-American Women of Mark," *AME Church Review* 8 (April 1892), 373, 384–386.

Era as their official voice. These organizations explicitly encouraged education and social activism for black women, fostering refinement and personal discipline associated with the mainline denominations to which so many of their leaders were loyal. "For turn-of-the-century club women... printed text served as both representation and promoter of language as political change agent," wrote Anne Ruggles Gere and Sara R. Robbins in their study of *Woman's Era*. "Club women who read printed texts composed by other club women could... inhabit new discourses, new ways of thinking about themselves and their positions in the social world."[1]

In "Some Afro American Women of Mark," a talk read before the Brooklyn Literary Union on February 16, 1892, Frazier constructed a scrapbook of great women reminiscent of Hallie Quinn Brown's *Homespun Heroines*. The section excerpted below follows passages where Frazier nominates Phillis Wheatley, Frances Ellen Watkins Harper, Mary Ann Shadd Cary, Charlotte Forten, and H. Cordelia Ray as "women of mark" for their contributions to literature and especially poetry. In this section Frazier moves beyond the literary into a rendition of leading figures in education, medicine, and sculpture. She takes pains to cite commencement exercises, to highlight financial and institutional constraints, and to note the particular aspects of character that allow these women to surpass the pervasive oppressions of their history. Frazier's speech highlights how important it was to record names and to canonize their accomplishments within the archival record, to lift women from obscurity to the nobility of documented race notice. "We young women of the race have a great work to do," Frazier concludes, pointing to these predecessors as the preface to that laboring future.

Some Afro-American Women of Mark (1892)

We have heard and read much of men of mark of our race, but comparatively little is known of able Afro-American women. It is my delight to present brief sketches of the lives of "Some Afro-American Women of Mark," having gained my information concerning them from libraries, public and private, from correspondence and from personal knowledge.

Notwithstanding the obstacles that presented themselves to Afro-American women, some of them, self-prompted, and in some cases self-taught,

---

[1] Anne Ruggles Gere and Sara R. Robbins, "Gendered Literacy in Black and White: Turn-of-the-Century African-American and European-American Club Women's Printed Texts," *Signs: Journal of Women in Culture and Society* 21:3 (Spring 1996), 658.

have removed obstacles, lived down oppression and fought their way nobly on to achieve the accomplishment of their aim.

Slavery was the greatest barrier in the way of progress to the African race. History records the fact that slavery was introduced in America in 1620, in Virginia. The slave trade then began by bringing slaves from Africa. This trade continued to grow, and gradually spread throughout the Middle and New England States, except Vermont. Boston, Mass., held her slave markets in common with other cities. In the year 1761, a time when slavery had reached its zenith, was seen one of the most pitiable sights ever witnessed in the Boston slave market, that of eighty girls, of various ages, brought from Africa, each snatched from a mother's fond embrace by hands most cruel, taken to a slave vessel, huddled together like cattle, with but little clothing to cover their nude forms, a dearth of food and nowhere to rest their weary bodies.

The portion assigned them, the hold of the ship, has been described as having been a room thirteen by twenty-five and five feet eight inches high. Can we imagine the trials, the tortures of these poor innocent girls so situated? As soon as the vessel reached the port of Boston, these girls were taken to the market and advertised for sale, to which sale purchasers flocked. Among the many attending this sale was a Mrs. Wheatley, wife of a Boston merchant. She, although in possession of a number of slaves, was desirous of finding a young slave girl with apparent docile qualities, in order that she might train her to be of service to her in her declining years.

Mrs. Wheatley carefully observed the various expressions of countenances, the many physical differences of this group, and was particularly moved by the meek and bright countenance of one half-sick, fatigued little girl about eight years old, who, to her mind, possessed the requisite qualities. She immediately purchased her, took her home, clothed and fed her, and gave her the name of Phillis Wheatley. Kind words, nourishment and warm clothing made such a marked change in the child that she was now a new being. Mrs. Wheatley, perceiving the child's improvement physically, still knew that by nature Phillis was unfit for heavy domestic work, and had her taught that which was lighter. Phillis knew no language save that of her native land, and so Mrs. Wheatley deemed it necessary for her welfare, as well as that of the child, to have her taught to speak the English language, and so requested her only daughter, Miss Mary Wheatley, to teach her to speak the English language and, what was most uncommon, to read it.

This was in opposition to the principles of slavery; but Mrs. Wheatley dared to do contrary to the slave owners of her time, doubtless through the Divine inspiration of the Almighty, for God moves in a mysterious way His wonders to perform." Miss Wheatley kindly consented to teach Phillis. Much to her surprise, she found Phillis very apt and thirsting for knowledge. Daily she progressed, and in less than two years was able to read the most difficult portions of the Bible with accuracy. Most of her knowledge of writing she acquired through her own efforts, scrutinizing good writing and copying with rude materials upon rough surfaces when paper and pencil were beyond reach. Phillis, unlike other children of her years, sought pleasure in close application to study. Mrs. Wheatley and family determined not to curb the child's ambition, but to provide her with books and writing material, which were to Phillis the means to procure the end.

Four years from the time Phillis was purchased in the slave market, she was able to write on many subjects that were hardly expected of one double her years. Her correspondence with some friends of Mrs. Wheatley, in England and with Obour Tanner, a fellow-slave, in Newport (supposed to be one of the girls brought from Africa with Phillis, also intelligent), evinced, from her power of expression and originality of thought, a mind of more than ordinary vigor.

Feeling that she had acquired sufficient knowledge of the English language, being then in her seventeenth year, she directed her attention to the study of Latin. In this, as in English, her efforts were crowned with success. In a short time she translated one of Ovid's tales so admirably that the writing attracted the attention of the learned people of Boston and England, who sought her at the home of the Wheatleys, and, conversing with her, found she was indeed a literary prodigy. This production, coming from a member of an enslaved race, gave rise to so many comments that all America, as well as England, was in a ferment, for it should be remembered that this period did not witness general culture among the masses of white people, and certainly no facilities for the education of the Negroes. The learned people of Boston invited her to their homes, loaned her books and papers. It is safe for me to say, that contact with the great minds of the time constituted one of the best parts of her education. Phillis was sensitive, and understood the prejudice existing against her race, and, while enjoying many privileges denied her kind, still maintained that meek manner characteristic of her when first seen in the slave market, and treated her fellow-slaves with the utmost consideration, winning from all affection. The inquisitive mind of Phillis was continually prompting her to seek the best works; from her study of the muses she acquired a taste for poetry, and successfully wrote many poems, which were characterized by a spirit of gratitude, simplicity, chastity, Christianity. Early she devoted herself to the service of the Lord, and was received in the Old South Church, Boston.

At the age of twenty Phillis was emancipated by her master. It was a source of great delight to her owners to see that, although Phillis had been declared free, she still remained the same, thanking God for His goodness in placing her in such considerate hands:

> 'Twas mercy brought me from my pagan land,
> Taught my benighted soul to understand
> That there's a God; that there's a Saviour, too.
> Once I redemption neither sought nor knew.
>
> Some view our sable race with scornful eye:
> "Their color is a diabolic dye."
> Remember, Christians, Negroes black as Cain
> May be refined, and join the angelic train.

Signs of precarious health, probably superinduced by too close application to study, became more marked and caused her mistress to become anxious about her. Mrs. Wheatley consulted her physician, who prescribed for Phillis a sea-voyage. Mrs. Wheatley's only son was about to sail for England on mercantile business, and arrangements were made for Phillis to go with him.

Her poem, entitled "A Farewell to America," dated May 7, 1773, is the day on which she is supposed to have sailed. George Williams, in his renowned "History of the Negro Race," says, "She was heartily welcomed by the leaders of the British metropolis and treated with great consideration." Under all the trying circumstances of high social life among the nobility and rarest literary genius of London, this redeemed child of the desert coupled to a beautiful modesty the extraordinary powers of an incomparable conversationalist. She carried London by storm. Thoughtful people praised her, titled people dined her, and the press extolled the name of Phillis Wheatley, the African poetess.

In England, her book of poems was republished through the earnest solicitation of her friends, and dedicated to the Countess of Huntington, with a picture of Phillis, and a letter of recommendation from her master, signed by many of the leading citizens of Boston. This letter was to repress all doubts that might arise concerning the authorship of the poems. Before she had regained her strength she received a letter from home, telling of the illness of Mrs. Wheatley and requesting her to return. As soon as possible, she was at the bedside of her loved one. Mrs. Wheatley expressed her relief at the presence of Phillis, and seemed perfectly satisfied. Day by day Mrs. Wheatley grew worse; finally the end came, March 3, 1774. This was, indeed, a sad hour for Phillis, for she realized that her best, her dearest friend was gone. Phillis remained in the Wheatley household and resumed her literary work.

When George Washington was appointed by the grand Continental Congress, in 1775, to be Generalissimo of the Armies of North America,

Phillis sent him a letter extolling his merits, and also a poem written in his honor, which brought forth the following reply from Washington:

CAMBRIDGE, February 28, 1776.
MISS PHILLIS:

I thank you most sincerely for your polite notice of me in the elegant lines you inclosed, and however undeserving I may be of such encomium and panegyric, the style and manner exhibit a striking proof of your poetical talents.

If you should ever come to Cambridge, or near headquarters, I shall be happy to see a person so favored by the muses, and to whom nature has been so liberal and beneficent in her dispensations.

I am,
With great respect,
GEORGE WASHINGTON.

No woman of the race, since the death of Phillis Wheatey, has attracted more attention by her poetic productions than Frances Ellen Watkins Harper. To her is given the honor of being the ablest female lecturer of her race. Frances Ellen Watkins Harper was born in Baltimore, of free parents, in 1825. She attended the school in Baltimore for free colored children, taught by her uncle, Rev. Peter Watkins, and continued there until her thirteenth year, at which time she was put out to work in a kind and respected family. Although free-born, she suffered much from the oppressive laws that bound her slave-brethren. Like Phillis Wheatley, she possessed an ardent thirst for knowledge. Before she had been employed in this family a year, her poetic productions, especially essays on "Christianity," attracted the attention of her employers, who encouraged her ambition by giving her the use of their library during her leisure moments. As a result of her communion with the best works, she was able to write many poems, as well as prose pieces, which she had published in a small volume called "Forest Leaves." This book attracted unusual attention as an earnest of what the writer could do. Feeling herself qualified, she took up teaching. In her own city the opposition was so bitter that she deemed it wise to go to a free State, and chose Ohio for her work.

Here she became dissatisfied and left for York, Penn., to resume her work. Blessed with a spirit of philanthropy, a generous mind and a sound judgment, understanding the wrongs perpetrated on her kind, she set to work to devise some means of ameliorating the condition of the race. In order that she might concentrate her efforts in this direction, she gave up teaching and found her way into the lecture field from the following circumstance: "About the year 1853, Maryland, her native State, had enacted a law forbidding free people of color from the North from coming into the State on pain of being imprisoned and sold into slavery. A free man, who had unwittingly violated this infamous statute, had recently been sold to Georgia, and had escaped thence by secreting himself behind the wheel-house of a boat bound northward; but before he reached the desired haven he was discovered and remanded to slavery. It was reported that he died soon after from exposure and suffering." In a letter to a friend referring to this outrage, Mrs. Harper thus wrote: "Upon that grave I pledge myself to the anti-slavery cause." Soon after she left York and went to Philadelphia, then to Boston, to New Bedford. Here she was called upon to deliver an address on the "Education and Elevation of the Colored Race." In this address she poured forth a stream of eloquence that astonished all present. This occasion marks the beginning of her public career. On she has continued, fearless in her outspoken opinions. She has lectured on freedom in every Southern city except in Arkansas and Texas; has held the position of Superintendent of Colored Work in the Woman's Christian Temperance Union for nearly seven years, and has lectured and written many poems on temperance, exerting a widespread influence.

None felt more keenly the death of John Brown, the noble hero who planned and died for the cause of emancipation, than Mrs. Harper. Tenderly she expressed her sympathy for Mrs. Brown in her bereavement, beseeching God to sustain her in the hour of affliction.

Mrs. Harper was married to Fenton Harper in Cincinnati, November, 1860. She still labored in the literary field, never giving up unless compelled to do so by other duties. On May 23, 1864, occurred the death of Mr. Harper. Some of her best productions are "The Slave Mother," "To the Union Savers of Cleveland," "Fifteenth Amendment." "Moses," a story of the Nile, deals with the story of the Hebrew Moses, beautifully portrayed by her from his infancy, when exposed on the Nile, found and adopted by Pharaoh's daughter; his gratitude to the princess; his flight into Midian and his return into Egypt; his nomadic life, by means of which God prepared him to be the means of deliverance to His people; to his death on Mount Nebo, and his burial in an unknown grave, following closely the account of the Scriptures.

Mrs. Harper is now engaged in writing a book called "Iola," which is a work on the racial question. May we not hope that the rising generation, at least, will take encouragement by her example and find an argument of race force in favor of mental and moral equality, and, above all, be awakened to see how prejudice and difficulties may be surmounted by continual struggles, intelligence and a virtuous character.

We also find in the lecture field, working for the best interest of her race, Mary Ann Shadd Carey, also an able writer and teacher. *Mary Ann Shadd Carey* was born in Delaware, and received a better education than was usually obtained by free colored people. As a speaker she ranks deservedly high; as a debater she is quick to take advantage of the weak points of her opponents, forcible in her illustrations, biting in her sarcasm.

The name of Charlotte L. Grimke, *nee* Forten, appears before me. A woman of rare intellectual gifts, a moral nature full of sympathy and benevolence for her race. Charlotte L. Grimke was born in Philadelphia. Like her predecessors, obstacles in the way of progress presented themselves to her. In her native city, then the most bitterly prejudiced of Northern cities, she was refused admission to institutions of learning, and was sent to school in New England—to Salem, Massachusetts. Here prejudice existed, but not so much as in Philadelphia. She was received into the grammar school at Salem. She was the only colored pupil in the school, and won the esteem of her teachers and fellow-pupils. A short time before graduation from this school, the principal requested each student of the graduating class, of which she was a member, to write a poem to be sung at the closing exercises, the successful competitor to be known only on that day. This proved a stimulus in drawing out the poetic genius of the young aspirants. The manuscripts were collected, each bearing a fictitious name. One of the many was selected and printed on the programme. This was the poem, entitled A PARTING HYMN.

To the surprise of all, this beautiful hymn was written by Charlotte L. Forten, the only colored pupil of her class, the only one of the school, convincing the prejudiced minds of the possibilities of her race.

She next entered the Normal School, from which she graduated, and was offered a position to teach in one of the schools, which offer she accepted, being the first colored woman to teach in a white school. She continued to teach until her health became impaired, and was advised, by her physician, to go South. After recuperating in Philadelphia for a time, she went farther South to teach the freedmen at Port Royal, on the coast of South Carolina, a deeply interesting work to her, and the years spent in that work the most delightful of her life; and while here, at the suggestion of her beloved and life-long friend, Mr. Whittier, she wrote some articles about life there. She afterward resided in Boston and Cambridge, where she became assistant secretary of the Teacher's Committee of the New England Freedmen's Aid Society. When this society disbanded, she went to Washington to reside, and there married Rev. Francis J. Grimke, who is well known to us as an eloquent divine. To him she has been a true minister's wife, and has done much to make his ministerial career successful. She has contributed to the *Anti-Slavery Standard, Boston Commonwealth, Boston Christian Register*. She has made some translations from the French, among them one of the Eickmann Chatrien Novels, entitled "Madame Therese," which was published by Scribner some years ago. Of late years Mrs. Grimke has been able to write but little, owing to her continued ill-health, which is the source of deep regret not only to herself, but to her many friends. One of her more recent writings, "A June Song," was read at the closing exercises of the "Monday Night Literary," at Cedar Hill, the residence of the Hon. Frederick Douglass.

H. Cordelia Ray, daughter of the late Rev. Chas. B. Ray, is a woman full of *savoir-faire*, and stands among our able women writers, not only in poetry, but in prose, excelling in poetry in the sonnet, in prose critical literature. Miss Ray was born and educated in New York City, and began to weave verses at the age of ten years. Among her poems are "The Mist-maiden," "The Hermit of the Soul," "Dante," "Antigone and Edipus," "Reverie," "Hour's Glory," "Lincoln" (written by request and recited for the unveiling of the Freedmen's monument at Washington in memory of Abraham Lincoln). This poem was quite widely copied in the papers.

Among the group of illustrative sonnets are, "Shakespeare, the Poet," "Raphael, the Artist," "Beethoven, the Musician," "Emerson, the Philosopher," "Sumner, the Statesman," "Toussaint L'Overture, the Patriot," "Wendell Phillips, the Philanthropist." Miss H. Cordelia Ray teaches in Grammar School No. 80, New York City, of which Professor Charles L. Reason is principal.

In June, 1891, the University of the City of New York held their commencement exercises. At this commencement, first in the history of education, university pedagogical degrees were conferred. An event of historic interest. Fourteen members of the University School of Pedagogy received the degree of Doctor of Pedagogy, and twelve the degree of Master of Pedagogy. Of the twelve, I am proud to say, three were colored—Miss H. Cordelia Ray, of whom I have just spoken, Miss Florence T. Ray and Miss Mary Eato. Miss J. Imogen Howard now attends the university, and will be the next to receive the degree of Master of Pedagogy.

Mrs. Sara J. S. Garnet has proved herself the pioneer for the maintenance of colored schools, and an advocate of the higher education of women. Mrs. Garnet is a teacher of varied experience. She has filled the positions from the lowest primary grades. She was an assistant in Grammar School No. 1, Mulberry Street, New York, principal of Primary Department No. 3, Brooklyn, and afterward appointed principal of Grammar School No. 81, Seventeenth Street,

New York, where she has served faithfully twenty-six years. Being a member of the National Teachers' Association for many years, and many times the only colored representative from this section of the country, she has enjoyed extensive travel over our own country and is well up in points of interest and information as regards the educational system and general development of our own country. As a philanthropist, nothing of interest to the race within her power and ability to be achieved has been lost. All opportunities are carefully watched and treasured for opportune development.

In Philadelphia, we find *Mrs. Fannie Jackson Coppin*, principal of the Philadelphia Institute for, Colored, Youth, an acute thinker, an eloquent speaker, a benefactress to her race. Mrs. Coppin was born in the District of Columbia about the year 1837, and was left an orphan when quite young. She was brought up by her aunt, Mrs. Clark. In Washington the opportunities for education were limited, that is to say for the race. Anxious to gain knowledge, she left and went to New Bedford, in her sixteenth year, where she began the studies of the higher branches. She entered Oberlin College and graduated with honor. Through her untiring efforts, the Philadelphia Institute for Colored Youth was founded for the purpose of giving Negro children an industrial as well as an intellectual education. This institution is a success. Says John Durham, now minister to Hayti, of Mrs. Coppin and her work: "Long before the industrial-training idea threatened to become a fad, she had introduced it into this institute for boys and girls. Had she been other than an American colored woman, or had she not had to struggle against the characteristic conservatism of the Society of Friends, she would have been one of the most famous of America's school reform instructors. As it is she works on modestly, indeed, too self-deprecating; eminent, but without notoriety."

It is said that the science of medicine has been regarded as ranking among the most intricate and delicate pursuits man could follow. Not long ago, woman began to feel that the science of medicine was not too intricate, not too delicate for her to follow, and so set herself to work to gain admission to some of the schools of medicine, that she, too, might become equipped with the necessary medical training, that would enable her to relieve the wants of suffering humanity. Nowhere was greater opposition to be found than in the profession and in the community.

It was doubted as to whether she was physically able to endure the hardships necessarily implied in an active practice. Slowly the portals of medicine opened to her, and earnestly she pursued her study. Afro-American women, best fitted by nature and education, have, like their white sisters, labored, although in the presence of more opposition, and met with success in the science of medicine. Those of mark are: Dr. Consuello Clark, Cincinnati; Dr. Caroline Anderson, Philadelphia; Dr. Hall Tanner and Dr. Susan McKinney. Dr. Susan McKinney leads the van in opening a sphere of usefulness. Dr. Susan McKinney, *nee* Smith, was born in Brooklyn, her father being the late Sylvanus Smith. The *Brooklyn Daily Eagle*, in mentioning and giving accounts of some able and noted colored people in Brooklyn, gave this interesting account of Dr. Susan McKinney:

"Dr. McKinney is a striking instance of force of character, conquering extraordinary, almost obdurate obstacles, and achieving success in the midst of difficulties that would dismay a giant. She not only had to overcome the prejudice against female practitioners, but those against her race. Her spirit was equal to the task, however, and at this moment her reputation is such that any woman, irrespective of color, might be proud of it. Dr. McKinney was a student in the Woman's Medical College, New York, under Dr. Clement Lozier, a professional woman of liberal ideas, a strong battler against the prejudice of caste, who first advocated the admission of colored women into the college. Shortly after Dr. McKinney's graduation she commenced to practice, an uphill course. Patients were slow in coming; her own race apparently mistrusted the skill of a colored medical woman. While she belongs to a class, that of Homeopathy, at that time discountenanced by the masses, she persevered and is now well established."

In former years she had sustained herself as a teacher in a public school, this city, out of the earnings of which position she defrayed her college expenses. That experience nerved her to struggle desperately for a standing in the medical profession at a juncture when to be courageous appeared foolish, so hopeless seemed the future. Dr. McKinney is one of the doctors on the medical staff of the Woman's Dispensary, on Classon Avenue, a member of the King's County and the New York Staff and City Society of Homeopathy, and a member of the Alumni Society. She has lectured on subjects bearing on her profession in several cities. One of the faculty of the college from which she graduated took the pains to look her up and engage her to attend a female member of his family, giving as his reason for so doing that she was, he thought, the brightest member of the class from which she was graduated. This was a high authority, and, therefore, complimentary to Dr. Susan McKinney.

The race points with pride to *Edmonia Lewis*, the greatest of her race in the art of sculpture. Her latent genius was stirred at the sight of a statue of Benjamin Franklin, in Boston. "I, too, can make a stone man," she said. She expressed her desire in this direction to William Lloyd Garrison, "that great Apostle of Human Liberty," and begged his advice. William Lloyd Garrison encouraged her and gave her a letter to the greatest sculptor of Boston, who, after reading the note, gave her a model of a human foot and some clay, and said, "Go home and make that; if there is anything in you it will come out." Delighted, she went, and worked out a copy. As soon as it was finished she returned to the sculptor. He was not pleased with it and broke it up, telling her to try again. She was not discouraged, for she was determined to achieve success in this art. Again she tried and obtained victory. "She has won a position as an artist, a studio in Rome, and a place in the admiration of lovers of art on two continents." Her studio in Rome is an object of interest to all European travelers. The most prominent of her works are, "Hagar in the Wilderness," a group of "Madonna with the Infant Christ and two adoring Angels," "Forever Free," "Hiawatha's Wooing," a bust of Longfellow the poet, a bust of John Brown, and a medallion portrait of Wendell Phillips. There are other Afro-American women of mark, brief accounts of whose lives I would be pleased to give, but the limited space will not permit.

We young women of the race have a great work to do. We have noble and brilliant examples of women, who, under all trying circumstances, have labored earnestly for the elevation of their race, their sex. Let us strive, with the advantages of a higher education, to carry out the aim of our noble predecessors—the success of the futurity of the race.

NINE § **Virginia W. Broughton**
(1856?–1934?)

NAMED AFTER THE STATE IN which her parents were once enslaved, Virginia W. Broughton was a leading Baptist minister and educator. After ten years of study, she graduated in 1875 from the first class of Fisk University. From Nashville she moved to Memphis where she taught in the public schools for twelve years, becoming principal of the North Memphis School and later assistant principal of the Kortrecht Grammar School for Colored Youth. While at Kortrecht she was introduced to Joanna Patterson Moore, a white missionary and Baptist organizer who was gaining a reputation throughout the South for her work with the Women's Baptist Home Mission Society and, in particular, her "Bible Bands." The principal object of these groups was to encourage among the laity a daily study of the Bible. Quickly these small gatherings became a primary networking mechanism for church growth, especially once Moore supplied regular lesson plans in the form of her periodical, *Hope*. Following her mother's death Virginia experienced a prolonged illness, possibly brought about by this devastation. Upon recovery, she decided to leave her job as a teacher and undertake full-time missionary work, joining Moore as her assistant editor and as secretary at Moore's first Fireside School. Together with *Hope* and the Bible Bands, the Fireside Schools established an institutional space to encourage family Bible study. As she would later recount in her autobiography, *Twenty Years' Experience of a Missionary* (1907), Broughton's days were consumed by missionary

Source: Virginia Broughton, "Woman's Work," *National Baptist Magazine* 1:1 (January 1894), 30–35.

meetings, children's meetings, Sunday school work, house-to-house visiting, bookkeeping, and housekeeping, the sort of work in which all "good women were expected to engage." Every aspect of her life was devoted to Christian care and women's improvement. Even her autobiography was distributed as a "contribution to the history of a race, whose true story must yet be told by members of the race would we give our young people the needed encouragement to make their lives what they should be."[1]

This was the sort of work advocated by Virginia in her public addresses, which she was frequently called upon to give as Moore's success became more widespread. "Woman's Work" was a speech delivered at the National Baptist Educational and Foreign Mission Convention in Washington, D.C., on September 14, 1893, and reprinted in the *National Baptist*. Eventually this talk, along with several other similar addresses, was collected in her *Women's Work, as Gleaned from the Women of the Bible* (1904). Nearly every idea articulated in Broughton's rhetoric was sourced in a Biblical passage, and each claim for women's unique status was legitimated through Biblical analogy. "As woman was instrumental in the fall," she explained, "God also used her in redeeming fallen humanity." Nothing was more important than her work of raising children, for "the mother transmits her virtues or her vices to her children." From Hannah, the mother of Samuel, to Yael, killer of Sisera; from martyred heroine Joan of Arc to the dressmaker Dorcas, Broughton uses women of the past to explain the spiritual utility of women in the present. Women need to be more than the "errand girl," Broughton proclaims, they must be brought to "work and plan" together with men. The message is both denominational, as Broughton encourages allowing women on executive missionary boards, and governmental, as she suggests their utility for the national security and legislation. Confirmed by scriptural sanction, Broughton preached the advancement of women in place and purpose.

Woman's Work (1894)

Delivered at the National Baptist Educational and Foreign Mission Convention, at Washington, D.C., September 14, 1893.

I come to you rejoicing in the fullness of the gospel, rejoicing for what God has wrought for the world, and above all, for what he has done for woman

---

[1] Virginia Broughton, *Twenty Year's Experience of A Missionary* (Chicago: The Pony Press, Publishers, 1907), 85 and Preface.

through the gospel of his dear Son. "Known unto God are all his works from the beginning of the world."—(Acts XV. 13.) And gradually has his works been made manifest to the world.

> "How firm a foundation, ye saints of the Lord,
> Is laid for your faith in his excellent word!
> What more can he say, than to you he has said,
> To you, who for refuge to Jesus hath fled."

To-day, with holy awe and reverence, we are to consider the gospel message which says, "There is neither Jew nor Greek; there is neither bond nor free; there is neither male nor female; for ye are all one in Christ Jesus."

In the beginning God created the heavens and the earth, and the earth was without form and void; and darkness was upon the face of the deep. Emerging from this state of chaos and darkness, God presented man, for his habitation, a beautiful garden fragrant with the perfume of flowers; resonant with the carol of birds, and supplied with all that was necessary for the well-being of man, and then said: "It is not good that the man be alone, I will make an helpmeet for him." Beginning with creation we find that woman has figured conspicuously, by proving herself a desirable help to man in every important dispensation of God's providence. As woman was instrumental in the fall, God also used her in redeeming fallen humanity. He gave us this, assurance in the first promise—"The seed of the woman shall bruise the serpent's head."

When God called out a peculiar people for himself, he made CHOICE of the MOTHER of Israel; thereby instituting the holy ordinance of matrimony and directing his children how to enter into it. But alas! as in other things, so in this all-important matter, we've left the commandment of God, and followed the doctrines of men—to the ruin and havoc of social blessedness. The following poetical strain applies to matrimonial bliss, as well as our Christian relation; in fact, Christ likens his love for his church to that which should exist between husband and wife:

> "Blest be the tie that binds
> Our hearts in mutual love,
> The fellowship of kindred minds
> Is like to that above."

No union, based upon anything than true love, as a result of real worth of character of the contracting parties, can be happy and productive of the great good God destined by the holy ordinance. In the deliverance of Israel from Egyptian bondage, it was the love and wisdom of woman that preserved, nourished and trained the man child that God called to be the leader, judge and priest for his people. Just here, as the care and training of children is preeminently the work of woman, we pause to say a few words concerning the influence and duty of women to children.

The fondest love and strongest ties of earth exist between mother and child.

> "At home or away, in alley or street,
> Wherever I chance in this wide world to meet
> A girl that is thoughtless or boy that is wild,
> My heart echoes softly, 't'is somebody's child.'
>
> No matter how far from the right she has strayed;
> No matter what inroads dishonor has made;
> No matter that sin and pain has tarnished the pearl;
> Though tarnished and sullied, she is some mother's girl.
>
> No matter how wayward his footsteps have been;
> No matter how deeply he has sunken in sin;
> No matter how low is his standard of joy;
> Though guilty and loathsome, he is some mother's boy."

The mother transmits her virtues or her vices to her children; in fact, she reproduces herself in her children, and she is exerting an influence for good or ill, in spite of her will, from the time the child is sensible of anything until it leaves the world. Oh, how careful ought she to be to make the most of herself, physically, mentally and morally, that her children might be a power in the world for good, and rise up and call her blessed! If there was no other reason favoring the higher education of women than the fact that they are to be the mothers of the nation, that one alone is all-sufficient; for the mother has almost the entire care of the child in early life. She is its first God-given teacher, and wields an influence no one else can. Let women see to it that they use every opportunity for development of all their powers.

A more important position is filled by no one than that held by the mothers of our country, not even the executive head of the government, for it is what the mothers make the boys that will give us a good or bad government; and the mothers control their children, while the executive head of this government is the servant of the people, since it is a government of the people, for the people and by the people.

We are learning now that we are responsible for the well-being of our children, and our neighbors' children, as to their bodies, minds and spirits, and feel the weight of this responsibility to the extent that we are trying by organized effort to prepare ourselves to meet it; that we may help on the onward march of all that is grand and glorious.

The story of Hannah leads us to understand how soon we should begin the training of our children. When the child was weaned, she carried him to the temple and gave him to the Lord, and God used Samuel as a powerful agency to reprove the wrong and defend the right.

In union there is strength, so the organizations of Christian women are giving them strength of character, and preparing them for effective service—such organization as the W. C. T. U., Missionary Circles, Kings Daughters, Bible Bands and Fireside Schools—the last named organization is a plan God has recently given our beloved sister J. P. Moore. It is so comprehensive that every woman in the land can enjoy its blessings. It is an organization for the improvement of the home life; the development of the women and the training of children. As the name indicates, it is a school around the fireside, and though it is of recent birth, God has wondrously blessed it, and there is already a host of women in the South-land as witnesses of its effectiveness in the elevation of our homes. Brethren and sisters, let me entreat you to encourage and foster the Fireside School, and as this sainted mother of Israel, who has given her life for our people, declines in strength, and step by step walks out of labor to reward, a halo of glory may crown her efforts, and she may go home rejoicing with the laurels of a victorious conqueror.

We believe that God meant what he said in Gen. ii. 18, as in Mark xvi. 16; and I'm sure you all agree that woman is a help along the line I've spoken; but we advance further, and affirm that it is not good for man to be alone any-where. Those places to which he goes, to the exclusion of women, such as saloons, club-rooms and legislative halls, are not suitable for him, and he is not safe, and we are sure it is not good for him, because God says that it is not good for man to be alone; and the wreck and ruin that result from his fre-quenting places of ill-repute, and the unjust and imperfect laws he makes are substantial proof that danger and death await those who disobey God's word. But what about man going alone to war? We answer by asking who was it that drove the nail into Sisera's temple? and what of the heroism of Joan of Arc? War is one of man's inventions; it is not good in itself, neither is it good for man to go to war alone, most especially in the Lord's work. "Neither is the man without the woman, neither the woman without the man in the Lord." 1 Cor. xi. 11. In the Lord we must be together. Esther and her people laboring together with God saved her nation. Anna and Simeon together welcomed Jesus when he was brought to the temple for the first time after his birth. In these perilous times, when our men's hearts are failing, and there are distress and perplexities of various kinds, there is the same need of the prayers of earnest Christian women that there was when Peter was in prison.

The power of prayer can not be over-estimated. "If ye abide in me and my words abide in you, ye shall ask what ye will, and it shall be done unto you." Many a husband, father, brother and son have been saved in answer to the faithful prayer of woman, and God has given you this evidence of woman's worth, that you might encourage her, and recognize her as your help-meet in evangelizing the world. We still have the poor and neglected, the widows and orphans, and hence Dorcas' work needs to be continued; the travelling servant of God are to be administered unto, and Lydias are in demand to entertain them, especially at such times as this; and since others need to be instructed in the way of the Lord more perfectly, Pricillas can find work to do.

We praise God that we all have the same blessed Savior, and Master, who has give us all the same blessed Gospel that he gave the Samaritan woman at the well, and Mary at the Sepulchre; and he is calling now; loudly calling you and me; calling by the lightning; by the storm and tempest; by persecution, famine, pestilence and death, and by the Gospel of his dear Son, ever from the mouths of women and children, do we hear this pleading voice, take the Cross and follow on.

We claim for woman her God-given name, help-meet, and insist that man needs her help in every department of life. He cannot be right to put woman in one corner and man in another. All of our church work stands greatly in need of the united effort of its members, and since the majority of the membership is women, unless they work, very little can be accomplished.

Isn't it strange, men will suffer women to do all the drudgery work, plow, plant, cultivate and gather the crop, draw water and split rails, and all other kinds of drudgery; but when it comes to mental or spiritual work, men wish to exclude women; as if they thought women had all the muscular strength and they had the brains and thinking powers.

Friends, we must come to the acknowledgment of this truth, "That it is not good for man to be alone," and our church work needs the wisdom of both sexes to carry it on as God ordains it.

The President has a Cabinet and an errand boy that stands by his side; both are his helpers; he needs both, but could better dispense with his errand boy than with his Cabinet. Now, we would like to whisper to man that he needs woman's help more in his cabinet than as an errand girl.

Did I say woman more needed in your cabinet than as an errand girl? Yes, brethren, you will find her of service upon your Executive Boards, both State and National. She'll do you good everywhere, all the days of your life; for God has said, "It is not good that man should be alone."

God help us to examine this subject in the light of his Word! Do it for the sake of the children, who need the united wisdom of men and women to guard their wayward feet in the path of righteousness; do it for the sake of our homes, where we want love, order, peace and purity; but know we cannot have them unless husband and wife work and plan together. Let us do it for the sake of our country, where good and just laws are so much needed for the protection and encouragement of both man and woman; and above all for the sake of the Lord Jesus, who has prayed the Father that we might be one even as he and his Father were one; that the World might believe he was sent of the Father.

What a glory shall follow in the wake of the acceptance of this glorious truth. God's Church will awake, Jews and Greeks; bond and free, male and female, and when awakened, a mighty host will be in action—stalwart men, women and children—and the Gospel Message shall soon extend throughout the earth, and we shall say no longer, one to the other, "know ye the Lord," but all shall know him, and

> "From Greenland's icy mountains,
> From India's coral stand;
> And Afric's sunny fountains,"

shall ascend songs of praise to the Lamb that was slain.

> "And Jesus shall reign, where'er the sun
> Doth his successive journeys run;
> His kingdom, spread from shore to shore,
> Till moons shall wax and wane no more."

In closing my thoughts on woman's work, as presented in God's word, Mr. Moody's four words necessary to the study of God's word are very suggestive, "ADMIT, SUBMIT, COMMIT, TRANSMIT." Admit—believe it all, from Genesis to Revelation; don't stop at the Jordan, but grow in grace and in the knowledge of the Lord Jesus Christ. Submit—yield to its requirements. Commit—learn it, treasure it—"Thy words have I hid in my heart." Transmit—"give it to others," (Deut. vi. 6–9.)—that we may all take heed thereto, and go forward as laborers together with God, seeking to save this lost world!

TEN

Gertrude Bustill Mossell

(1855–1948)

G ERTRUDE BUSTILL MOSSELL, WHO PUBLISHED under the name Mrs.
N. F. Mossell, was born into the elite of black Philadelphia. Her great-grandfather was a baker for George Washington's troops before he founded the first black mutual aid society in America, the Free African Society. Gertrude continued the social consciousness of her forebearer. She showed early signs of literary aptitude when her high school commencement speech, "Influence," was chosen by Bishop Henry McNeal Turner to be published in the AME *Christian Recorder*. During the 1870s, she taught public school in Philadelphia and Camden, New Jersey, while writing on a part-time basis for the *Philadelphia Echo* and the *Philadelphia Independent*. In 1883 she married a leading Philadelphia physician, Nathan F. Mossell, with whom she had two daughters. It was during the early years of her marriage that she launched the career for which she is best known, namely as an editor for the woman's section of local papers. In 1885 she became woman's editor of the *New York Freeman* (later the *New York Age*), and then the *Indianapolis World*. The major forum for her voice was her weekly column, "Our Woman's Department," which was the first woman's column in the history of the African-American press. In 1889 *The Journalist* said of Mossell, "On matters pertaining to women and the race, there is no better author among

Source: Mrs. N. F. Mossell, "A Sketch of Afro-American Literature," *The Work of the Afro-American Woman* (New York: Oxford University Press, 1988), 48–66.

our female writers. Her style is clear, compact and convincing."[1] Like analogous columns of counsel in white newspapers, "Our Woman's Department" doled out helpful hints on everything from money management to child-rearing, keeping vegetables fresh to making use of leftover meat. Nothing was too minor for her consideration, nor was any topic disconnected from the core principles of chastity, thrift, and practicality. Raising children and running a home were defined by Mossell as virtuous businesses of the highest order. As a correspondent for *Woman's Era*, and a contributor to magazines like *Colored American Magazine*, the *AME Church Review*, and the *Philadelphia Times*, Mossell concentrated more explicitly on political and social issues, endorsing thoughtful agitation and civilized disobedience to achieve desegregation and genuine equality.

The Work of the Afro-American Woman (1894) was Mossell's singular accomplishment, compiling some of her journalistic commentary while also supplying a narrative of black women in the nineteenth century. From their leadership in antebellum reform to their professional ascendance in many fields, black women were, to Mossell, the agents of race progress. The following selection emphasizes the literary aspect of their accomplishments, focusing on how the "intellectual history of a race is always of value in determining the past and future of it." Despite the documentary silences imposed by slavery, Mossell believes the race's history can be found in its poets, its preachers, and its political pursuits. "The first written works of the Afro-American," Mossell explains, were issued "to form a liberal sentiment that would favor the abolition of slavery." Here Mossell supplies one of the first pieces of African-American literary criticism, distilling themes in textual production and nominating heroes (like Gustavus Vassa) for the race's rereading. She even names "recent" publications that would, in her mind, have an enduring effect, including "Aunt Lindy" by Victoria Earle Matthews, a story that gives "a strong refutation of the charges made against the race." Finally, in her list of publications at the end, Mossell not only echoes a bibliographic impulse widespread among contemporaneous publications, but also offers to the reader a sense of the intellectual itinerary of her class, gender, and educational cohort, including histories by Methodist leaders, offerings by familiar women (like Cooper and Wheatley), tales of ancient history, race history, poems, "Negro melodies," and prominent sermons. Preserving the past required preserving its texts.

———— ✕ ————

[1] Rodger Streitmatter, *Raising Her Voice: African-American Women Journalists Who Changed History* (Lexington: University Press of Kentucky, 1994), 46.

The Work of the Afro-American Woman (1894)

A SKETCH OF AFRO-AMERICAN LITERATURE

THEY *who have their eyes fixed in adoration upon the beauty of holiness are not*

far from the sight of all beauty. It is not permitted to us to doubt that in Music, in

Painting, Architecture, Sculpture, Poetry, Prose, the highest art will be reached in

some epoch of its growth by the robust and versatile race sprung from those practical

idealists of the seventeenth century, those impassioned seekers after the invisible

truth and beauty of goodness.

—Moses Coit Tyler.

The intellectual history of a people or nation constitutes to a great degree the very heart of its life. To find this history, we search the fountain-head of its language, its customs, its religion, and its politics expressed by tongue or pen, its folklore and its songs. The history of the Afro-American race in this country may be divided into three epochs—the separation from native land and friends, and later arrival in this land of forced adoption. Next follows two hundred and fifty years of bondage and oppression mitigated only through the hope thrown upon life's pathway by the presence of hundreds of freemen of the race eking out an existence hampered on all sides by caste prejudice. Later, an era of freedom covered by twenty years of emancipation, holding in name citizenship, but defrauded of its substance by every means that human ingenuity could devise. Again, the intellectual history of a race is always of value in determining the past and future of it. As a rule, a race writes its history in its laws and in its records. Not so the Afro-American: he could make no law; deprived of the opportunity to write, he could leave no written word; he could only protest against the injustice of his oppressors in his heart, in his song, and in his whispered consolations to the suffering and dying.

The heredity and evironment of a people fix their intellectual limitations as they do their moral and physical. Therefore, perhaps it would be said, these people can have no real literature; but in yet another sense let its successful achievement convince us of the accomplished fact. Every human attempt must have had its first, feeble, rudimentary steps, must have one day been the era of small things. The first tiny stream that at last swells to a broad river having therefore its own important place in the future life of that fact, so these faint, tottering intellectual steps must be worthy of record. With all its drawbacks the race has built up a literature of its own that must be studied by the future historian of the life of the American nation. Afro-American literature in the United States, and by this we mean literature which has originated with the Afro-American, must be largely tinctured with the history of three great happenings in their lives. Torn from their home and kindred, they soon lost all memory of their native tongue, except as here and there some idiom survived. Their first faint gropings in the language of the new world were recitals of the woes they had suffered and the longing for home and loved ones. The soul felt desire to see again the land of their birth and look once more upon its beauty. But as memory of the fatherland became dimmed by time, the experiences of the life of bondage, its hardships and sufferings, its chastened joys and its future out-look toward the longed-for day of freedom that all believed would some day come, the ties of love and friendship formed, became the burden of their song.

At the time the slave trade started in this country, the possibilities of the new continent were new to the master; he had not become adjusted to his own novel environment. The newly imported Africans were largely descendants of the lowest type of African barbarism—history telling us they were mostly drawn from the coast tribes, who were easiest of capture, the white man fearing to go into the interior. The few belonging to the mountain tribes brought to this land were only such as had been held as prisoners of war by the coast tribes. The slaves were located in the warmest section of the New World, employed in the lowest forms of labor. Their environment was from every point of view hostile to intellectual development. They had been captured and enslaved that their toil might enrich another nation; they were reared in the midst of a civilization from whose benefits they were largely debarred; they were taught two things—reverence and obedience to authority as embodied in the master, and next in all of his race, and lastly to fear God. In spite of all impediments to intellectual advancement, here and there faint searchings after knowledge appeared among them. With a nature keenly alive to inquiry, the stories of the Bible took fast hold upon their imagination. The history of the children of Israel they made their own. As Moses through God became the deliverer of the Israelites, so would He give the oppressed ones of that day a deliverer. This seems to have been the first germ of intellectuality that appeared among them; this thought they wove into verse and sung and crooned as a lullaby. In their first attempts at literature may be found their origin—native Africans made Americans against their will—the tribes to which they belonged giving a clue to the differences in their powers of physical endurance or strength of character, when drawn from mountain or coastland. Their place of residence in their new home, largely a sojourner in the sunny South; their fear of the rigor of the northern and eastern climes; the troubles they had to contend with from within were those caused by the jealousy and suspicion implanted by their cunning masters, from without by the lack of opportunities for educational or spiritual growth, it being at that day against the law for an Afro-American to be found with a book, and a felony to teach one the alphabet. In the course of time, however, by stealth in the South and through the philanthropy of individuals of the North, largely members of the Society of Friends, they gained a foretaste of education. It has been said that oratory is the art of a free people, but this race even in the days of bondage and at the first faint breath of freedom, seem to have given birth to those who could rank with the masters of this art. The matchless oratory of Frederick Douglass, Samuel Ruggles Ward, Jabez Pitt Campbell and Joseph C. Price, has never been surpassed by men of any race on this continent. Scattered through every State in the Union, the Afro-American unconsciously imbibed the traits of character and order of thought of those among whom he dwelt. He became the Chesterfield of the South; his courtliness even in his master's cast-off belongings put that of the master to shame. The slave-mother's loving kindness to her own and her foster child became a proverb; her loving, wifely spirit of devotion and self-sacrifice dimmed the lustre of these virtues in her more favored sister of a fairer hue.

The preacher of this race has never been surpassed for his powers of imagery, his pathos, his abundant faith in the future states of reward and punishment. His faith in the word of God, even as a bondsman, made soft the dying pillow of many a passing soul; the quaintness and originality of his speech delighted many an auditor in the home circle, and his abounding love of great titles and high-sounding names has never ceased to amuse the student of this impressionable son of Ham.

The first written works of the Afro-American were not issued to make money, or even to create a literature of their own, but to form a liberal sentiment that would favor the abolition of slavery, or at least, the gradual emancipation of the slaves, and thus laboring they assisted the Anti-Slavery workers in the advancement of their cause. Thus, the speeches of Frederick Douglass, his "Life of Bondage," and other like writings were given to the world. At a later day, as opportunities for education advanced, and readers among their people increased, various weekly, annual, quarterly and monthly publications appeared. Here and there some more cultured and learned member of the race gathered into book-form scattered sermons, church history and poems. Within the past twenty years they have become, to a large extent, their own journalists, gathering and compiling facts about the race, forming plans to erect monuments to their heroes, recording the deeds of these heroes both in prose and verse. The despised Afro-American is learning daily to honor himself, to look with awe upon the future possibilities of his people within the life of this nation.

The first two books written by members of the race in America were by native Africans, who had for a time drifted to the shores of Europe, and there in that purer light of freedom published the outpourings of their burdened spirits, and at that early day, as at the present, the song was in the minor key, never rising to a glad and joyous note. Both books were well received, their merit recognized, and their authors honored with the love and confidence of those who had minds liberal enough to recognize the worth of a brother, although of sable hue. The first attempt at book-making by an Afro-American in the United States was, strange to say, from the pen of a woman, and was entitled "Poems on Various Subjects, Religious and Moral," by Phyllis Wheatley, servant to Mr. John Wheatley of Boston. The volume was dedicated to the Right Honorable the Countess of Huntington, by her much obliged, very humble and devoted servant, Phyllis Wheatley, Boston, June 12, 1773. A meekly worded preface occupies its usual place in this little book. Mr. Wheatley's letter of explanation of the difficulties encountered follows the preface. Fearing, as often occurred in those days of bitter race-hatred, that the authenticity of the poems would be questioned, an attestation was drawn up and signed by a number of worthy gentlemen.

Afro-Americans are born idealists; in them art, poetry, music, oratory, all lie sleeping. To these the first dawn of hope gave utterance. The little slave girl, in the safe, quiet harbor of her mistress' boudoir, takes heart of grace and tunes her lyre. Her verse shows the shadow of her unhappy lot, but rises above these sorrows and on the uplifted wings of song, floats to the starry heavens and consoles the afflicted, gives praise to the faithful ruler, breaks forth in love for the new home.

Phyllis Wheatley, from all accounts given of her from every source, was of a sweet, loving disposition, attaching herself readily to those with whom she came in contact by this especial trait in her character. Her book was written under the pleasantest auspices, surrounded by loving and appreciative friends, with a bright fire and friendly lamp in her room that she might get up at any moment and jot down the thought. The point is often discussed whether the poems of Phyllis Wheatley are of literary merit or simply curiosities as the work of an African child. That this gifted one died in her early womanhood would lead us to feel that longer life might have left to the world poems of greater strength and beauty. Yet, scan as often as we will or may the verses of Phyllis Wheatley, we claim for her the true poetic fire. In the poem to the Right Honorable the Earl of Dartmouth, the perfect rhythm, the graceful courtesy of thought, the burning love for freedom capture the heart. The

"Farewell to America," the "Tribute to New England," have a sweetness and grace, a sprightliness and cheer all their own. Another proof of the genius of this young poetess may be found in the poem beginning, "Your Subjects Hope, Dread Sire." How these verses must have won the heart of His Most Excellent Majesty the King! what a flood of sympathy must have gone out to this young maiden in bondage, who could forget her sorrows in his joy!

A narrative by Gustavus Vassa, published October 2d, 1790, was the second volume written by an African made by force a resident of America. Prejudice being so great, this volume, as was Phyllis Wheatly's, was first published in England. The second edition was welcomed in his American home. The writing of this little narrative, unlike the first, was accomplished under many hardships and difficulties, pursued by troubles and trials and dire calamities, yet it is a true and faithful account, written in a style that deserves respect. The following memorial to the English Parliament will give an idea of the style of the volume.

To the Lords spiritual and temporal, and the Commons of the Parliament of Great Britain.

My Lords and Gentlemen:—Permit me, with the greatest deference and respect, to lay at your feet this genuine narrative, the design of which is to excite in your august assemblies a sense of compassion for the miseries which the slave trade has entailed on my unfortunate country. I am sensible I ought to entreat your pardon for addressing to you a work so wholly devoid of literary merit, but as the production of an unlettered African who is actuated by the hope of becoming an instrument towards the relief of his suffering countrymen, I trust that such a man pleading in such a cause will be acquitted of boldness and presumption. May the God of Heaven inspire your hearts with peculiar benevolence on that important day when the question of abolition is to be discussed, when thousands in consequence of your decision are to look for happiness or misery.

I am, my Lords and Gentlemen,

Your most obedient and devoted humble servant,

Gustavus Vassa.

"I believe it is difficult," writes Vassa, "for those who publish their memoirs to escape the imputation of vanity. It is, therefore, I confess, not a little hazardous in a private and obscure individual, and a stranger too, to thus solicit the indulgent attention of the public. If then the following narrative does not prove sufficiently interesting to engage general attention, let my motive be some excuse for its publication. I am not so foolishly vain as to expect from it either immortality or literary reputation. If it affords any satisfaction to my numerous friends, at whose request it has been written, or in the smallest degree promotes the interest of humanity, the end for which it was undertaken will be fully attained and every wish of my heart gratified. Let it therefore be remembered that in wishing to avoid censure, I do not aspire to praise." Says the Abbe Gregoire in his volume entitled "An Inquiry Concerning the Intellectual and Moral Faculties, or a Literature of Negroes:" "It is proven by the most respectable authority that Vassa is the author of this narrative, this precaution being necessary for a class of individuals who are always disposed to calumniate Negroes to extenuate the crime of oppressing them." Says the good Abbe in conclusion, "The individual is to be pitied who, after reading this narrative of Vassa's, does not feel for him sentiments of affection and esteem."

The second class of writers were natives of America, living in liberal communities, such as could be found in the New England and some of the Middle States. "Walker's Appeal" is one of the most notable of these volumes, as it counselled retaliation. The author's reward was a price upon his head. Writers, such as William Wells Brown, of "Rising Sun" fame; William C. Nell, with "Colored Patriots of the Revolution;" Frederick Douglass, Francis Ellen Watkins Harper, with other like workers, labored for the Anti-Slavery cause. Inspired with a hope of greater privileges for themselves and emancipation for their brethren in the South, they wrote with a burning zeal which had much to do with securing the end desired. After this came twenty-five years of freedom with its scores of volumes, such as Williams' "History of the Negro Race in America," Fortune's "Black and White," Bishop Gaines's "African Methodism in the South," Albery Whitman's "Poems," Crummel's "Greatness of Christ," Penn's "Afro-American Press," Scarborough's "Greek Grammar," Johnson's "Divine Logos," Bishop Payne's "History of African Methodism," Steward's "Genesis Reread."

This era produced history, narrative, fiction, biography, poetry and scientific works varying in grade of excellence, but yet all of invaluable interest; for in them is garnered that which must give inspiration to the youth of the race. Each had its effect of gaining the hearts of their enemy, winning respect and admiration, thus strengthening the bands of a common humanity. Simple and unadorned, these writings have a force and eloquence all their own that hold our hearts, gain our sympathies, fill us with admiration for the writers, for their persevering energy, their strong love of freedom, the impartiality of their reasoning. With what sincerity they bear testimony to the good they find even in their enemies. With what clear judgment they state the difficulties that surround their path. With what firm faith they look ever to the Ruler of all nations to guide this one to justice. Yes, this race is making history, making literature: he who would know the Afro-American of this present day must read the books written by this people to know what message they bear to the race and to the nation.

Of volumes of a later date all are more or less familiar. But we cannot forbear in closing to say a word of three recent race publications: "Iola, or The Shadows Uplifted," by Mrs. F. E. W. Harper, and "A Voice from the South, by a Black Woman of the South" (Mrs. A. J. Cooper). "Iola, or The Shadows Uplifted," is in Mrs. Harper's happiest vein. The scene is laid in the South, and carries us through the various stages of race history from slavery to this present day. All of the open and settled questions of the so-called Negro problem are brought out in this little volume. In the opening and closing of many chapters Mrs. Harper has risen to a height of eloquent pleading for the right that must win for the race many strong friends. Mrs. A. J. Cooper has done for her people a great service in collecting her various essays into book form. Together they make one of the strongest pleas for the race and sex of the writer that has ever appeared. In this little volume she proves that few of the race have sung because they could but sing, but because they must teach a truth; because of the circumstances that environed them they have always been, not primarily makers of literature, but preachers of righteousness.

The third volume, "Aunt Lindy," by (Victoria Earle) Mrs. W. E. Matthews, the last to appear, is a beautiful little story and is deserving of careful study, emanating as it does from the pen of a representative of the race, and giving a vivid and truthful aspect of one phase of Negro character. It shows most conclusively the need of the race to produce its own delineators of Negro life.

The scene is laid in Georgia. A Cotton Exchange has taken fire, the flames spreading to a neighboring hotel, many of the inmates are wrapped in the flames of the dread tyrant. One, a silver-haired stranger, with others is carried to neighboring homes for quiet and careful nursing.

"Good Dr. Brown" thinks of no other nurse so capable as "Aunt Lindy."

The old lady had been born in slavery, suffered all its woes, but in the joys of freedom had come to years of peace.

She welcomed the wounded sufferer, laid him in a clean, sweet bed that she had kept prepared hoping that some day one of her own lost children might return to occupy it.

As she stands by his side suddenly some feature, some word of the suffering one, brings back the past. Peering closely into the face of the restless sleeper she exclaims, "Great Gawd! it's Marse Jeems!"

Then begins the awful struggle in the mind of the poor freedwoman. The dreadful tortures of her life in bondage pass in review before memory's open portal. Shall vengence be hers? Shall she take from him the chance of life? Shall she have revenge, swift, sure and awful?

In these beautiful words Mrs. Matthews shows us the decision, how the loving forgiveness of the race, as it has always done, came out more than conqueror:

"Soon from the portals of death she brought him, for untiringly she labored, unceasingly she prayed in her poor broken way; nor was it in vain, for before the frost fell the crisis passed, the light of reason beamed upon the silver-haired stranger, and revealed in mystic characters the service rendered by a former slave—Aunt Lindy.

"He marvelled at the patient faithfulness of these people. He saw but the Gold—did not dream of the dross burned away by the great Refiner's fire."

In this little story, and especially in its sequel, Mrs. Matthews has given a strong refutation of the charges made against the race by Maurice Thompson in his "Voodoo Prophecy," where he makes the poet of wild Africa to say:

> "A black and terrible memory masters me,
> The shadow and substance of deep wrong.
>
> I hate you, and I live to nurse my hate,
>   Remembering when you plied the slaver's trade
> In my dear land.....How patiently I wait
>   The day,
>   Not far away,
> When all your pride shall shrivel up and fade!
>
> As you have done by me so will I do
> By all the generations of your race."

Only the race itself knows its own depth of love, its powers of forgiveness. In the heart of this race, if the American nation will only see it so, they have the truest type on earth of forgiveness as taught by the Redeemer of the world.

This blood-bought treasure, bought with a Saviour's love, a nation's dreadful agony, is yet spurned and trampled on by professed followers of the meek and lowly Jesus.

As we remember that the one novel written in America that captured the hearts of the world sung the wrongs of this people; that the only true American music has grown out of its sorrows; that these notes as sung by them melted two continents to tears; shall we not prophesy of this race that has so striven, for whom John Brown has died, with whom one of Massachusetts' noblest sons felt it high honor to lie down in martial glory, to whom a Livingstone bequeathed to their ancestors in the dark continent that heart that in life beat so truly for them? Shall we not prophesy for them a future that is commensurate with the faith that is in them?

LIST OF AFRO-AMERICAN PUBLICATIONS

Phyllis Wheatley's Poems, 1773.
Narrative, by Ouladal Ecquino or Gustavus Vassa.
Walker's Appeal.
Light and Truth, Lewis, Boston, 1844.
Whitfield's Poems, 1846.
Martin Delaney's Origin of Races.
My Bondage and Freedom, Frederick Douglass, 1852.
Autobiography of a Fugitive Negro, 1855.
Twenty Years a Slave, Northrup, 1859.
Rising Son and Black Man, William Wells Brown.
William C. Nell. Colored Patriots of the Revolution.
Tanner's Apology for African Methodism.
Still's Underground Railroad.
Colored Cadet at West Point, Flipper.
Music and Some Highly Musical People.
My Recollections of African Methodism, Bishop Wayman.
First Lessons in Greek, Scarborough.
Birds of Aristophanes, Scarborough.
History of the Black Brigade, Peter H. Clark.
Higher Grade Colored Society of Philadelphia.
Uncle Tom's Story of His Life, by Henson.
Greatness of Christ. Black Woman of the South.
Future of Africa, Alexander Crunnell, D. D.
Not a Man, and Yet a Man, Albery Whitman.
Mixed Races, J. P. Sansom.
Recollections of Seventy Years, Bishop D. A. Payne, D. D.
Memoirs of Rebecca Steward, by T. G. Steward.
In Memoriam.
Catherine S. Beckett, Rev. L. J. Coppin.
A Brand Plucked from the Fire, Mrs. Julia A. J. Foote.
Thoughts in Verse, George C. Rowe.
Cyclopædia of African Methodism, Bishop Wayman.
Night of Affliction and Morning of Recovery, J. H. Magee.

The Negro of the American Rebellion, William Wells Brown.

African Methodism in the South, or Twenty-five Years of Freedom, Bishop Wesley J. Gaines.

Men of Mark, Wm. J. Simmons, D. D.

Afro-American Press, I. Garland Penn.

Lynch Law, Iola. (Ida B. Wells.)

Women of Distinction, L. A. Scruggs, M. D.

Genesis Reread; Death, Hades and the Resurrection, T. G. Steward, D. D.

Corinne, Mrs. Harvey Johnson.

A Voice from the South, by a Black Woman of the South, Mrs. A. J. Cooper.

Two volumes written by whites, yet containing personal writings by the Negro Race.

A Tribute to the Negro.

An Inquiry Concerning the Moral and Intellectual Faculties, or a Literature of the Negroes, by Abbe Gregoire.

The Cushite, Dr. Rufus L. Perry.

Noted Negro Women, Majors.

"Aunt Lindy," Victoria Earle.

Tuskegee Lectures, Bishop B. T. T. Tanner, D. D.

The Rise and Progress of the Kingdoms of Light and Darkness, or the Reigns of the Kings Alpha and Abaden, by Lorenzo D. Blackson.

History of the Negro Race in America, Geo. Williams.

History of the A. M. E. Z. Church.

History of the First Presbyterian Church, Gloucester.

History of St. Thomas' Protestant Episcopal Church, Wm. Douglass.

History of the A. M. E. Church, D. A. Payne.

Black and White, T. Thomas Fortune.

Liberia, T. McCants Stewart.

Bond and Free, Howard.

Poems, Novel Iola, Mrs. F. E. W. Harper.

Morning Glories (Poems), Mrs. Josephine Heard.

Negro Melodies, Rev. Marshall Taylor, D. D.

The New South, D. A. Straker.

Life of John Jasper, by himself.

Church Polity, Bishop H. M. Turner.

Digest of Theology, Rev. J. C. Embry, D. D.

Sense and Method of Teaching, W. A. Williams.

Brother Ben, Mrs. Lucretia Coleman.

The Divine Logos, H. T. Johnson, D. D.
The Relation of Baptized Children to the Church, L. J. Coppin, D. D.
Domestic Education and Poems, D. A. Payne.
The Negro in the Christian Pulpit, Bishop J. W. Hood.

We should be glad if authors would send us the names of omitted volumes to be used in a possible future edition.

ELEVEN | Hardie Martin

IN *THE CYCLOPEDIA OF THE Colored Baptists of Alabama* (1895), Charles Octavius Boothe included over thirty photographs of prominent Baptist citizens of Alabama. For most of these individuals, Boothe offered additional biographical detail within the text of the volume. However, in the case of one image, an 1895 photograph of Hardie Martin, the only information Boothe supplied was to describe her as a "Teacher in Public School, Montgomery, Ala."[1] This placement, when coupled with her address on the twenty-ninth anniversary of the Columbia Street Church in Montgomery, could tell us something about her position. The talk, reprinted below, offers a powerful plea for the role of the church in the countering of illiteracy and depravity in modern society. Martin used an impressive array of historical precedents to emphasize the extent of the problem and its potential solutions. "In the days of Polycarp, Roger Williams, Martin Luther, John Knox, and John Wesley no evil that endangered the interests of the masses was winked at," Martin preached, establishing a Protestant apostolic succession that created the "march of civilization" from Mars Hill to Montgomery. The church should take over the school, take over the press, and take over the homes, permeating the lives of common people with knowledge of Paul and his acolyte pulpits. Martin was the teacher who saw in history the ecclesiastical destiny of man's uplift. Conspicuously absent from her writings was any invocation of race. Martin perhaps supposed that in

Source: Miss Hardie Martin, "How the Church Can Best Help the Condition of the Masses," National Baptist IV/V:4/1 (October 1896/January 1897), 279–281.
[1] Charles Octavius Boothe, The Cyclopedia of the Colored Baptists of Alabama: Their Leaders and Their Work (Birmingham: Alabama Publishing Company, 1895), 82.

Christ's eyes, all humans were equal. By mirroring His holy agents, Martin's listeners could, she believed, make this world as He aspired.

How the Church Can Best Help the Condition of the Masses (1896)

The importance of the subject assigned me is commensurate with the condition of the masses and the state of civilization to which they might attain. The subject of the elevation of the masses from a state of illiteracy and moral depravity has been to the minds of the pure and good, the all-absorbing subject that took the Apostle Paul of the first century through the trying ordeals of his day, and amid the perils of ancient superstition, rose to the height of the ancient Demosthenes upon Mars Hill, and stated in language burning with hallowed fire that, "God has made of one blood, all nations of men to dwell upon the face of the of the earth." It was there at that ancient seat of learning where all of the Grecian literature got its trend and sentiment, and where the frame work of religious and political ideas were matured that the apostle puts in the leaven that would raise the loaf which would bless the nations. His miraculous call to Europe and the miracles that attended his labors there never blessed the cause of the Redeemer, ne'er so much as his visit to Athens. From Athens, all Greece and the adjacent countries looked for information. Whatever emanated from there was in the sight of the people right, whatever did not, was at least questioned, if not objected to as totally wrong.

If the Church would hasten the blessings purchased by the Lord Jesus Christ to the masses of humanity, it must lay hold upon the great centers of education. The stoics and philosophers with their encyclopedias of information must be consecrated to God and the use of humanity to bless the masses of the people. All freely admit that knowledge is power; and consecrated knowledge is supernatural power. Let the Church therefore, lay its hands upon the great centers of education; let the Church get the Bible into the school-houses. All over our land and country there are large masses of children of every grade and kind with minds to be trained; characters to be formed. They are assembled daily at the feet of the stoics. Now, consecrate this teacher; lay hold upon his or her heart and mind the one great object, that of the elevation of the masses, and in two generations the world will be transformed.

2. Let the Church see to it that able, consecrated, godly men occupy the pulpits; too much importance cannot be laid upon the importance of an

educated, trained, and consecrated minisistry. It has pleased God the Divine Governor, of the universe with his infinite knowledge to call men known as ministers, to lead, govern, and control the masses of his people. The masses therefore eventually will be what their leaders are—no more, no less. I think no age since the days of the Apostles has suffered more for the need of true and brave ministers than the nineteenth century. In the days of Polycarp, Roger Williams, Martin Luther, John Knox, and John Wesley no evil that endangered the interests of the masses was winked at. Though years have gone since these heroic divines have passed from the stage of action, yet their foot prints are as visible upon the surface of our religious literature as if they were yet living. Spain, Germany, France, and all the other countries of the old world will never forget Luther for his stand against the power of popery. Roger Williams has immortalized his name by his stand against states' interference with religious worship, and his undying arguments for the privilege of worshipping the Creator according to the dictates of one's own conscience.

3. If the Church would help the masses in this, able men must occupy the pulpits, who love the souls of the people more than they do their own lives. Now, it is a fact in our day that there are many evils which constitute the nations word, and in some places have completely stopped the march of civilization, and the pulpits of this country are in a great measure silent as to these most potent evils. First is the whiskey traffic; next, is immorality, which is a natural result of alcoholic trade, and other things. If the Church would employ a powerful force in the abolition of these evils, let it employ preachers, who like John the Baptist, John Knox, Roger Williams, and others, who would die rather than see evils triumphing that are blighting and ruining every interest of the people.

4. Let the Church take charge of the press of this country. I believe the press a divine institution; for some of the greatest missionary movements of this century, too—it is well known—have had their beginning in the reading of truth on the printed page. Nothing can exert so powerful an influence on the mass of humanity as the printing press of the country. If it were possible for the Church to get consecrated, evangelical, spirited men in all of the editors' chairs, behind all of the great newspapers, I believe that in twenty-five years every saloon and every thing, that would tend to degrade us as a race, would be a thing of the past. The press is one of the potential educational forces of this age. As a moral power it ranks with the pulpit in its influence on the public mind. The great center-acting force to this pernicious agency, is the religious *press*, and from it the friend of truth may hope for the happiest results. Apostles used the pen as well as the pulpit, and employed written

truth to guide the faith and intelligence of the people. Let us suppose that all the great papers of the country were being used in the elevation of the masses; what an upward stride would be made by the people. But it is to be regretted, however, that this very important factor which could be used in the elevation of the masses by the Church is neglected.

The Church must see to the religious, moral, and intellectual training of the homes. I think that well-trained, strong, intelligent women visiting the homes of the common people would be a source of great blessings to the masses. For there is work to be done for women that women alone can do. Then let us sit not idly dreaming, when thousands are waiting for us to help them. We must learn to work for the happiness of others. Our work may seem like casting one's bread upon the waters, and there may be little probability of ever hearing from it again. Truth is not always lost, but in its material embodiment will sometimes live for many long decades.

> Dare to do right! dare to be true,
> The failing of others can never save you;
> Stand by your conscience, your honor, your faith,
> Stand like a hero, and battle till death!

TWELVE ∮ **Victoria Earle Matthews**
(1861–1907)

THE YOUNGEST OF NINE CHILDREN, Victoria Earle Matthews was born a slave in Fort Valley, Georgia. Her mother fled the plantation at the outset of the Civil War and returned after emancipation to take Victoria and her sister to New York City. Educated in the public schools of New York, she had to leave high school before graduation in order to support her family, becoming briefly a household domestic. Throughout these hardships, she sought out free lectures and the new public libraries. In 1879 she married and moved to Brooklyn and began to write for the *Brooklyn Eagle* and *Waverly Magazine* under the pen name Victoria Earle. Eventually she would be hired by several New York newspapers, including the *Times*, the *Herald*, and the *Sunday Mercury*, as well as African-American newspapers such as the *Boston Advocate* and the *New York Globe*. Among her literary contributions, perhaps most significant was her 1893 story "Aunt Lindy: A Story Founded on Real Life," in which Matthews tracked a slave who decided to heal her former master rather than seek vengeance upon him.[1]

Praised in her lifetime as a signal work of racial reconciliation, "Aunt Lindy" and the creativity it bespoke was secondary to Matthews' relentless club work. In 1892 she formed and served as president of the Woman's Loyal

Source: Victoria Earle Matthews, "The Awakening of the Afro-American Woman," *With Pen and Voice: A Critical Anthology of Nineteenth-Century African-American Women*, edited by Shirley Wilson Logan (Carbondale: Southern Illinois University Press, 1995), 149–155.

[1] Amina Gautier, "African American Women's Writings in the Woman's Building Library," *Libraries & Culture* 41:1 (Winter 2006), 64–67.

Union of New York. In 1895 she helped found the National Federation of Afro-American Women and was later instrumental when this organization and the National Colored Women's League merged with the National Association of Colored Women, serving then as the first national organizer of the combined group from 1897 until 1899. Meanwhile, she founded the White Rose Industrial Association, a resource group that, in 1900, organized the White Rose Mission, a settlement house for young black working women.

In her 1926 biographical profile of Matthews, Hallie Brown described Matthews as a chimera in the annals of African-American womanhood, writing that "her enthusiasm and quick grasp of any situation, together with a certain dramatic quality gave her a forceful, decided manner of speaking that was not always understood."[2] This "decided" manner is on full display in "The Awakening of the Afro-American Woman," a talk delivered at the annual convention of the Society of Christian Endeavor in San Francisco on July 11, 1897. The talk names the "awakening" as the "history of the race lifting out of its original condition of helplessness" through Christian forces and female fortitude. That history was a "sullied" bleakness: "What a past was ours!" The "horrors of the past" would only be overcome with the "joyous labor" of a Christian mother. The home is hallowed as "the noblest, the most sacred spot in a Christian nation." Her climactic call for support to the service of this Christian model for nurturing includes a recommendation not only for a reformation of law, but also an empathetic spirit. To overcome such a treacherous past would require present patience.

———— ∞ ————

The Awakening of the Afro-American Woman (1897)

The awakening to life of any of the forces of nature is the most mysterious as it is the sublimest of spectacles. Through all nature there runs a thread of life. We watch with equal interest and awe the transformation of the rosebud into the flower and the babe into manhood. The philosopher has well said that the element of life runs through all nature and links the destinies of earth with the destinies of the stars. This is a beautiful and ennobling thought; while it binds to earth it yet lifts us to heaven. It gives us strength in adversity, when the storms beat and the thunders peal forth their diapason and confusion

---

[2] Cited in Hallie Quinn Brown, *Homespun Heroines and Other Women of Distinction* (Xenia, OH: Aldine Publishing Company, 1926), 215.

reigns supreme everywhere; it tempers our joys with soberness when prosperity hedges us about as the dews of the morning hedge about with gladness the modest violet shyly concealed by the wayside. Life is the most mysterious as it is the most revealed force in nature. Death does not compare with it in these qualities, for there can be no death without life. It is from this point of view that we must regard the tremendous awakening of the Afro-American womanhood, during the past three decades from the double night of ages of slavery in which it was locked in intellectual and moral eclipse. It has been the awakening of a race from the nightmare of 250 years of self-effacement and debasement. It is not within the power of any one who has stood outside of Afro-American life to adequately estimate the extent of the effacement and debasement, and, therefore, of the gracious awakening which has quickened into life the slumbering forces and filled with hope and gladness the souls of millions of the womanhood of our land. To the God of love and tenderness and pity and justice we ascribe the fullness of our thanks and prayers for the transformation from the death of slavery to the life of freedom. All the more are we grateful to the moral and Christian forces of the world, the Christian statesmen and soldiers and scholars who were the divine instruments who made it possible for this womanhood to stand in this august presence to-day, this vast army laboring for the upbuilding of the Master's kingdom among men; for it is true as Longfellow said;

> Were half the power that fills the world with terror,
> Were half the wealth bestowed on camps and courts,
> Given to redeem the human mind from error,
> There were no need of arsenals and forts.

The auction block of brutality has been changed into the forum of reason, the slave mart has been replaced by the schoolroom and the church.

As I stand here to-day clothed in the garments of Christian womanhood, the horrible days of slavery, out of which I came, seem as a dream that is told, some horror incredible. Indeed, could they have been, and are not? They were; they are not; this is the sum and substance, the shame and the glory of the tale that I would tell, of the message that I would bring.

In the vast economy of nature, cycles of time are of small moment, years are as hours, and seconds bear but small relation to the problem, yet they are as the drops of rain that fall to earth and lodge in the fastnesses of the mountain from which our rivers are formed that feed the vast expanse of ocean. So in the history of a race lifting itself out of its original condition of helplessness, time is as necessary an element as is opportunity, in the assisting forces of humankind.

When we remember that the God who created all things is no respector of persons, that the black child is beloved of Him as the white child, we can more easily fix the responsibility that rests upon the Christian womanhood of the country to join with us in elevating the head, the heart and the soul of Afro-American womanhood. As the great Frederick Douglass once said, in order to measure the heights to which we have risen we must first measure the depths to which we were dragged. It is from this point of observation that we must regard the awakening of the Afro-American womanhood of the land. And what is this awakening? What is its distinguishing characteristics? It would seem superfluous to ask or to answer questions so obvious, but the lamentable truth is, that the womanhood of the United States, of the world, knows almost absolutely nothing of the hope and aspirations, of the joys and the sorrows, of the wrongs, and of the needs of the black women of this country, who came up out of the effacement and debasement of American slavery into the dazzling sunlight of freedom. My friends, call to mind the sensations of the prisoner of Chillon, as he walked out of the dungeon where the flower of his life had been spent, into the open air, and you will be able to appreciate in some sense our feelings in 1865,

> When the war drums throbbed no longer,
> And the battle flags were furled.

What a past was ours! There was no attribute of womanhood which had not been sullied—aye, which had not been despoiled in the crucible of slavery. Virtue, modesty, the joys of maternity, even hope of mortality, all those were the heritage of this womanhood when the voice of Lincoln and the sword of Grant, as the expression of the Christian opinion of the land, bade them stand forth, without let or hindrance, as arbiters of their own persons and wills. They had no past to which they could appeal for anything. It had destroyed, more than in the men, all that a woman holds sacred, all that ennobles womanhood. She had but the future.

From such small beginnings she was compelled to construct a home. She who had been an outcast, the caprice of brutal power and passion, who had been educated to believe that morality was an echo, and womanly modesty a name; she who had seen father and brother and child torn from her and hurried away into everlasting separation—this creature was born to life in an hour and expected to create a home.

> Home, sweet home;
> Be it ever so humble,
> There's no place like home.

My friends, more, home is the noblest, the most sacred spot in a Christian nation. It is the foundation upon which nationality rests, the pride of the citizen and the glory of the Republic. This woman was expected to build a home for 4,500,000 people, of whom she was the decisive unit. No Spartan mother ever had a larger task imposed upon her shoulders; no Spartan mother ever acquitted herself more heroically than this Afro-American woman has done. She has done it almost without any assistance from her white sister; who, in too large a sense, has left her to work out her own destiny in fear and trembling. The color of the skin has been an almost insurmountable barrier between them, despite the beautiful lines of the gentle Cowper, that—

> Skin may differ,
> But affection
> Dwells in black and white the same.

I am not unmindful, however, of the Northern women who went into the South after the war as the missionary goes into the dark places of the world, and helped the Afro-American women to lay the foundation of her home broad and deep in the Christian virtues. For years they did this in the schoolroom and their labors naturally had their reflex in the home life of their pupils.

Broadly speaking, my main statement holds, however, that these women, starting empty handed, were left to make Christian homes where a Christian citizenship should be nurtured. The marvel is not that they have succeeded, not that they are succeeding, but that they did not fail, *utterly fail*. I believe the God who brought them out of the Valley of the Shadow, who snatched them from the hand of the white rapist, the base slave master whose unacknowledged children are to be found in every hamlet of the Republic, guided these women, and guides them in the supreme work of building their Christian homes. The horrors of the past were forgotten in the joyous labor that presented itself. Even the ineffaceable wrongs of the past, while not forgotten, were forgiven in the spirit of the Master, who even forgave those who took His life.

If there had been no other awakening than this, if this woman who had stood upon the auction block possessed of no rights that a white man was bound to respect, and none which he did respect, if there had been no other awakening of the Afro-American woman than this, that she made a home for her race, an abiding place for husband, and son, and daughter, it would be glory enough to embalm her memory in song and story. As it is, it will be her sufficient monument through all time that out of nothing she created something, and that something the dearest, the sweetest, the strongest institution in Christian government.

But she has done more than this. The creation of a home is the central feature of her awakening, but around this are many other features which show her strong title to the countenance and respect of the sisterhood of the world. She has meekly taken her place by her husband, in the humble occupations of life as a bread winner, and by her labors and sacrifices has helped to rear and educate 50,000 young women, who are active instructors in the Christian churches of the land. In the building up of the Master's kingdom she has been and she is an active and a positive influence; indeed, in this field she has proven, as her white sister has proven, the truth of Napoleon Bonaparte's sententious but axiomatic truth, that "The hand that rocks the cradle rules the world." It is not too much to say that the 7,000,000 Afro-American church memberships would fall to pieces as a rope of sand if the active sympathy and support of the Afro-American women were withdrawn. It is demonstrable that these women are the arch of the Afro-American temple. But these women who came out of slavery have done more than this. They have not only made Christian homes for their families, and educated 50,000 Sunday-school workers, but they have given to the State 25,000 educated school teachers, who are to-day the hope and inspiration of the whole race. The black women who came out of slavery in the past thirty years, have accomplished these tremendous results as farm-laborers and house servants, and they deserve the admiration of mankind for the glorious work that they have accomplished. In the past few years the educated daughters of these ex-slave women have aroused themselves to the necessity of systematic organization for their own protection, and for strengthening their race where they find it is weak, and to this end they have in the several States regularly organized and officered clubs in the Afro-American Women's National Association; there are besides hundreds of social clubs and temperance organizations working in their own way for a strong Christian womanhood. Indeed, the impulse of aspiration after the strong and the good in our civilization is manifest on all hands in our womanhood. It is all so grounded in Christian morality that we may safely conclude that it is built upon a rock and cannot be shaken by the fury of the storms.

The awakening of the Afro-American woman is one of the most promising facts in our national life. That she deserves the active sympathy and co-operation of all the female forces of the Republic, I think I have sufficiently shown. We need them. We have always needed them. We need them in the work of religion, of education, of temperance, of morality, of industrialism; and above all we need their assistance in combating the public opinion and laws that degrade our womanhood because it is black and not white; for of a truth, and as a universal law, an injury to one woman is an injury to all women. As long as the affections are controlled by legislation in defiance of

Christian law, making infamous the union of black and white, we shall have unions without the sanction of the law, and children without legal parentage, to the degradation of black womanhood and the disgrace of white manhood. As one woman, as an Afro-American woman, I stand in this great Christian presence to-day and plead that the marriage and divorce laws be made uniform throughout the Republic, and that they shall not control, but legalize, the union of mutual affections. Until this shall have been done, Afro-American womanhood will have known no full and absolute awakening. As the laws now stand, they are the greatest demoralizing forces with which our womanhood has to contend. They serve as the protection of the white man, but they leave us defenceless, indeed. I ask the Christian womanhood of this great organized Army of Christ, to lend us their active co-operation in coercing the lawmakers of the land in throwing around our womanhood the equal protection of the State to which it is entitled. A slave regulation should not be allowed to prevail in a free government. A barbarous injustice should not receive the sanction of a Christian nation. The stronger forces of society should scorn to crush to the earth one of the weakest forces.

Next to these degrading marriage and divorce laws which prevail in too many States of the Republic, the full awakening of the Afro-American woman to her rightful position in society, are the separate car regulations which prevail in most of the States of the South. They were conceived in injustice; they are executed with extraordinary cowardice. Their entire operation tends to degrade Afro-American womanhood. None who are familiar with their operation will dispute this statement of facts. From this exalted forum, and in the name of the large army of Afro-American women, I appeal to the Christian sentiment which dominates this organization, to assist us in righting the wrongs growing out of these regulations, to the end that our womanhood may be sustained in its dignity and protected in its weakness, and the heavenly Father, who hath declared, "righteousness exalteth a nation, but sin is a reproach to any people," will give His benediction to the laws made just.

I am moved here further to invoke your patience and sympathy in the efforts of our awakening womanhood to care for the aged and infirm, for the orphan and outcast; for the reformation of the penal institutions of the Southern States, for the separation of male and female convicts, and above all for the establishment of juvenile reformatories in those States for both races, to the end that the shame of it may be removed that children of tender age should be herded with hardened criminals from whose life all of moral sensibility has vanished forever.

I feel moved to speak here in this wise for a whole race of women whose rise or fall, whose happiness or sorrow, whose degradation or exaltation are the concern of Christian men and women everywhere. I feel moved to say in conclusion that in all Christian and temperance work, in all that lifts humanity from its fallen condition to a more perfect resemblance of Him in whose image it was made, in all that goes to make our common humanity stronger and better and more beautiful; the Afro-American women of the Republic will "do their duty as God shall give them light to do it."

THIRTEEN 🔗 Amelia Etta Hall Johnson
(1858–1922)

A MELIA ETTA HALL JOHNSON WAS born on the eve of the Civil War to parents who had migrated from Maryland to Toronto, Canada. Educated in Montreal, Johnson moved to Boston in 1874 and three years later to Baltimore, where she married Harvey Johnson, minister of the Union Baptist Church and a rising star in black Baptist circles. From then on her life was defined by her work on behalf of children and her church. Taking the pen name "Mrs. A. E. Johnson," the aspiring writer and mother of three children began writing short poems and essays for black periodicals in the late 1880s. She was especially devoted to Sunday School publications, contributing children's columns to local papers and founding two short-lived monthly journals, *The Joy* (est. 1887) and *The Ivy* (est. 1888).

Johnson's literary reputation, however, came from her novels for young people. *Clarence and Corinne, or God's Way* (1890), written expressly for use in Sunday schools, was published by the American Baptist Publication Society, one of the largest publishing enterprises of its time. Johnson's didactic work was only the second novel by a black woman to be published in book form, and the first to be used as Sunday school literature for mixed audiences. Johnson's works shied away from overt mention of race, instead focusing on generic social problems of poverty, alcoholism, and abuse. These were problems which Johnson argued could only be remedied through Christian piety, temperance, and the inculcation of proper morals. Johnson also upheld the

Source: A. E. Johnson, "Some Parallels of History," *National Baptist Magazine* 7:1 (July 1899), 1–5.

importance of women's work within the home, and expressed a muted protest of the social forces that limited the ability of black women to properly fulfill domestic duties.

Johnson's nonfiction writings, including the essay reprinted here, reveal an aspect of her racial commitments that diverged sharply from the mild piety of her children's literature. Like her husband, who published articles that upheld the importance of black self-development and race pride, Mrs. A. E. Johnson recognized the limitations placed on her writings by the dearth of African-American institutional support. She felt keenly the frustration of rejection at the hands of white publishers who continued to publish racist depictions of blacks while rejecting the work of black authors. Caught up in the struggles to establish a black Baptist denominational publishing house in the mid-1890s, Johnson understood the need for African Americans to take pride in their accomplishments and, if necessary, to create separate institutions that would allow them to flourish.

"Some Parallels of History" appeared as the lead article in the young *National Baptist Magazine* in July 1899. Johnson uses history to argue for the validity—indeed the necessity—of separate black institutions such as a denominational publishing house. She likens the situation of contemporary blacks to that of Saxons in the eleventh century and the British colonists on the eve of the American Revolution. Like those forebears, African Americans are a freedom-loving people who have a God-given right to flourish. If white oppressors want to keep them down, they have just as much right as the conquered Saxons or the burdened American colonists to seek liberty and independence. Echoing the call for self-help voiced by Booker T. Washington and other black leaders of the day, Johnson asserts that blacks must work "peaceably, if we can, but none the less firmly." Sounding here less like a meek Christian homemaker and more like a crusader for racial justice, Johnson concludes that only through collective self-assertion can the race "fill our place in the world."

Some Parallels of History (1899)

The title I have chosen for this paper is not meant to carry the idea that it is a strict chronicle of data, or a systematic record of happenings. I mean merely to refer to such historical events as are necessary to the desired treatment of the subject.

That "history repeats itself," may be an ancient and well-worn axiom; nevertheless, it is a very true and expressive one.

Some people seem to have a strong aversion to the idea advanced by Solomon, the Wise, that "there is no new thing under the sun," and prefer to fancy that what exists at the present time, or may exist in the future, has never had its parallel. But, for my part, I like to trace the resemblance between one object and another. I like to think that no matter what *is*, or *is to be*, has, in its essential points, *already been*.

Now, to our subject, Historical Parallels. For the first example to be considered, it will not be necessary to go back further than the birth of the English nation, which really took place at the time of the Norman Conquest. Twice before had England been under the control of other powers, but she had shaken them off, only to fall into the hands of the Normans in 1066. The Saxons, as we know, were, up to this date, a rude, bluff people, and were indebted to the parties who invaded their shores for any amount of refinement they may have imbibed; and to the Romans, their first conquerors, for Christianity, for until then they were heathen and idolaters.

When, in 1066, the battle of Hastings was fought, and the English King, Harold, was defeated, and William of Normandy took his place on the throne, there was a decided change in England—a change that lasted; things were never the same after the advent of the Norman rule. The yoke fell heavily upon the shoulders of the Saxon, or English, people, and they were frowned upon, and put down on every occasion. Their lands and possessions were taken from them on the slightest pretext and given to the conquerors. They were taxed heavily, and yet allowed no voice in the adjustment of affairs. In fact, they were reduced, many of them, to a state of serfdom, which is a polite term for slavery. But they did not submit tamely to this treatment. They had been conquered, but they refused to remain conquered; and, so, after a long series of wars and uprisings they succeeded in again wresting the English crown from the intruders, and the tables were turned. It took, however, so many years before this was accomplished, that the two nationalities had unconsciously become assimilated, and merged into each other, that, as I have said, the Saxons, as they had been in the old, rude days, were never replaced; but the English nation as it is now understood, came through this evolution. What I want to emphasize in this instance is that it was the love of liberty and independence born in the hearts of the English people that made it impossible for them to content themselves under the despotic rule of their conquerors; and they were determined to win back their birthright. Liberty and independence are every man's birthright, and should not be taken from him.

To be sure, the English nation was indebted to the Norman French for a great deal; for, as I said, they had no refinement or culture worth speaking of, but in the many years that elapsed before they regained their rule, they had undergone so many changes from contact with the French, that they were never again exactly the same people; and yet, they did not hesitate to fight them with all their might until they had everything again in their own hands.

"History repeats itself" in the birth of the so-called American nation. Up until perhaps about 1738 there was no American nation; all in America owed allegiance to England, from whence came the Puritans, or colonists. Oppressed and downtrodden, their claim to liberty of thought and action was crushed by the English ruling powers, and they were forced to seek foreign shores. Still, they were English subjects; their homes, parents and children were English, and politically they were loyal adherents to the crown; but they were rebels against the religious oppression to which they had been subjected.

No loyalty can long survive the iron heel of tyranny; no loyalty will long stand being crushed to earth, every liberty curtailed, every effort snubbed or threatened; hence the first grumbling of the thunder that bespoke the war storm that began to break forth in fitful gusts until its final culmination in 1775, when the famous War of the Revolution regularly opened. From this time, the different battles were fought, lost and won, until at last, in October, 1781, came the final engagement which determined the victory in favor of the Americans, and in 1783, the treaty was made that recognized the independence of the United States. Thus, had another nation freed itself, as it had a right to do. I cannot be so patriotic that I may blindly admire any nation that claims the right of arbitrary government, or utterly disregards the opinions and rights of a people, and this was the most general cause of the American Revolution.

I will not stop to draw the parallel between the oppression of the Puritans by the English in their mother country, and the oppression of their fellow countrymen by the Americans in their new home; because all who are acquainted with the history of this country know how certain religious sects were branded, hounded and tormented; of the shameful page in Massachusetts' history that bears the account of the drowning of inoffensive old women as witches, and the hanging "in batches" of unfortunate creatures, many of whom were said to be "men of education and standing, and tenderly nurtured women who had done nothing to offend their neighbors, and who were convicted under the direction of apparently sober-minded judges, upon the most frivolous tales." It is sufficient to say that the parallel exists, and again "history repeats itself" in the story of the colored race in America. They were introduced into this country and it became their home. They grew in numbers, and changed in character and condition until they became a distinct people; and the usual fermentation and restlessness under oppression and restraint gradually began, making its first public outbreak in the John Brown Raid. And when the Union was threatened and there was a call for colored men to take up arms in the defense of the country of their adoption, and for them the reward of success was to be the abolition of slavery, how eagerly did they respond! How bravely and faithfully did they fight! Without them would the cause have been won? Did they not deserve the right of citizenship that could not honestly be withheld? The colored Americans then became a part of the country. And that is about where the matter stands to-day.

The Saxons and Normans were two distinct peoples or nations; but they inhabited one country. As the years went by they blended and coalesced until now there is in England, under the name of English, but one people. They share and share alike, having the same interests, the same pursuits, and all goes well.

In America there are two peoples: the colored Americans and the white Americans. But here, I am afraid, my parallel does not come as straight as I could wish, for they do not share and share alike; they have not the same interests nor the same pursuits; and all does not go well.

When the American nation insisted upon adding the colored people to their number, they took upon themselves the responsibility of a people. When the war ended there was this great mass of human beings to be settled-down and assimilated. It had to be done. The Americans were responsible for their presence and their condition, which was, to say the least, not creditable to the nation. These people had toiled hard and faithfully all these years, and were now turned loose upon the world with no money, no homes, and no education. Something must be done. The Americans argued: "We cannot allow this host of people to roam the country, untaught and unchecked, or our lives will not be safe. It is our fault that they are ignorant and untrained, and it is but just that we do what we can to remedy the evil we have wrought, although we cannot rub out all traces of it." And, so, they put forth efforts to help the already eager people to fit themselves for the exigencies of life. They founded schools to teach them to teach themselves, and things began to look bright for the newly fledged people. That these efforts of the citizens of the United States were successful we have but to remember that the war that brought freedom to the colored people closed in 1865, and that only thirty-four years have elapsed since then. Take up any book of reference pertaining to their progress, and the most skeptical must be convinced of their wonderful development, although he may not openly admit the fact.

A strange phase of the matter is, that, while all along, the understanding has been that the colored people were, as soon as prepared, to help in the educating, uplifting and upbuilding of their own people, and to do generally for themselves what had been done for them, the white portion of the nation is inclined to refuse them the right to do this, and only allows them to work under protest. But "history repeats itself:" the Saxons refused to be set aside by the Normans; the Americans refused to be set aside by the English and the colored people of the United States can be altered by human hands. It is but right that we should work for the religious, moral, financial and educational advancement of ourselves and people, and if our white brethren close their avenues to us because of this determination, we must create avenues for ourselves. Others have been forced to do the same and have succeeded, and why not we? "What man has done man can do." It is God's ruling, too; not man's, and while the "earth is the Lord's, and the fullness thereof," we have the same right to make the most of ourselves as any others of his creatures, for we, too, are of his creation.

Then let us labor to advance ourselves, and assist our people to improve themselves in every possible way, and stick to those who are steadily marching on. Let us cease trying to prove to the world that we were born into it for the sole purpose of admiring the white people of the United States, and that this is all we will ever be fit for. This is not a very laudable or attractive prospect to look forward to, I am sure.

It goes without saying that if we are to develop, expand, improve or advance, we must launch out for ourselves, and help ourselves, if none will help us just because we refuse to be regarded as nonenities. We must do as others have done before us: make a way for ourselves through the ranks of opposing forces—peaceably, if we can, but none the less firmly. We must fill our place in the world if we are to furnish our true and complete parallel to its history.

FOURTEEN

Katherine Davis Tillman

(1870–?)

B ORN IN MOUND CITY, ILLINOIS, to Laura and Charles Chapman, Katherine Davis Chapman Tillman published her first poem, "Memory," in the *Christian Recorder* when she was eighteen. Besides her publication record, biographical details about Tillman's life are hard to find. She attended high school in Yanktown, South Dakota, and attended the State University of Louisville in Kentucky and Wilberforce University in Ohio. In some of her writing, she alludes to a Reverend G. M. Tillman, who historians have assumed was her husband. In addition to these skeletal specifics, Tillman has left behind a long resume of novellas, plays, poetry, and essays, published in the *A.M.E. Church Review*, the *Christian Recorder*, and by the A.M.E. Book Concern. To illustrate her recitations, Tillman drew upon black cultural history for motivational iconography and collective inspiration. Included in her topical array were essays recommending professions for black women, advocating African-American poetry and the writings of Pushkin, poems on Richard Allen and the history of slavery, and several short works of fiction, including the pageant reprinted here. *Heirs of Slavery* offers a series of monologues testifying to the assaults of enslavement. The wooden caricatures of the "Gladiator" and the "Slave Woman" are intentional contrivances, bent to make the past commensurable and to compel listeners to an obvious moral conclusion. As Claudia Tate has explained, Tillman's plays "literally talk the black characters out of frustration and into

Source: Katherine Davis Tillman, "Heirs of Slavery: A Little Drama of Today" *A.M.E. Church Review* 17:7 (January 1901), 199–203.

hopefulness."[1] With references to contemporary social concerns (like the Hero's allusion to "the Negro-hater"), Biblical imagery, and the ancient world, the play reminds its audience that slavery was neither new nor inescapable. Through familiar heroes, and a study of history ("thou glittering torchlight of the Age"), Tillman hopes to end the "bloody strife" of slavery's inheritors.

Heirs of Slavery. A Little Drama of Today (1901)

DRAMATIS PERSONAE

Hero: A Negro youth attired as an American citizen.

Father Time: An old man leaning on his staff, with an hour-glass in his hand.

History: A tall, beautiful woman in a robe of purple velvet, with a crown upon her head and an Aladdin's lamp in her left hand.

Miriam: Jewish maiden in national costume.

Gladiator: A Greek in a Greek garb.

Virginia: A maid in ancient Roman attire.

Anglo-Saxon Digger: A man in workman's garb of early English period. Yoke around his neck and spade in one hand.

Slave Woman: A beautiful Negro woman in a costume of rich fantastic colors.

Poesy: A slender girl in robe of delicate pink and green, flowers in her hair and scroll in left hand.

Art: A girl in dark crimson robe, cream colored girdle and roses, which she carries in her left hand.

Chorus of Singing Girls: White robes with long, flowing sleeves. Wreaths upon their heads.

HEIRS OF SLAVERY

Scene: A beautiful wood. A rustic seat appears in the background. Soft
　　music is heard in the distance.

(Enter Hero.)

---

[1] Claudia Tate, "Introduction," *The Works of Katherine Davis Chapman Tillman* (New York: Oxford University Press, 1991), 44.

Hero:

Tired out with life and color-blinded men,
I'll rest me in the shade of this attractive glen
And think, what brought me to this restful place,
And of the woes of my unhappy race.
Born of a race of slaves, my father paid
Our ransom and us freemen made;
And when great Lincoln signed the Black Man free,
We northward came to breathe true liberty,
And upward ever have we struggled since,
Our world of snarling critics to convince
Man's merit on no color's shade depends;
And here and there, we've found some honest friends.
Up from the depths and studious nights I've come,
No loud acclaims proclaimed my welcome home,
The little children cry me on the street,
And taunting words my tingling ears must greet.
In market-place, in courts and all by-ways
The Negro-hater dams my gates of praise;
In every way, our foe this thought would teach:
Manhood in highest forms above the Negro's reach,
Then why should I contend when all seems vain?
I'm down, why struggle sore to rise again?
My state, my hue, my race, all keep me back
From equal chance with others on life's track.

(*Hero sinks down on seat and falls asleep.*)
(*Enter Father Time.*)

Father Time:

Hot-blooded youth must have some time to cool.
I'll patience have with this misguided fool,
And flag his spirits with historic wine—
Till light upon his struggling soul shall shine.

(*Time stamps on ground. Enter History.*)

Time:

History, thou glittering torchlight of the Age,
My idle whims must for the time engage,
Show to this youth of sunny Afric race
What other nations have been made to face.
Discouraged by his seeming sad young fate,

Teach him himself at proper worth to rate,
Disadvantages proudly to despise
And to the utmost heights in spite of all to rise;
For I have been e'er since existed Man,
And e'en before, and I know his race can
Prove to the world, despite their lowly birth,
Of one blood, hath God made all nations of the earth.

   History:
Thy wish my law, oh, Father Time,
Man's history in every clime
I keep alone, and he shall see
Some other heirs of slavery.

   (*History rubs lamp. Enter Miriam.*)
   Miriam:
Upon the Nile we've laid our pretty boy,
Our little Moses of our hearts the joy;
Oh, woe to us, proud Egypt's daily scorn,
Oh, woe that e'er an Israelite is born;
Abused and scourged, with backs kept raw,
We now must make bricks, without straw.

   (*Miriam goes out weeping. Enter Gladiator.*)
   Gladiator:
Alas! that I, a freedom-loving Greek,
Must now of shameful ignominy speak.
Rome's wretched slave I at Nero's behest
Must stake my life; strength against strength must test.
'Mid scenes of slaughter all my days are sped,
When shall I reach the realms of the dead?
The gods attend my unpropitious life
And grant this day may end its bloody strife!

   (*Gladiator goes out. Enter Virginia.*)
   Virginia:
A slave! Oh, Venus, hear; I'm Marcus' slave.
Oh dark the hour that birth unto me gave.
Oh Father, haste Virginia's cries to hear;
Oh haste thee and relieve Virginia's nameless fear!

   (*Virginia rushes out. Enter Saxon.*)
   Saxon Digger:
'Neath Norman yoke, the Anglo-Saxons bend

Their homes, their lives upon their lords depend,
Sad to relate, four oxen equal all
The value of the life of an unhappy thrall!
   (*Saxon goes out. Enter Slave Woman.*)
   Slave Woman:
All gone, my children gone,
And I am left alone;
All auctioned off for gold—
May curses deep untold
Fall on this Slavery's cursed mart
That tears me from my own apart.
   (*Slave Woman goes out weeping. Enter Poesy.*)
   Poesy:
I inspired song of Miriam's heart
When Jordan's waters rolled apart
I guided David's gracious song,
And dwelt with patient Job full long;
From classic hills of Greece and Rome
Homer and Sappho's strains have come;
In England, Shakespeare's soul I filled
Till he the passing years had stilled;
Longfellow and Whittier well I loved,
Their poet-hearts 'gainst Wrong I moved;
And I have not forgotten thee—
The Negro's harps of minstrelsy
        Shall ring with strength throughout the land
Till laurel-crowned thy poets stand.
   (*Poesy remains standing over Hero. Enter Art, who scatters roses over Hero
      as she speaks.*)
   Art:
Egypta, Rome and mighty Greece
The fabled land of Golden fleece—
Their marble pillars, temples grand
Despairing joy of every land,
The painting of old masters great,
The works of man ancient and late,
Are due to Art's inspiring love.
And now thy petty fears remove,

I love thy bright warm-hearted race,
And high o'er all thy name shall trace.
   (*Art steps beside Poesy. Enter Chorus of Singing Girls, who form a circle*
      around Hero and chant.)
   Singing Girls:
Arouse, oh youth, from thy slumber deep,
Too long have ye lain in enchanted sleep,
Arouse to conquest, great and vast,
Arouse, for thou the power hast.
   (*All leave. Hero starts up and yawns.*)
   Hero:
In faith, I've had a long and curious dream,
For it somehow to me in sleep did seem
I saw Semitic slaves 'neath Hamite rule!
Romans and Greeks I saw in Slavery's school.
And much do I despise my childish speech.
If we to loftiest heights aspire to reach,
We must both toil and suffer; 'tis the way
All nations conquered in the heated fray.
Allen and Douglass shame my sorry plight
Toussaint and Dumas star my gloomy night.
Resolved am I no little part to play;
Upon our night must dawn a fairer day.
I'll do my best, proving where'er I can
Despite his skin, a man is but a man!
   (*Curtain.*)

FIFTEEN | # Pauline Hopkins
(1859–1930)

P AULINE ELIZABETH HOPKINS WAS AN editor, short-story writer, novelist, actress, singer, and supporter of black political activism. She was born in Portland, Maine, the only child of William A. Hopkins, a Civil War veteran, and Sarah A. Allen, and lived most of her life in Boston. After graduating from Boston's Girls' High School, Hopkins pursued an interest in drama and musical theater. She wrote plays and performed in the 1870s and 1880s with her family's ensemble group, the Hopkins' Coloured Troubadours, and was billed as "Boston's Favorite Colored Soprano" in 1882. The Troubadours performed sketches and musicals that highlighted black history and critiqued political concerns in the post-Reconstruction era. In the 1890s, financial exigency forced her to suspend her dramatic interests to study stenography. While she continued to deliver lectures and write essays, Hopkins supported herself as a stenographer in the Massachusetts Bureau of Statistics for much of that decade.

Only at age 40 was Hopkins able to devote herself full time to writing, when a group of black businessmen in Boston established the *Colored American Magazine*, the first African-American literary journal. Its inaugural editorial statement asserted that the magazine was intended to strengthen communal bonds among African Americans. Hopkins proved to be one of its most consistent contributors in its early years, and its goals meshed perfectly with her own artistic and political commitments. Over

Pauline Hopkins, *Of One Blood: Or, the Hidden Self, in Colored American Magazine* (Nov. 1902–Nov. 1903); "Famous Women of the Negro Race: Educators," *Colored American Magazine* 5:1 (May 1902), pp. 41–46; 5:2 (June, 1902), pp. 125–130; 5:3 (July 1902), pp. 206–213.

the next four years, in an astonishing outburst of creative activity, she published three serial novels, including *Hagar's Daughter: A Story of Southern
Caste Prejudice* (1901–1902), *Winona: A Tale of Negro Life in the South and
Southwest* (1902), and *Of One Blood: Or, the Hidden Self* (1902–1903), seven
short stories, two series of biographical articles, and a variety of commentaries and editorials protesting race and gender proscriptions and advocating uplift. She also published a protest novel, *Contending Forces* (1900),
under the aegis of the publishing company that produced the magazine.
This four-year period would prove to be the apex of her literary career. By
1904, colleagues of the more conciliatory Booker T. Washington gained
ownership of the *Colored American*, moved its headquarters to New York,
and shifted its tone to a less overtly political stance. As editor of the *Colored
American*, Hopkins was perceived as too radical, and was forced out upon
the arrival of this new guard.

The two pieces reprinted here demonstrate the range of her literary talents as both a writer of fiction and an essayist, reflecting her abiding concern
to provide a usable history, both ancient and modern, for her readers. The
serialized novel *Of One Blood* explores the links between past and present in
the lives of contemporary African Americans. In the scene excerpted, Reuel
Biggs, a researcher who is passing as white, has embarked on an expedition
to Africa. He listens as one of his colleagues describes the glorious, lost civilization of Meroe, founded by ancient Ethiopians. The party is searching for
a mysterious and hidden city that will prove the link between Ethiopia and
ancient Egypt, and in turn will silence white scholars who have long denied
that Egyptian civilization was in any way indebted to Ethiopian roots. Using
the form of a fantasy time-travel return to that original Ethiopian culture,
Hopkins' story suggests that the Anglo-Saxon race owes many of its scientific
and artistic achievements to the Negro race.

The second document reprints one of Hopkins' many essays on black history, specifically, famous black educators. She begins by detailing the
systematic attempt by whites under the slave system to deny education to
African Americans, and surveys, state by state, antebellum efforts to establish schools for blacks. She then highlights the work of educators, especially
women, who have labored for the cause of African-American schools.
Hopkins does not excuse northern states for their original commitment to
slavery: Her narrative highlights the slave traffic in Massachusetts as well as
that in Mississippi. But she also lauds the revolution in public consciousness
that led to reform efforts in the north, efforts sparked, as she notes, by
African-American leaders. Their work, she asserts, while it does not rival the
achievements of a Tennyson or a Hume, has profound significance: "By the

lives of those men and women who have shown the slightest spark of the divine fire in the color of their life work, we have proved our origin."

Of One Blood: Or, the Hidden Self (1902–1903)

CHAPTER XII

Late one afternoon two weeks later, the caravan halted at the edge of the dirty Arab town which forms the outposts to the island of Meroe.

Charlie Vance stood in the door of his tent and let his eyes wander over the landscape in curiosity. Clouds of dust swept over the sandy plains; when they disappeared the heated air began its dance again, and he was glad to re-enter the tent and stretch himself at full length in his hammock. The mail was not yet in from Cairo, consequently there were no letters; his eyes ached from straining them for a glimpse of the Ethiopian ruins across the glassy waters of the tributaries of the Nile which encircled the island.

It was not a simple thing to come all these thousand of miles to look at a pile of old ruins that promised nothing of interest to him after all. This was what he had come for—the desolation of an African desert, and the companionship of human fossils and savage beasts of prey. The loneliness made him shiver. It was a desolation that doubled desolateness, because his healthy American organization missed the march of progress attested by the sound of hammers on unfinished buildings that told of a busy future and cosy modern homeliness. Here there was no future. No railroads, no churches, no saloons, no schoolhouses to echo the voices of merry children, no promise of the life that produces within the range of his vision. Nothing but the monotony of past centuries dead and forgotten save by a few learned savans.

As he rolled over in his hammock, Charlie told himself that next to seeing the pater and Molly, he'd give ten dollars to be able to thrust his nose into twelve inches of whiskey and soda, and remain there until there was no more. Then a flicker of memory made Charlie smile as he remembered the jollities of the past few months that he had shared with Cora Scott.

"Jolly little beggar," he mentally termed her. "I wonder what sort of a fool she'd call me if she could see me now whistling around the ragged edge of this solid block of loneliness called a desert."

Then he fell asleep and dreamed he was boating on the Charles, and that Molly was a mermaid sporting in a bed of water-lilies.

Ancient writers, among them Strabo, say that the Astabora unites its stream with the Nile, and forms the island of Meroe. The most famous historical city of Ethiopia is commonly called Carthage, but Meroe was the queenly city of this ancient people. Into it poured the traffic of the world in gold, frankincense and ivory. Diodorus states the island to be three hundred and seventy-five miles long and one hundred and twenty-five miles wide. The idea was borne in upon our travellers in crossing the Great Desert that formerly wells must have been established at different stations for the convenience of man and beast. Professor Stone and Reuel had discovered traces of a highway and the remains of cisterns which must have been marvellous in skill and prodigious in formation.

All was bustle and commotion in the camp that night. Permission had been obtained to visit and explore the ruins from the Arab governor of the Province. It had cost money, but Professor Stone counted nothing as lost that would aid in the solution of his pet theories.

The leaders of the enterprise sat together late that night, listening to the marvellous tales told by the Professor of the city's ancient splendor, and examining closely the chart which had remained hidden for years before it fell into his hands. For twenty-five years this apostle of learning had held the key to immense wealth, he believed, in his hands. For years he had tried in vain to interest the wealthy and powerful in his scheme for finding the city described in his chart, wherein he believed lay the gold mines from which had come the streams of precious metal which made the ancient Ethiopians famous.

The paper was in a large envelope sealed with a black seal formed to resemble a lotus flower. It was addressed:

To the student who, having counted the cost, is resolute to once more reveal to the sceptical, the ancient glory of hoary Meroe.

Within the envelope was a faded parchment which the Professor drew forth with trembling hands. The little company drew more closely about the improvised table and its flickering candle which revealed the faded writing to be in Arabic. There was no comment, but each one listened intently to the reader, who translated very fully as he went along.

"Be it known to you, my brother, that the great and surpassing wealth mentioned in this parchment is not to be won without braving many dangers of a deadly nature. You who may read this message, then, I entreat to consider well the perils of your course. Within the mines of Meroe, four days' journey from the city toward Arabia, are to be found gold in bars and gold in flakes, and diamonds, and rubies whose beauty excels all the jewels of the earth. For some of them were hidden by the priests of Osiris that had adorned the crown of the great Semiramis, and royal line of Queen Candace, even from ancient Babylon's pillage these jewels came, a spectacle glorious beyond compare.

There, too, is the black diamond of Senechus's crown (Senechus who suffered the captivity of Israel by the Assyrians), which exceeds all imagination for beauty and color.

"All these jewels with much treasure beside you will gain by following my plain directions.

"Four days' journey from Meroe toward Arabia is a city founded by men from the Upper Nile; the site is near one of its upper sources, which still has one uniform existence. This city is situated on a forked tributary, which takes its rise from a range of high, rocky mountains, almost perpendicular on their face, from which descend two streams like cataracts, about two miles apart, and form a triangle, which holds the inner city. The outer city occupies the opposite banks on either side of the streams, which after joining, form a river of considerable size, and running some five miles, loses itself in the surrounding swamps. The cities are enclosed within two great walls, running parallel with the streams. There are also two bridges with gates, connecting the inner and outer cities; two great gates also are near the mountain ranges, connecting the outer city with the agricultural lands outside the walls. The whole area is surrounded by extensive swamps, through which a passage known only to the initiated runs, and forms an impassible barrier to the ingress or egress of strangers.

"But there is another passage known to the priests and used by them, and this is the passage which the chart outlines beneath the third great pyramid, leading directly into the mines and giving access to the city.

"When Egypt rose in power and sent her hosts against the mother country, then did the priests close with skill and cunning this approach to the hidden city of refuge, where they finally retired, carrying with them the ancient records of Ethiopia's greatness, and closing forever, as they thought, the riches of her marvelous mines, to the world.

"Beneath the Sphinx' head lies the secret of the entrance, and yet not all, for the rest is graven on the sides of the cavern which will be seen when the mouth shall gape. But beware the tank to the right where dwells the sacred crocodile, still living, although centuries have rolled by and men have been gathered to the shades who once tended on his wants. And beware the fifth gallery to the right where abide the sacred serpents with jewelled crowns, for of a truth are they terrible.

"This the writer had from an aged priest whose bones lie embalmed in the third pyramid above the Sphinx."

With this extraordinary document a chart was attached, which, while an enigma to the others, seemed to be perfectly clear to Professor Stone.

The letter ended abruptly, and the chart was a hopeless puzzle to the various eyes that gazed curiously at the straggling outlines.

"What do you make of it, Professor?" asked Reuel, who with all his knowledge, was at sea with the chart. "We have been looking for mystery, and we seem to have found it."

"What do I make of it? Why, that we shall find the treasure and all return home rich," replied the scholar testily.

"Rubbish!" snorted Charlie with fine scorn.

"How about the sacred crocodile and the serpents? My word, gentlemen, if you find the back door key of the Sphinx' head, there's a chance that a warm welcome is awaiting us."

Charlie's words met with approval from the others, but the Professor and Reuel said nothing. There was silence for a time, each man drawing at his pipe in silent meditation.

"Well, I'm only travelling for pleasure, so it matters not to me how the rest of you elect to shuffle off this mortal coil, I intend to get some fun out of this thing," continued Charlie.

There was a shout of laughter from his companions.

"Pleasure!" cried one. "O Lord! You've come to the wrong place. This is business, solid business. If we get out with our skins it will be something to be thankful for."

"Well," said Reuel, rousing himself from a fit of abstraction, "I come out to do business and I have determined to see the matter through if all is well at home. We'll prove whether there's a hidden city or not before we leave Africa."

The Professor grasped his hand in gratitude, and then silence fell upon the group. The curtains of the tent were thrown back. Bright fell the moonlight on the sandy plain, the Nile, the indistinct ruins of Meroe, hiding all imperfections by its magic fingers. It was wonderful sight to see the full moon looking down on the ruins of centuries. The weird light increased, the shadows lengthened and silence fell on the group, broken only by the low tones of Professor Stone as he told in broken sentences the story of ancient Ethiopia.

"For three thousand years the world has been mainly indebted for its advancement to the Romans, Greeks, Hebrews, Germans and Anglo-Saxons; but it was otherwise in the first years. Babylon and Egypt—Nimrod and Mizraim—both descendants of Ham—led the way, and acted as the pioneers of mankind in the untrodden fields of knowledge. The Ethiopians, therefore, manifested great superiority over all the nations among whom they dwelt, and their name became illustrious throughout Europe, Asia and Africa.

"The father of this distinguished race was Cush, the grandson of Noah, an Ethiopian.

"Old Chaldea, between the Euphrates and Tigris rivers, was the first home of the Cushites. Nimrod, Ham's grandson, founded Babylon. The Babylonians early developed the energy of mind which made their country the first abode of civilization. Canals covered the land, serving the purposes of traffic, defense and irrigation. Lakes were dug and stored with water, dykes built along the banks of rivers to fertilize the land, and it is not surprising to learn that from the earliest times Babylonia was crowded with populous cities. This grandeur was brought about by Nimrod the Ethiopian."

"Great Scott!" cried Charlie, "you don't mean to tell me that all this was done by *niggers*?"

The Professor smiled. Being English, he could not appreciate Charlie's horror at its full value.

"Undoubtedly your Afro-Americans are a branch of the wonderful and mysterious Ethiopians who had a prehistoric existence of magnificence, the full record of which is lost in obscurity.

"We associate with the name 'Chaldea' the sciences of astronomy and philosophy and chronology. It was to the Wise Men of the East to whom the birth of Christ was revealed; they were Chaldeans—of the Ethiopians. Eighty-eight years before the birth of Abraham, these people, known in history as 'Shepherd Kings,' subjugated the whole of Upper Egypt, which they held in bondage more than three hundred years."

"It is said that Egyptian civilization antedates that of Ethiopia," broke in Reuel. "How do you say, Professor?"

"Nothing of the sort, nothing of the sort. I know that in connecting Egypt with Ethiopia, one meets with most bitter denunciation from most modern scholars. Science has done its best to separate the race from Northern Africa, but the evidence is with the Ethiopians. If I mistake not, the ruins of Meroe will prove my words. Traditions with respect to Memnon connect Egypt and Ethiopia with the country at the head of the Nile. Memnon personifies the ethnic identity of the two races. Ancient Greeks believed it. All the traditions of Armenia, where lies Mt. Ararat, are in accordance with this fact. The Armenian geography applies the name of Cush to four great regions—Media, Persia, Susiana, Asia, or the whole territory between the Indus and the Tigris. Moses of Chorene identifies Belus, king of Babylon with Nimrod.

"But the Biblical tradition is paramount to all. In it lies the greatest authority that we have for the affiliation of nations, and it is delivered to us very simply and plainly: 'The sons of Ham were Cush and Mizraim and Phut and Canaan and Cush begot Nimrod and the beginning of his kingdom was Babel and Erech and Accad and Calneh, in the land of Shinar.' It is the best interpretation of this passage to understand it as asserting that the four races—Egyptians, Ethiopians, Libyans and Canaanites—were ethnically connected, being all descended from Ham; and that the primitive people of Babylon were a subdivision of one of these races; namely, of the Cushite or Ethiopian.

"These conclusions have lately received important and unexpected confirmation from the results of linguistic research. After the most remarkable of Mesopotamian mounds had yielded their treasures, and supplied the historical student with numerous and copious documents, bearing upon the history of the great Assyrian and Babylonian empires, it was determined to explore Chaldea proper, where mounds of considerable height marked the site of several ancient cities. Among unexpected results was the discovery of a new form of speech, differing greatly from the later Babylonian language. In grammatical structure this ancient tongue resembles dialects of the Turanian family, but its vocabulary has been pronounced to be decidedly Cushite or Ethiopian; and the modern languages to which it approaches nearest are thought to be the Mahen of Southern Arabia and the Galla of Abyssinia. Thus comparative philology appears to confirm old traditions. An Eastern Ethiopia instead of being the invention of bewildered ignorance, is rather a reality which it will require a good deal of scepticism to doubt, and the primitive race that bore sway in Chaldea proper belongs to this ethnic type. Meroe was the queenly city of this great people."

"It is hard to believe your story. From what a height must this people have fallen to reach the abjectness of the American Negro," exclaimed a listener.

"True," replied the Professor. "But from what a depth does history show that the Anglo-Saxon has climbed to the position of the first people of the earth today."

Charlie Vance said nothing. He had suffered so many shocks from the shattering of cherished idols since entering the country of mysteries that the power of expression had left him.

"Twenty-five years ago, when I was still a young man, the camel-driver who accompanied me to Thebes sustained a fatal accident. I helped him in his distress, and to show his gratitude he gave me the paper and chart I have shown you tonight. He was a singular man, black hair and eyes, middle height, dark-skinned, face and figure almost perfect, he was proficient in the dialects of the region, besides being master of the purest and most ancient Greek and Arabic. I believe he was a native of the city he described.

"He believed that Ethiopia antedated Egypt, and helped me materially in fixing certain data which time has proved to be correct. He added a fact which the manuscript withholds,—that from lands beyond unknown seas, to which many descendants of Ethiopia had been borne as slaves, should a king of ancient line—an offspring of that Ergamenes who lived in the reign of the second Ptolemy—return and restore the former glory of the race. The preservation of this hidden city is for his reception. This Arab also declared that Cush was his progenitor."

"That's bosh. How would they know their future king after centuries of obscurity passed in strange lands, and amalgamation with other races?" remarked the former speaker.

"I asked him that question; he told me that every descendant of the royal line bore a lotus-lily in the form of a birthmark upon his breast."

It might have been the unstable shadows of the moon that threw a tremulous light upon the group, but Charlie Vance was sure that Reuel Briggs started violently at the Professor's words.

One by one the men retired to rest, each one under the spell of the mysterious forces of a past life that brooded like a mist over the sandy plain, the dark Nile rolling sluggishly along within a short distance of their camp, and the ruined city now a magnificent Necropolis. The long shadows grew longer, painting the scene into beauty and grandeur. The majesty of death surrounded the spot and its desolation spoke in trumpet tones of the splendor which the grave must cover, when even the memory of our times shall be forgotten.

Famous Women of the Negro Race

VI. EDUCATORS

By the toleration of slavery, the great American government lowered its high standard and sullied its fair fame among other nations. Though slaves were introduced by the fathers across the seas, this was not accepted as an apology for crimes worse than murder. Great minds of every clime condemned American slavery. It was felt that no possible excuse could be offered for the crime of chattel bondage being fostered by a government so proudly heralding its championship of human liberty and equality.

Slavery was the sum of all villanies, and the slave-holder the greatest of villains.

It may be truly said that through the intellect speaks the soul, proving man's kinship with God and his heirship to immortality. Nature gives to the immature mind and unseeing eye matter already formed and boundaries set which are accepted blindly until the intellect, aroused by cultivation, penetrates the form and passes the boundaries seeking the First Principle of these things. Before the resistless restlessness of this cultured intellect, the intricate laws of Nature become but accessories to aid man in his search for the how and why of his own existence and of the entire universe. By it he adds fullness and richness to life; and if he pursue the development of the mind along the lines which bring nearness to Divinity, then he soars above the sordidness of earth and exemplifies in body and mind those characteristics resembling our Creator which we are taught should be the end of every well-directed life. All this a state of servitude denies to man.

For the elevation of humanity, and that man may begin here that primary development of the soul to be continued beyond the grave, let us hope, the common school was founded. In ancient times, Aristotle held and taught that "the most effective way of preserving a State, is to bring up the citizens in the spirit of the Government; to fashion, and as it were, cast them in the mould of the Constitution." Indeed, all thinkers agree that principles of right, equity, and justice must underlie all ideas of progressive civilization; and that a true conception of individual and mutual rights of property, contract, and government can never be successfully propagated except through the medium of the public school.

The slave-holder of the South early saw and appreciated the power of the God-given maxim "Mind is the glory of man;" he knew the power of a general diffusion of knowledge by the common school. What would become of this institution if the manhood of the Negro were not denied? He had read, too, the Declaration of Independence: "All men are created equal." So, to logically follow the Declaration it was necessary to prove the Negro a brute, that it might not be said that the government was based on the social, educational, moral and religious extinction of the rights of millions of immortal beings.

With the subtleness of Satan they proclaimed the inferiority of the Negro intellect, and to prove their reasoning correct began to bring about the state they desired by special enactment of laws which should sufficiently degrade the helpless beings in their control. The mind befogged and mentality contracted was more effectual than manacles and scourges in giving safety to the "peculiar institution," and would furnish ample excuse for all atrocities.

To the Negro then, bond or free, all school privileges were denied. At the opening of the war between the States, Mr. Phillips agitated disunion as the only road to abolition. To him, the Constitution that in a measure protected, even partially, the master who held property in human beings, was but a "covenant with death and an agreement with hell," and as such, the constitution became odious in his eyes. When, however, the first gun, was fired at Fort Sumter, he changed his condemnation of the Union to support of it, and accepted war as a means to the end he had in view. In 1863–64, he advocated the arming, educating and enfranchising the freedman. Then came into life the colored school-mistress, and of her heroic efforts to lighten the intellectual darkness which enveloped the ex-slave, no eulogy that we can write would half tell the story of her influence upon her race in building character, inculcating great principles, patiently toiling amidst the greatest privations far from home and pleasant surroundings. The colored teacher grasped the situation in its entirety,—that education is the only interest worthy the deep, controlling anxiety of the thoughtful man. The struggle that these women made for an independent, self-respecting manhood for their race was against desperate odds.

The ex-slave was totally unfit to cope with life's emergencies. The first necessity of human endeavor—a true home—simply did not exist. There was no room in that desert of mental blackness for the practice of even the common arts of life.

To these people, erstwhile counted as the beasts of the field, the colored teacher gave an awakened intelligence with which to secure their further education along industrial lines and the art of right living; fostered a delight in duty which gave them the habit of sustained endeavor; stability of character; warmth of heart to keep them true to family and social pieties; a sense of obligation which made them good citizens; an awakening to joy in their birthright of universal liberty.

It was providential that previous to the war, private schools were established in all the large Northern cities; and under the most stringent laws in slave-holding States, the ambitious Negro would somehow contrive to learn to read and write; consequently, when the call came for colored teachers many were found sufficiently well-equipped. It is instructive as well as interesting to study the laws affecting the education of the Negro as applied in each State, and how bravely the struggle for learning was waged in the very teeth of oppression.

In Alabama, 1832: "Any person or persons who shall attempt to teach any free person of color or slave to spell, read, or write, shall upon conviction thereof be fined a sum not less than $250, nor more than $500."

In Arkansas instruction was practically denied.

Connecticut's history tells a sad tale of New England prejudice against the Negro. Outrage was sanctioned in that State, sanctified and supported by laymen and churchmen of great but warped intellectuality. What wonder that slavery with all its attendant horrors continued so long to curse the land!

The well-known devotion of New England to popular education encouraged a hope that a collegiate school on the manual-labor plan might be established in New Haven, but the cruel prejudice of Connecticut people defeated the plan September 8, 1891, at a public meeting, it was resolved, by the mayor, common council, and legal voters to resist the establishment of such a school by every legal means.

Miss Prudence Crandall, a member of the Society of Friends, established a school for young ladies in Canterbury, Conn., in the autumn of 1832. A few months after her school opened, she admitted Sarah Harris, a colored girl, a member of the village church. This young woman attended the district school and desired to become better educated in order to teach among the children of her race. Although a classmate of some of Miss Crandall's pupils, objections were immediately raised to her remaining in the school.

All Miss Crandall's property was invested in the building, and the alternative of dismissing the colored girl or losing her white pupils was a bitter trial, but she met the issue grandly, rising above all personal interest in devotion to principle.

Having determined upon her course, she advertised at the beginning of her next term, her school would be opened to young ladies and misses of color, and others who might wish to attend. The people of Canterbury, greatly enraged, called a town meeting to abate the threatened "nuisance." Notwithstanding all opposition the school opened with fifteen or twenty pupils, but they were insulted upon the streets, the stores closed against them and her, their well filled with filth and the house assailed. The Legislature passed an act making the establishment of schools for colored youth illegal, and this act was received by the citizens of Canterbury with firing of cannon, ringing of bells, and demonstration of great rejoicing. Physicians refused to attend the sick of her family. The Trustees forbade her to come with them into the house of God. Miss Crandall was finally arrested for the crime of teaching colored girls, but in July, 1834, after many trials, the case was quashed, the court declaring it "unnecessary to come to any decision on the question as to the constitutionality of the law."

Soon after this an attempt was made to burn Miss Crandall's house. In spite of all difficulties, however, she continued to struggle on in her work of benevolence. But her enemies were determined and implacable, and on September 9, 1834, assaulted her house with clubs, rendering, it untenantable, and then acting upon the advice, of friends, the project was abandoned.

How great must have been the degradation of New England when upon this delicate, lovely woman the torture was inflicted of social ostracism, insult, exclusion from God's house, a criminal trial, and confinement in a murderer's cell,—all inflicted by the church, the county, the State!

Delaware taxed free colored persons for the fund to educate white children, but in 1840 the Society of Friends formed the African School Association, at Wilmington, and established two schools for boys and girls of color.

In the District of Columbia prejudice was rampant, and the laws very stringent against the education of Negroes, for slaves formed a large part of the population of the capital. But the colored people of the District were eminently progressive; they determined to have schools and to educate their children, and in the face of persecution that might well have daunted the most daring, instituted private schools where the children were taught the rudiments of learning. Among the many energetic women who opened these schools we mention Mrs. Anne Maria Hall, Anne Eliza Cook, Nannie Waugh, Louisa Parke Coston, Martha Costin, Martha Becraft, and the members of the Wormley family.

One of the most successful schools was operated by Miss Myrtilla Miner, for four years. She received applications from more pupils than she could admit. Her work was done in a quiet, unostentatious manner, but she possessed a rare union of qualifications,—good sense, tact, industry, energy—all of which wait upon successful ventures. Her school attracted the attention of philanthropists everywhere and finally led to the establishment of the Normal School for Colored Female Teachers under the care of the "Washington Association for the Education of Free Colored Youth." We append an extract from the appeal for aid which Miss Miner sent out to the friends of the oppressed.

"While good men send forth shiploads of bread to feed the famishing of other lands, and the country sends free equipments of ships, money and men to bear home the oppressed of other nations; why not remember the suffering at home, who suffer for want of soul-food; for enlightenment of mind, such as a Christian nation should be careful to bestow.

"Shall the colored people of Washington be allowed the instruction necessary to enlighten their minds, awaken their consciences, and purify their lives." We fear some will answer 'No,' but there are others who will say 'Yes,' and to these we earnestly look for aid.

"We would at this time considerately inquire, can we be sustained in our efforts to perfect an Institution of learning here, adequate to the wants of the people, worthy the spirit of the age, and embodying those religious principles and moral teachings which, by their fruits shall be found to purify the heart, rendering it 'first pure, then peaceable?'

"We earnestly urge this appeal. We entreat all ministers of Christ to care for these lost sheep; we entreat the women of our country to aid in rescuing their sex from the extremity of ignorance, dishonor and suffering; we entreat the happy mothers of our land to pity and relieve the sorrows of mothers compelled to see their children growing up in ignorance and degradation."

In Florida and Georgia white children alone were educated. Georgia was very strict in establishing a penal code in 1833, against persons employing any slave or free person of color to set type or perform any other labor about a printing office, requiring knowledge of reading, writing, etc.

The laws of Illinois and Indiana were cruel in relation to the education of Negroes; a free mission institute at Quincy, Ill., was mobbed because a few colored persons were admitted to the classes.

In Kentucky and Louisiana the laws provided imprisonment for all persons teaching Negroes. The close of the war found the ex-slaves of New Orleans in a lamentable condition, and among those who were moved to tender their services to ameliorate this situation the name of Mrs. Louisa De Mortie ranks deservedly high.

She came to Boston in 1853, we believe, from Norfolk, Va., where she was born free. In 1862 she began as a public reader in Boston, where her rare ability gained her many admirers and friends among leading men and women of the country, and a successful public career seemed to be before her.

About this time—hearing of the distress amongst the colored children of New Orleans, left orphans by the war, she resolved to go there and devote her life to their welfare. While there the yellow fever broke out, and although urged by relatives and friends to return to the North until it had abated somewhat, she refused to desert her post of duty among the helpless little ones.

In 1867 Mrs. De Mortie succeeded in raising enough money to erect a building for an orphans' home; but her useful career was cut short at last by yellow fever, and she died October 10, 1867, in her thirty-fourth year.

The news of her death created profound regret among all classes at the North where her name was a household word, and the newspapers of New Orleans spoke of her in the most eulogistic terms.

Mrs. De Mortie was a remarkably brilliant and gifted woman. Richly endowed by nature with the qualities that please and fascinate, it may be said with truth that she was one of the most beautiful women of her day.

Negro children were excluded from the benefits of school training in Maryland, but God opened a way.

St. Frances Academy for colored girls was founded in connection with the Oblate Sisters of Providence Convent, in Baltimore, June 5, 1829, receiving the sanction of the Holy See, October 2, 1831. The convent originated with the French Fathers, who came to Baltimore as refugees fleeing from the revolution in San Domingo. The colored women who formed the original society which founded the convent and seminary, were from San Domingo, though some of them had been educated in France.

The Sisters of Providence renounce the world to consecrate themselves to the Christian education of colored girls. This school under their control has developed in importance until the good it has accomplished can hardly be estimated. Teaching as the Sisters do the solid principles of domestic virtues and pure religion, a legacy is passed on of inestimable value to the unborn thousands yet to come.

Miss Fanny M. Jackson (wife of Bishop Levi B. Coppin) was born in Washington, D.C., about 1837, and was left an orphan at an early age. She was brought up by her aunt, Mrs. Sarah Clark, but the opportunities for acquiring education were limited in the District, and she went to New Bedford with her aunt Mrs. Orr. When Mrs. Orr removed to Newport, R.I., Miss Jackson took up her residence with the family of Mayor Caldwell. At this time Miss Jackson had begun to give her friends glimpses of her rare gifts of mind which have since ripened into scholarship of the most profound nature. When we consider Miss Jackson's early struggles for education and the high position she occupies to-day in educational circles, we must acknowledge her to be one of the most remarkable women of the century just closed.

Her rare genius attracted the attention of ripe scholars everywhere, and it is interesting to hear Hon. Geo. Downing, of Newport, tell of his first meeting with the lady, when they crossed swords in public debate at a citizens' meeting to consider the question of colored schools.

Mayor Caldwell was so strongly impressed by her ability that by his aid she was able to enter the school at Bristol, R.I., and begin the study of the higher branches. After preparation here, Miss Jackson went to Oberlin College, where she soon took the highest rank with other progressive students. To assist her in meeting the bills for tuition, she taught music in families in the village, and also was entrusted with the musical training of the children of the professors at the college. Miss Jackson is a fine performer on the piano, harp, guitar and organ, often serving as organist in her vacation time in the church where Minister Van Horn was so long the pastor.

Irreproachable in reputation, with rare gifts and great moral aspirations, Miss Jackson was and always has been of untold value and benefit to her race. She easily won the highest respect and sympathy from her Oberlin teachers, and she was selected as a teacher for the Institute at Philadelphia, long before graduation.

The Institute for colored youth was founded by Richard Humphrey, of Philadelphia, a member of the Society of Friends; a people whose sympathy and charity for the oppressed Negro are proverbial, and who have earned our heartfelt gratitude and respect.

Mr. Humphrey left a fund of ten thousand dollars, a legacy coming under the guidance of the Society amounted to sixteen thousand two hundred and ninety dollars in 1838. With this sum a charter was secured from the Legislature of Pennsylvania in 1842. Its object the education of colored youth, male and female, "to act as teachers and instructors in the different branches of school learning, or in the mechanical arts and agriculture."

The Institute was permanently located on Lombard street, in 1851.

Graduating with honors, Miss Jackson at once took her position in this school, where she was principal until she resigned in 1902. Her ability in governing this institution of learning has given her world-wide fame; she is respected by parents and guardians, and loved by her pupils.

Miss Jackson has appeared on the platform where her rhetoric has dazzled the listener. As a writer she is a keen reasoner and a deep thinker, handling live issues in a masterly manner.

We would compare her to Madame De Stael, but that cultured woman was the product of centuries of education and refinement. Miss Jackson is a unique figure among women of all nationalities,—a standing monument of the handiwork of the Great Architect, whose masterly creations man can never hope to approach.

VII.   EDUCATORS (*CONTINUED*)

As we have said, one necessary condition of American slavery was ignorance. By the inexorable laws of Mississippi and South Carolina the Negro was doomed to hopeless moral and mental abasement.

In 1843, Mississippi ordered all free persons of color to remove from the State. There was, of course, no provisions allowed for the education of the Negro.

North Carolina allowed free persons of color school privileges until 1835, when they were abolished by law.

South Carolina allowed privileges of no kind, and only the most rigid and extreme laws prevailed; owing to the great demand for slave labor, thousands of unhappy blacks were imported, and the slave code reached the maximum of cruelty in that State.

On the contrary, in the Northern New England States—Maine and Vermont—slavery never existed at any time, and Negroes enjoyed the same privileges as did the Anglo-Saxon. New Hampshire possessed very few slaves at any time, and at an early period passed laws against their importation. There, also, education was free to all regardless of color.

Outside of this small section, efforts were made to establish institutions for the culture of colored youth, for years they failed signally; the tree of slavery "overshadowed the whole land, shedding its blighting influence on Northern as well as Southern hearts."

The condition of the Negroes in New York was about the same as in Virginia, although their privileges were more. They were admitted to membership in the churches, and no law was passed against educational methods.

A school for Negro slaves was opened in New York in 1704, by Elias Nean, a native of France. The New York African Free School was founded in 1786, located between Beekman and Ferry Streets. After many struggles and vicissitudes, in 1815, a commodious brick building was erected, large enough, to accommodate 200 pupils, and Miss Lucy Turpin took charge of the sewing with other branches. She was followed by Miss Mary Lincrum, Miss Eliza J. Cox, Miss Mary Ann Cox and Miss Caroline Roe, all of whom sustained the high character of the enterprise.

When General Lafayette visited the United States, he visited this school and examined the children in geography and other studies. He professed himself much pleased with the progress the children had made.

The New York schools advanced steadily, and in 1853 the colored schools of the Board of Education of New York City and County were established. The schools were graded, and Miss Caroline W. Simpson was made principal of Colored Grammar School, No. 3, and Miss Nancy Thomas principal of No. 4 (in Harlem).

From that time until the present, the advancement of the race in New York has been inspiring. The business men of the State are second to none in the country, leading the race in many instances. Along the lines of social and educational life we find the same cheering aspect. The social life is enjoyable and refining; the schools among the best in the United States, embracing teachers honored and respected for faithfulness and ability, culture and refinement.

In Puritan Massachusetts, a traffic in human beings was carried on for over a century. Thousands were sold; and the profit accruing from the sale of Negroes in all parts of the country laid the foundation of the wealth of many an old Massachusetts family. Slaves were classed as property, being valued as "horses and hogs." They were not allowed to bear arms nor be educated. The church, too, discriminated against them in every way.

But, although Massachusetts may commit a wrong, she is not persistent in evil when the public conscience is once aroused.

It was Judge Sewall, who delivered his warning words in 1700, to the New England colonies, cautioning them against slavery and the ill-treatment of Negroes in these words: "Forasmuch as Liberty is in real value next unto Life, none ought to part with it, but upon most mature consideration." People and slaves were aroused by this speech; sermons and essays continually excited the inhabitants. When the Revolution broke out and the war with England was on, the slaves fought in defence of the colonies, and thus by courage and patriotism loosened the chains of bondage in the North.

The first colored schools in Boston was held in the house of Primus Hall; the second, in the basement of the Belknap-Street church (St. Paul's Baptist church), and in 1835 a school-house was erected known as "Smith Schoolhouse" from the name of Abdiel Smith, who left a fund for that purpose. Added to this fund the city of Boston allowed two hundred dollars annually, and parents were charged twelve and one-half cents per week for each child.

William C. Nell, a well-known Negro agitator of Massachusetts, was instrumental in opening Boston schools to the Race, and in 1855, after a hard fight, in accordance with a law passed by the Legislature, colored schools were abolished.

The first colored teacher appointed in the mixed schools of Boston was Miss Elizabeth Smith, daughter of Hon. J. J. Smith,—well-known as an abolitionist, and closely associated with Messrs. Garrison, Phillips, Sumner, Hayden, Nell and E. G. Walker.

Miss Smith was born in Boston on the old historic "hill," and educated at the "old Bowdoin school" on Myrtle St., graduating from the famous Girls' High School, of Boston. The Smith family is well and favorably known all over the country, having a large circle of friends and admirers in every city. One sister, Mrs. Adelaide Terry, is a well-known vocalist and teacher of music; another sister, Miss Florence Smith, is a successful teacher in the schools of Washington, D.C. Miss Harriet Smith, the youngest, is a valuable assistant of the Bowdoin school, Boston, Mass. The only brother is Mr. Hamilton Smith, of Washington, D.C. Miss Elizabeth was the eldest living child of this interesting family.

After graduation, Miss. Smith taught in the South for a time, but was appointed to the Joy-Street school in 1870, where she remained four years. Retiring from this position, she was employed in the evening schools for a number of years, being re-appointed, finally, to a permanent position in the

Sharpe school. While in the active performance of her duties there, looking forward hopefully, to holding the position of principal, by promotion, she died in the latter part of 1899, deeply regretted by friends and associates.

Miss Smith was a remarkably good woman, who easily won the love and respect of her associates—teachers, pupils and companions, by her quiet, unostentatious manner, and who used her wide influence among the young of both races for their elevation and advancement.

Most men and women of the African race who have become famous because of a talent above the ordinary, are content to draw their ancestry' from our common father Adam, and their talent from the bestower of all good things—our Creator. So it is with the subject of this school.

Miss Maria Louise Baldwin was born in Cambridge, Mass. Her parents were well-known and highly respected citizens of the "city across the Charles," who, like many other parents struggled hard to give their children all the advantages which parental love could bestow.

Miss Baldwin is the eldest of three children,—Miss Gertrude, her sister, has been for years a teacher in the public schools of Wilmington, Delaware: the only brother, Louis, is engaged in the real estate business at Cambridge, and has been very successful. He is a genial, popular man, much liked by his associates and business friends. Miss Baldwin's early education embraced the plain, straightforward curriculum of the New England public school,— passing from primary grade to grammar, to high, to training, imbibing grace of mind and body together with comprehensive Christianity and orderly deportment from her cultured teachers, many of them descendants of the best New England stock; acquiring depth of thought, activity in business and the value of method in all life's duties from this association.

Leaving a happy childhood behind her, the young girl entered upon the serious work of bread-winning very soon after graduation, at Chester County, Maryland, teaching there two terms. Active in mind and body, possessing great energy and executive ability, Miss Baldwin, in this probationary stage of her work, developed into a successful teacher.

In 1882 came the turning point in her life-work—she was appointed a teacher in the Cambridge public schools. This gave her the fulcrum, the one thing demanded by humanity—opportunity. Without this, aspiration and ability may be said to resemble "silent thunder;" youthful and unknown, deprived of opportunity, genius is baffled and sinks to earth never to realize its "noble aspirations." But upon her favorites Fortune is wont to smile and give first place.

We give the story of Miss Baldwin's appointment as nearly as possible in her own words:

"I was given at first an, 'overflow' class to teach, with the assurance that I would be kept while that class continued to be a necessity; I was, in short, a temporary teacher. Mr. Francis Coggswell, superintendent of schools, said he could not tell how long I would stay, but the next year I was called to the same place, and was confirmed in my position by the Board.

The Louis Agasszziz school is on Sacramento St., corner of Oxford St., and not far from the Agassiz Museum; it is in an aristocratic corner of Old Cambridge, and beneath the shadow of 'Fair Harvard's' wings.

"For seven years I taught in all the lower grades of the school, gaining thereby invaluable experience. In 1889 Miss Ewell, then the principal of the school, and greatly beloved, resigned in June, the resignation being kept secret until after vacation, and the school opened in September without a head, remaining so until the middle of October.

"One Friday Mr. Coggswell asked me how I would like the position of principal. I immediately answered, 'Not at all.' 'Why?' he inquired. I replied, 'I am happier with the little children, and prefer to remain where I am. If I failed in the position you mention, it would be a conspicuous failure.'

'Saturday morning, Mr. Coggswell called at my home, and sitting in this room where we are now, said, 'Miss Baldwin, you are neglecting an opportunity to show to Cambridge more than you have already done.' He added, 'The committee have every confidence in your executive ability and desire you to accept the place.'

"I was confused and somewhat dazed, and begged that he would give me until afternoon to decide. Directly he was gone I hastened to Miss Ewell's house and asked her advice. She said, 'I knew you would be asked and I want you to take it.'"

"That afternoon I told Mr. Coggswell that I would accept for two weeks, and for thirteen years I have been principal of the school, being appointed in October, 1889. There are eight assistants and three hundred and fifteen pupils. In October, 1902, I round out twenty happy years spent in teaching in the public schools of Cambridge."

As a woman of letters, Miss Baldwin's career is full of interest. She is distinctly a product of to-day, in this pursuit.

The entire colored population was happily surprised and greatly cheered when it was announced that she was chosen to deliver the address on Harriet Beecher Stowe before the Brooklyn Institute of Arts and Sciences, February 22, 1897. It was a distinctive triumph, in which Miss Baldwin stood alone beneath the searching light of public curiosity, and, in some instances, we doubt not, incredulity among the educated whites unacquainted with her ability. She arose to the occasion grandly and fulfilled our fondest hopes, covering herself and us with new honors. We do not hesitate to say that if she had distinguished herself in no other way save in compiling and delivering this lecture, her name would have gone down to posterity as a literary genius.

Brooklyn Institute of Arts and Sciences originated as far back as 1823; it early assumed a notable place in the intellectual life of Brooklyn. In 1888, it was re-organized under Prof. Franklin W. Hooper, as director, and its past history, almost phenomenal in its brilliancy, is due to the fact and foresight of that gentleman.

It has to-day a splendid new Museum Building, 600 yearly lectures, 3,000 yearly classes and special meetings; its extension courses, its schools of art, its summer biological schools, its library, and its collections. Members of the Institute enjoy the precious privileges, and in addition to ordinary lectures, the Institute conducts special courses and entertainments. Thus, for example, the Boston Symphony concerts in Brooklyn are conducted under the auspices of its department of music at low cost to the members. The Institute has twenty-seven, departments, including anthropology, archology, architecture, astronomy, botany, chemistry, domestic science, electricity, engineering; entomology, fine arts, geography, geology, law, mathematics, microscopy, mineralogy, music, painting, pedagogy, philology, photography, physics, political science, psychology, sculpture, and zoology.

Augustus Graham, benefactor of the Institute, provided the fund that pays for the "Washington Anniversary," February 22, being set aside to commemorate the life of some great American. Washington, Garrison, Summer, Curtis, Lowell, and others had been taken. The February following Mrs. Stowe's death she was the subject of commemoration,—the first woman to be so distinguished. The committee wrote to Miss Baldwin, and in "fear, and trembling" she accepted the honor. For this lecture Miss Baldwin was paid one hundred dollars. Among the noted men who have been called to address the members of this Institute we mention a few: Mr. Russell Sturgis; Dr. Burt G. Wilder, of Cornell; Col. Thos. W. Higginson; Charles Kendall Adams, L.L.D., of the University of Wisconsin; Hon. Charles A. Boutelle, of Maine.

Prof. Booker T. Washingon lectures there in 1902.

The popularity of Miss Baldwin's lecture has been unparalleled from its first delivery. It has been repeatedly given by its talented author before associations and clubs of the highest literary repute; among them we may mention the Brooklyn Institute of Arts and Sciences; Cantabrigia Club, Cambridge; the Old South course of historic lectures; the Municipal Lecture Course, Boston.

In complexion, Miss Baldwin is a dark mulatto; features well-defined, and an intelligent and refined countenance; her figure is well developed, inclined to embonpoint; her head is round, the organs well-balanced, and about it is coiled black, silky hair, clustering in waves over the thoughtful brow. Upon the platform she is a pleasant picture, dignified in her carriage and polished in her address; her full, softly modulated, contralto voice easily reaching the most distant corners of a hall.

We do not claim to number among our men of letters and public speakers a Tennyson or a Dickens, a Carlyle or a Hume, nor subtle diplomats of the Disraeli school, but by the lives of those men and women who have shown the slightest spark of the divine fire in the color of their life-work, we have proved our origin.

To the favored few among us who have enjoyed exceptional advantages of obtaining knowledge, and thereby cultivation, together with that nice perception which distinguishes easily between the polished achievements of inherited scholarly traits as defined by the masterpieces of fiction, scientific work or exquisite art creations of the Anglo-Saxon, and the ambitious strivings of our own people toward the same goals,—to this class our efforts may seem pathetic, and altogether vain, but let us remember,—whether the window through which the glory of sunlight comes to us is circular, square or oval, or whether it be set in the Egyptian, the Grecian, the Gothic or the architecture of the lowly cabin of the South with its mud flooring, the form of the medium does not concern us, it is the light itself,

> "As sunshine broken in the rill,
> Though turned aside, is sunshine still."

The Anglo-Saxon came not to his present state of perfection fully equipped; he is the product of centuries of constant practice in the arts and graces of educated civilization. If we go back a few centuries we find his ancestors described by Csar and Tacitus. Csar, writing home, said of the Britons, "They are the most degraded people I ever conquered." Cicero advised Atticus not to purchase slaves from Briton, "because," said he, "they cannot be taught music, and are the ugliest people I ever saw."

Macaulay says: "When the Britons first became known to the Tyrian mariners, they were little superior to the Sandwich Islanders" (meaning, of course, their most savage state).

Rome got her civilization from Greece; Greece borrowed hers from Egypt, thence she derived her science and beautiful mythology. Civilization descended the Nile and spread over the delta, as it came down from Thebes. Thebes was built and settled by the Ethiopians. As we ascend the Nile we come to Meroe the queen city of Ethiopia and the cradle of learning into which all Africa poured its caravans. So we trace the light of civilization from Ethiopia to Egypt, to Greece, to Rome, and thence diffusing its radiance over the entire world.

The query:—What is the best course for the Negro in education to mould him into a useful self-supporting citizen? has as many sides as a chameleon has shades—in whatever light we view it, fresh complications arise, and because of these very complications we ought not to utter a wholesale condemnation of our leaders and their opinions, neither should we utter harsh words of censure against the patriotic band of thinkers who stand jealously guarding the rights of the race from dangerous encroachment.

Twenty years hence we can better judge the motives of our leaders, for Time is a true leveller; twenty years hence we can applaud with fervor the iron-hearted men who bar Oppression's way. Until then, let us exercise the virtue of charity that suffereth long and is kind; that beareth all things, believeth all things, hopeth all things, endureth all things. More and more are we led to say: "Events are God's, let Him sit at His own helm, that moderateth all."

In the careers of Miss Baldwin and our other New England teachers, the section has sustained its reputation.

Miss Baldwin is honored, respected and loved by all who know her. From pupils and parents she has always received the treatment that we delight to lavish upon those whom we love.

Intermarriage between Northern and Southern white families, the introduction of Southern teachers into the schools, and a natural feeling of kinship between the Northern and Southern Anglo-Saxon, may cause happenings in New England which smack of prejudice towards us as a race. But such things are as nothing when we remember that New England principles gave us a free Kansas way back in 1857: that New England blood was first shed in the streets of Baltimore when the toxin of war sounded the call to save the Union: that New England cemented the Proclamation of Emancipation in the death of Col. Shaw: and, greater than all, stern New England Puritanism in the persons of Garrison, Summer, Phillips, Stearns, Whittier, Francis Jackson, and others, gave the black man the liberty that the South would deny even to-day, if possible: gave to the Negro all over this broad land his present prosperity, no matter how inconsiderable it may appear to us: gave us Douglass and Langston, Robert Elliott and Bruce, and Booker T. Washington, with his world-famous Tuskegee Institute.

May my tongue cleave to the roof of my mouth and my right hand forget its cunning when I forget the benefits bestowed upon my persecuted race by noble-hearted New England.

VIII. EDUCATORS (*CONCLUDED*)

A half-century or more ago among the earnest workers of the great city of Boston, counted with those of prominence and refinement, of open hospitality and culture, was the family of the Howards.

For many years they lived at the homestead on Poplar St., in the then aristocratic quarter of the old West End. The house, a four-story brick edifice, was well-kept, and differed in no one particular from its flourishing neighbors, albeit its owners were colored, and it was a most unusual thing to find a Negro family so charmingly located as were the Howards, in those days when the trials endured by the race to-day were but child's play by comparison with the terrible sufferings then imposed upon the entire race.

One of the sons of this family, Edwin Frederick, brought to his home as his loving wife, Joan Louise Turpin of New York. By her genial manners and sympathetic heart this lady soon made herself a valued member of the household, and a valued friend to a large circle among members of her own race, as well as that class of broad, liberal-minded lovers of humanity among whom may be numbered such revered names as Garrison, Sumner, Wilson, Phillips, Higginson, and Lydia Maria Child, for the Howard family was identified closely with the anti-slavery movement from its inception. Married in New York, the eldest daughter of Edwin and Joan Howard, Adelaine Turpin, was born in that city, and claims it as her birthplace; while Dr. Edwin Clarence and Joan Imogen are a son and daughter who delight ever that almost under the shadow of the "gilded dome" of Massachusetts' capitol building, their infancy and early youth were passed.

All three, reared under the finest moral influences, amid surroundings tended to foster a taste for literature, science, and that which is in the highest degree aesthetic, it is not surprising that we find these representatives of an honest mother and a universally beloved father, shedding sunshine and light through a long experience of private and public usefulness, in a service for the betterment of the children of our race, and for the alleviation of the sufferings of mankind.

As a physician, a graduate of Harvard Medical School, Dr. Howard is known as the senior and among the most skilful of the doctors of Philadelphia, Pa., a city where he has won his enviable professional reputation, and among whose people he is ever accorded every honor by the citizens at large and by the highest officials who administer the affairs of the Quaker city.

In early life, during a residence of five years on the "Dark Continent" he first evinced his tendency towards the medical profession. As an observer and a student, a season was passed in the hospitals and institutions of a kindred nature in England and France. He is a valued member of the Philadelphia County Medical Society, the Pennsylvania Medical Society, and the American Medical Association, frequently being a delegate chosen to represent the first in the State and National Societies. Not among the least of the many services rendered to his adopted city is that which for eleven years was given as a member of the Board of Education.

Miss Adeline Turpin Howard, early in life offered herself as an instructor in that field of educational work where the torch frequently followed closely upon the opening of a school for that class among us then known as "Freedmen." In Virginia, that State of whose historic name every white American is proud; in Maryland's remote country hamlets; and in far away Louisiana along the banks of the Red River, unselfishly, with patience, perseverance and that spirit of self-renunciation that many have known in their efforts to lift to better lives those from whom slavery had taken God's greatest blessings, she labored for years. That many among the young and the vigorous, the old and down-trodden, long looked up to and honored her must, in these years, be a choice memory. To-day we find her active, progressive and most capable as the highly esteemed principal of the Wormley Building in West Washington, D.C., where, as the administrative head and the practical teacher, she has under her charge and that of able assistants, over six hundred girls and boys who rank well in their literary subjects, as well as in those branches of domestic art, and moral and aesthetic training which lead to good citizenship.

Joan Imogen Howard was the first colored pupil of the grammar schools of Boston to graduate and then knock at the door of the Girls' High and Normal School (then located on Mason St.) for entrance. This was accomplished without "conditions" as to her examinations; but since, hitherto, no dark-hued student had ever been seated in its halls, some apprehension was felt as to the effect on the classes. To the honor of the head-master, Mr. Seavey, and the grandly broad-minded Miss Temple, nothing of this objection was ever known or felt during the three years' course. Graduating with honor, an opening presented itself in New York City, and there until the close of the year 1901, we knew her, ever striving to take a step higher in her profession as a teacher. Knowing "The mill will never grind with the water that has passed," courses in "Methods of Teaching" were taken at short intervals at institutions of the first rank, and in 1892, she was graduated from New York University receiving a diploma and the well-earned degree of "Master of Pedagogy."

The University of the State of New York is an innovation in educational circles, embracing, as it does, all the chartered colleges and secondary schools in the State; it is an institution unique in its organization and its methods of work.

There has been scarcely any educational reform in the State of which the University has not been the promoteor. In the training of teachers it has been especially active. Its field has so been extended to include the charterings of high schools, academies, and colleges and also of libraries, museums, summer schools, corresponding schools, permanent lecture courses, and all other institutions for promoting higher education.

When one considers that political issues have become in these years mainly economic, the merits of a general education of the people in the scientific aspects of their individual life becomes clear. When we consider the fact that all classes and all races in a cosmopolitan population such as ours must understand the effect that a change of governmental policy may have upon the commercial life of our Republic, it becomes plain to the dullest intellect that our future legislation, executives, and judicial officers, must have always before them the economic welfare of the people, white and black; it is, therefore, necessary that all education, professional as well as business, shall embrace a clear understanding of the relations between the industrial life of the people and the laws and policy of the government.

More and more must women enter into a knowledge of all these questions in order to be fitted to teach the embryo man the duties of good citizenship. Recognizing this need, the sociological student must bow to the increasing demands of higher education. Under the broadening influence of such educational methods, Miss Howard has developed into a perfect womanhood.

In 1892, Governor Flower of New York, through the enthusiastic advocacy of Judge Jas. C. Matthews (one of the most prominent in the legal fraternity of Albany) appointed her a member of the Board of Women Managers of the State of New York, for the Columbian Exposition. Far from being a place of embarrassment on account of its being without a parallel on any other State Board for the same grand event, Miss Howard's experiences were made a joy to her by the Governor of the State, the Mayor of Albany, and by the choice specimens of New York's most liberal-minded and aristocratic gentlewomen who formed the Board. As a result of her efforts and of the untiring, painstaking and executive sub-committee that were formed throughout the State, statistics of women's work were tabulated, exhibits gathered, and the literary works of Lydia Maria Child—almost a martyr in the cause of abolition—were gathered nearly in their entirety. These became a valued part of the rare collection of books in the artistic library of the Woman's Building in the dreamily beautiful "White City" at Chicago in 1892 and 1893. Now, they and an exhaustive account of the "Distinguished Work of the Colored Women of America" are among the treasures in the "many-millioned-dollared" capitol at Albany.

Miss Howard feels herself one with the many in this vast country for she frequently says that she never could and never can know sectional differences. That she never could, she owes to the teachings of a revered mother; that she never can is but a return for the spirit of loyal support of indomitable energy, enthusiastic outpouring of money, and above all, the unanimity of effort which placed ballot after ballot to her credit, until a shower, which knew no ceasing, poured votes into the New York Telegram Office in the "Trip to Paris Contest" for sixteen months, until when the announcement of the five successful candidates was made in June, 1900, her name was the third, and the trip to France and Belgium was the result.

This she considers the crowning event in a career in which only a little has been done by her, but that little she hopes is a part of "God's great plan."

After teaching every grade required by the curriculum in the grammar departments of New York's schools, an indisposition of a serious nature compelled her to resign her position as the teacher of the graduating class of Public School No. 80, Manhattan, and reluctantly retire from active service.

Now, as a companion to her deceased mother's sister, Mrs. Bowers, and of her esteemed brother, Dr. Howard, she resides in Philadelphia, where it is hoped a complete family circle will be formed by the addition, at no future day, of the sister who is still claimed by our old Bay State as one of its honored daughters.

Apropos of the fact that numbers of famous Negro women have been signally honored by white institutions of renown in various communities, it is profitable to pause a moment and consider the position taken by the General Federation of Women's Clubs in its recent convention at Los Angeles, Cal.

The application of the Women's Era Club, Boston, for admission to the General Federation, was made at a time when a club could only be admitted by a majority vote of the Board of Directors. The dues were sent to the Treasurer, and Mrs. Ruffin was in Milwaukee expecting to be seated in the convention. June 4, 1900, a motion was made to admit the club to membership.

The fact that the admission of a colored club would establish a precedent made the Board unwilling to act, and the dues were returned to Mrs. Ruffin, and a motion to lay it on the table was made and carried.

During the two years which have elapsed since then there has been constant agitation over the "color question." Political "wire-pulling" of every sort has been resorted to by the Southern women and their Northern sympathizers to keep out the colored sisters, and at last success has crowned their efforts.

Mrs. Dimies T. Denison of New York placed herself on record by making the following statement to the reporter of the "Los Angeles Times."

"The newspapers seeking for 'copy' have magnified the matter. It really is only a side issue although it is important. I am sure the delegates will act wisely. The Civil War is past; the old wounds have been healed; the North and the South are re-united, and we cannot afford to take any action that will lead to more bitter feeling. The South is represented strongly in the federation, and the effect on those members is obvious if colored women are admitted on a social equality with white members. We must not, and I feel that the delegates will not, do anything that threatens disruption of the federation of which we are all so proud."

As a result of a vote taken on May 5, 1902, by the General Federation of Women's Clubs, it became practically impossible for colored clubs to get into the federation. The decision was for the Massachusetts-Georgia compromise, by which State rights are maintained, in that no restrictions are placed upon State Federations: but the way to membership in the General Federation is blocked by the necessity of passing two boards and the Membership Committee of the General Federation, the unanimous vote of which last committee is required for admission. The victory is thus to the South.

In the discussion preceding the casting of ballots. Mrs. Gallagher of Ohiluo said:

"This is not a question of color, it is a question of an embryonic race, not yet strong enough to stand with us.... The Negroes are by nature imitators. If we admit them to associations with us, they will lose their power of independent development and become merely followers of the whites. They have not yet reached a plane on which they can compete with us and maintain their own independence. The best thing we can do for them is to let them go on developing along their own lines. Then, when they have fought their fight and won their way up, where they can stand on an equal footing with us, let us consider their admission."

In the discussion of the color question, Miss Jane Addams (Hull House, Chicago) aroused the most interest by declaring herself a partisan of colored clubs and holding the opinion that "no race can uphold a race integrity apart from other races, and that it lies with the stronger people to stand with the weaker." The final call for the previous question carried the amendment by an overwhelming vote.

The power of organization among women is a sociological study. Women were narrow mentally; it is supposed that they have been broadened by their educational opportunities and their growing influence which has, hitherto, commanded the respect of the world. We had hoped that as a race, we should receive the fair treatment, the sympathy, the loyalty, that their reputation guaranteed, but the Biennial at Los Angeles has given us a rude awakening.

> "They find their fellows guilty of a skin
> Not colored like their own, and having power
> To enforce the wrong, for such a worthy cause
> Doom and devote them as their lawful prey."

At the World's Congress of Representative Women from all Lands, in 1892–3, under the superintendeance of such women as Mrs. Potter Palmer, Mrs. Charles Henrotin, Mrs. May Wright Sewall, Mrs. Avery, Miss Frances E. Willard, and others, such notable women of color as Frances Ellen Harper, Fanny Jackson-Coppin, Annie J. Cooper, Fanny Barrier Williams, and Hallie Q. Brown delivered addresses which drew the eyes of the entire world upon them and their race.

In connection with the same great Exposition, Miss Imogen Howard, as we have stated in the above sketch, was signally honored by being appointed a member of the Board of Women Managers of the State of New York for the Columbian Exposition, the only Negro so honored by any other State. Miss Howard's a peculiar fitness for the position to which she was called, added additional lustre to her fame, and her race stepped up a rung on Ambition's ladder.

In Massachusetts, we may mention that, added to her fame as a teacher and lecturer, Miss Maria L. Baldwin has for years been a member of the Cantabrigia Club of Cambridge, than which no wealthier, no more highly cultured, no club of wider fame exists in the entire country. No token of esteem has been too high for this club of noble-minded women to bestow on their admired colored member.

In connection with the famous Boston Political class under its president, the great parliamentarian, Mrs. Harriet P. Shattuck, we may mention the fact that Mrs. Mary J. Buchanan, a beautiful and cultured woman of color, has been a member for years; has filled every office; and was for a number of seasons honored as the vice-president of the club.

Mrs. J. St. Pierre Ruffin's career as a club woman is too well known to need rehearsal, and we doubt not that many other colored women, of whom we have no knowledge, are connected with similar white institutions of wealth and influence.

In the face of this testimony to the superior work being done by all classes of Negro women, in every State in the Union where their ability has been given an opportunity to materialize, we are justly indignant that our women are branded as the intellectual inferiors of the whites in such words as were used by Mrs. Gallagher: "When they have fought their fight and won their way up where they can stand on an equal footing with us, let us consider their admission."

We know that we shall be pardoned the assertion that jealousy has something do with the decision of the great Biennial Convention of 1902.

We have felt and argued always against unrestricted and universal suffrage, feeling that mentally woman is as narrow to-day as ever, that behind windy, grandiloquent speeches of belief in the equality of the human species, dwelt a spirit of perverseness that might at any moment break forth to our undoing.

So must Mrs. Harper have felt when during her speech at the Women's Congress 1892, she uttered the following words, which implied a doubt of the temper of the great majority of our white female population toward the Negro.

"Political life in our country is plowed in muddy channels, and needs the infusion of cleaner and clearer waters. I am not sure that women are naturally so much better than men that they will clear the stream by the virtue of their womanhood; it is not through sex, but through character that the best influence of woman upon the life of the Nation must be exerted.

"I do not believe in unrestricted and universal suffrage for either men or women. I believe in moral and educational tests. I do not believe that the most ignorant and brutal man is better prepared to add value to the strength and durability of the government than the most cultured and upright woman. I do not think that willful ignorance should swamp earnest intelligence at the ballot box, nor that educated arrogance, violence and fraud should cancel the votes of honest men. The hands of lynchers are too red with blood to determine the political character of the government for even four short years."

The ballot in the hands of woman means power added to influence. How well she will use that power I cannot foretell. Great evils stare us in the face that need to be throttled by the combined power of an upright manhood and an enlightened womanhood.

"American women!" What a sublime opportunity to create healthy public sentiment for justice, and to brand lawless cowardice that lynches, burns and tortures humanity! To grapple the evils which threaten the strength and progress of the United States! Have they the grand and holy purpose of uplifting humanity?

SIXTEEN

Leila Amos Pendleton

(1860–?)

L IKE MANY AFRICAN-AMERICAN WOMEN OF her day, Leila Amos Pendleton channeled her political, intellectual, and social ambitions into women's auxiliary associations and educational institutions. As the founder and president of the Alpha Charity Club of Anacostia and the Social Purity Club of Washington, D.C., as well as a secretary and vice president in several other women's race organizations, Pendleton labored to relieve and inspire her community. She was especially devoted to race improvement through the education of children. Pendleton served as a public school teacher for many years in Washington, D.C., and during her tenure there she synthesized her pedagogical experience and racial activism in a volume written expressly for African-American youth, *Narrative of the Negro* (1912).

In this sweeping textbook, Pendleton provides a pageant of black history, describing African heroes from several continents and eras in vivid detail. Throughout the text, Pendleton highlights the importance of recorded history; for example, in the passage below she mourns the lost Alexandrian library. "There can be no doubt," she writes, "that many now disputed points of race origin, relationship, and achievement might have been settled by the facts recorded upon the parchments and scrolls with which the shelves of the Alexandrian Library were filled." Pendleton argued that historical narratives of racial unity and accomplishment would fuel contemporary achievement and pride. History was thus both a demonstration of collective endurance

Source: Leila Amos Pendleton, *A Narrative of the Negro* (Washington, D.C.: Press of R. L. Pendleton, 1912), pp. 5–6, 13–18, and 27–37.

and an exercise in communal maintenance. These excerpts underline the importance of a resuscitated ancient past, one that emphasized African superiority and civilization. Nevertheless, Pendleton sustains a Christian wariness toward wealthy nations, noting that certain sinful excesses (for example, slavery) were inevitably punished. Finally, unlike other race historians, Pendleton incorporates the courageous work of women into her narrative, illustrating the critical role of women—as activists, soldiers, and mothers—in the historical success of Africans and African Americans.

A Narrative of the Negro (1912)

CHAPTER ONE, "A TALK WITH THE CHILDREN"

Most girls and boys, who are from twelve to fourteen years old can tell, if one should ask them, many interesting things about America, the country in which we live and most children whose foreparents came from Europe or Asia have been taught to love those countries just because their kinfolk once lived there. Many little colored children can draw a map of Africa, tell some of its products and describe some of its people; I wonder how many have been taught to think of Africa with interest and affection, because our great, great grandparents came from that continent? Perhaps if we talk awhile about our Motherland and some of the notable things which have happened there, we shall all learn to love that wonderful country and be proud of it.

In these talks, though sometimes the adjective "colored" will be used just as the word "white" is frequently made use of, we shall, as a rule speak of ourselves as "Negroes" and always begin the noun with a capital letter. It is true that the word Negro is considered by some a term of contempt and for that reason, many of us wince at it; but history tells us that when England had been conquered by the Normans, centuries ago, and the Norman barons were beating, starving and killing the natives, the name "Englishman" was considered an abusive term, and the greatest insult one Norman could offer another was to call him an "Englishman." You know that now all who claim England as home are justly proud of it, and no Englishman is ashamed of that name.

If history repeats itself, as we are often told it does, the time will come when our whole race will feel it an honor to be called "Negroes." Let us each keep that hope before us and hasten the time by living so that those who know us best will respect us most; surely then those who follow will be proud of our memory and of our race-name.

There are some of us who feel that, pitifully small though it be, we have given the very best and done the very most it is possible for us to give and to do for the race, and we are looking to you, dear children, to perform the things which we, in our youth had hoped and planned. We beg that you will not fail us. In order to realize our hopes for you, there is one thing which you must do: While you are still too young to be earning money, while you are yet at the beginning of your education, you, each, may be building up a strong and beautiful character, an honest, truthful, brave and upright character; it is THE ESSENTIAL thing and without it either money or education or both will be worse than wasted.

After leaving Africa we shall take a glance at the past and the present of the Negro in other lands, especially in our own country of America.

CHAPTER THREE, "ANCIENT CIVILIZATION"

Thousands of years ago, far up the river Nile and near the modern Senaar, flourished the Ethiopian kingdom of Meroe. Many statues and monuments have been unearthed in this region from time to time, and it is from the writings, pictures and carvings upon these that most of our knowledge of this ancient country comes.

These statues were erected to the idols or gods whom the people worshipped because they did not know the true God; the monuments were built with passages and chambers and were used as temples for the worship of their gods; so while no trace is now found of the dwellings of the people their temples covered with pictures show plainly their manner of living and of worship as well as many other things of interest.

The city called Meroe was the seat of government, or as we say in these days the capital, and the rulers were chosen from among the priests. Some very interesting things are told of the manner of choosing a king and the rules by which he was governed. As in most ancient countries, the men who were by nature the cleverest made themselves priests and whenever a new king was selected, they pretended their gods had selected him. As soon as the choice was made known the people fell down before the king and gave him all honor. He was beautifully clothed and given great power but he could not go beyond what the laws of the country allowed, so that Meroe was what is called a limited or constitutional monarchy.

When the priests felt that the king had reigned long enough, they sent to him a messenger with the emblem of death; as soon as the poor king saw this emblem he was compelled to retire at once and kill himself. So you see that even in those days to be a king was not always to be either safe or happy.

The city of Meroe was a lively, bustling place, for its streets were crowded with caravans bringing in from the surrounding regions, gold, silver, copper, salt, iron, frankincense, etc. These articles were sent down to Egypt and along with them went ideas which were even more valuable than the articles of commerce. The Egyptians enlarged upon and continued the civilization which was begun in Ethiopia, especially in the kingdom of Meroe and even the pyramids of Egypt are merely larger and elaborated copies of those whose remains are dug up around the site of Meroe.

Remember that in this old, old kingdom king and court, priests and worshipers, merchants and householders were Negroes.

On both sides of the Nile have been found the ruins of ancient cities, at least twenty on either side, and learned men have taken great pleasure in bringing to light the buried evidences of what was once the busiest and most prosperous part of the world; these ruins stretch from beyond Meroe down to Egypt. We shall be able to take, here, but a glance at Egypt for you may find many books on that country. Many persons have devoted their lives to the study of ancient Egypt, and it has been made so important a branch of human knowledge as to have a name of its own—Egyptology.

Some historians tell us very plainly that the Egyptians were not Africans at all and so Negroes need not be proud of what they did, but it is not reasonable to suppose that the natives had obligingly left that most fertile region uninhabited to await the coming of strangers and as there is so much uncertainty as to whom the Egyptians were and whence they came and as to which were Negroes and which were Egyptians proper in those dim and distant days, it is just as well to believe that we were and are all related though we cannot tell exactly the degree of our cousinship.

Alexandria in Egypt contained the largest and most remarkable library of the ancient world, for that city was the seat of learning and culture. This library, gathered through hundreds of years before the advent of Christ, by the rulers of Egypt was burnt when the fleet of Julius Cæsar caught fire in the harbor. If any books escaped, or were subsequently replaced they must have perished when the whole quarter of the city was burnt by Aurelian.

While the destruction of the library was a tremendous loss to the whole human family, the Negro was by far the heaviest loser; for there can be no doubt that many now disputed points of race origin, relationship, and achievement might have been settled by the facts recorded upon the parchments and scrolls with which the shelves of the Alexandrian Library were filled.

It is very certain that the Egyptians and other peoples of northern Africa were, as has been said, far ahead of the rest of the continent, but nevertheless it is also certain that the neighboring countries of Europe obtained their first instruction in the arts and sciences and received their first ideas of a written language from what has been in modern times called the Dark Continent, but which was in olden days a light which lighted the world. Civilization moved northward into Europe rather than southward into the heart of Africa for the reason that travel in the interior, on account of the jungles, deserts, mountains, swamps and ravines, was unsafe and uncomfortable.

The most ancient rulers of Egypt were called Pharaohs and they governed the country for hundreds of years. A Pharaoh was ruling when Joseph was sold by his brothers into Egypt and another Pharaoh reigned when the Jews, who had been held in bondage many years, were led by Moses out of the country over the Red Sea into the Promised Land in Asia. The Persians conquered the country about 520 B.C.; after them it was ruled by Alexander the Great; next by a line of kings called Ptolmies; then by Rome; next by the Mohammedans and today it is largely under the government of England. Egypt played a wonderful and important part in the world's history for thousands of years. It was to this country that the child Jesus was carried to be saved from wicked King Herod who would have killed him. There is near the site of ancient Heliopolis, the City of the Sun, a sycamore tree about which the legend runs that it once sheltered the Holy Family; here, also, at Heliopolis, it is said that Moses taught and Jeremiah wrote.

It was when Alexandria was the fountain of the learning of the ancient world that the Christian religion took root in northern Africa. There were men from Africa present in Jerusalem on the Day of Pentecost, when hundreds testified to the wonderful works of God, each in his own tongue. These men and others first took the Gospel to Africa, and it flourished there unhindered for nearly three centuries, but while Diocletian was Emperor of Rome, Christians suffered great persecution.

In the Church in Africa, as elsewhere, many died—young girls and women among them—rather than betray their faith. "Among those who thus perished was Leonidas, the father of Origon; Potimicæna, who was put to death by being slowly dipped into burning pitch; Felicitas, a beautiful slave girl, who was torn to pieces by wild beasts; Perpetua, a young woman of high birth, and many others."

When Constantine became Emperor, these persecutions ceased, but, as you see, African Christians had their share in the glory of martyrdom....

Finally, a great rivalry arose between Carthage and Rome and after a time these two countries went to war. For the space of nearly one hundred and twenty-five years these countries were enemies. There was first war, then peace between them, but in 146 B.C. Rome conquered and many thousands of the Carthagenians were killed by the sword or buried under the burning ruins of their homes; the remainder were sold into slavery, the Romans razed what was left of the city to the ground, plowed up the, earth and sowed salt in the furrows as a sign of utter desolation. Hannibal, the great general, was a Carthagenian who did his part in his country's service. He won many great victories and finally killed himself rather than fall into the hands of the enemy.

All the pomp and pride of these ancient countries, their wealth and power, the things for which they killed themselves or killed each other have melted into nothingness, have become "as a tale that is told." Yet we learn from their story how important a part Africa played in ancient times.

CHAPTER FIVE, "MODERN AFRICA"

In modern times Africa has been little more than a big, rich grab bag for the great powers of the world. By might not by right have they divided her territory among them, and small indeed is the portion to which the natives may lay claim. Thoughtful people agree that there are two reasons for this state of affairs. First, the lack of unity, or oneness among native Africans, which is the most important reason, and second, inferior knowledge of modern warfare and lack of modern arms. Says one English writer, "No single separate African race or tribe has yet felt anything like unity with the black race in general; otherwise Europe and Asia could not continue to govern Africa." As it is, England, France, Germany, Italy, Portugal, Belgium and Turkey claim large portions of African soil.

Friends of Africa have often been discouraged by some of the barriers to progress which have been unnecessarily placed in the way. A white American missionary has recently written: "I wonder that the Africans do not shoot with poisoned arrows, every white man that lands on their coast, for he has brought them rum, and is still bringing it; and in a few decades more, if the rum traffic continues, there will be few left in Africa to be saved. The vile rum, in that tropical climate, is depopulating the country more rapidly than famine, pestilence and war. Africa, with the simple gospel of Jesus is saved, but Africa with rum is eternally lost."

In modern times there have been a few of the native kingdoms which have attracted the attention of the world by their tribal unity and their ability to resist the stealthy advance of civilized nations. . . .

Yorubaland is a large tract in the hinterland of Lagos, West Africa. The Yorubas are said to vary in color from jet black to quite light, and in features, from the heavy, thick cast of countenance to the more delicate and refined.

There is among them a tradition that their forefathers were of Oriental origin, and a large number of American Negroes are said to be of Yoruba stock. The nation comprises many tribes and they are both city-dwelling and farming people. It is said that the houses of the chiefs often contain as many as fifty rooms, decorated with carvings representing symbolic devices, fabulous animals, and hunting or warlike scenes. They have an excellent system of government, the power being in the hands of a Council of Elders, presided over by a chief. The chief must always be taken from members of one or two families and owes his position to a combination of the principles of heredity and election. Yoruba is now divided into semi-independent states, placed under British protection by the treaty of 1893. The country extends from Benin on the east to Dahomey on the west, and contains several large cities, some with a population of 40,000.

In 1821, Adjai, a boy of about eleven years, was captured in Yorubaland and sold into slavery. The next year, he was rescued by a British ship and landed at Sierra Leone. The missionaries cared for and educated him and in December, 1825, he was baptised and given the name, Samuel Adjai Crowther. He became a teacher at Furah Bay and afterwards an energetic missionary in the Niger country. In 1842, he went to England and entered the Missionary College, and in June, 1843, was ordained by Bishop Blomfield. Returning to Africa, he went first to Yorubaland and afterwards to Abookuta where he labored earnestly. At the latter place, he translated the Bible and the Prayer Book into Yoruba and other dialects and also prepared school books for the people. He showed the natives how to improve their way of farming and how to trade their cotton for other things. He went on several expeditions up the Niger and afterwards went to England, where on St. Peter's Day, 1864, he was consecrated first Bishop of the Niger. Bishop Crowther, upon reaching Africa again, established several missions and turned many to Christianity. He died of paralysis on December 31, 1891, having for many years displayed as a missionary, untiring industry, great practical wisdom, and deep piety.

Benin was another powerful native kingdom. It was first visited by the English in 1553 and for many years carried on a trade in ivory, palm oil, pepper, etc. The Beni are said to be a pure Negro tribe, speaking a distinct language and having a well-organized government. In the seventeenth century, it was known to Europeans as Great Benin. The King of Benin was a puppet in the hands of the priests, who were the real rulers. The people are skilled in weaving cloth, ivory carving and working in brass, and much of the work of the native artists is to be seen.

In 1897 the English consul general sent to ask for an audience with the king. The latter requested the English to remain away until after the annual "customs," but in spite of this request, the consul, with eight others started for Benin and were massacred on the way, only two escaping. A large English force was sent against Benin and after a long, hard fight the city was conquered and partly burned. The king and chiefs were tried, the king deported to Calabar and the chiefs executed. The whole country is now governed by a Council of Chiefs, under supervision of a British resident.

The kingdom of Dahomey, like those of Benin and Ashanti was a purely Negro and pagan state. King Gezo, its most famous ruler, reigned forty years and under him the country was exceedingly prosperous. He reorganized the women warriors, or Amazons, for which Dahomey is famous. The strongest and best looking women were drafted into the Amazon regiments and they were the pride of Dahomy. Each of these regiments had its own peculiar uniform and badges and the Amazons took the post of honor and danger in all battles.

"Sir R. F. Burton, who saw the army marching out of Kano on an expedition in 1862, computed the whole force of female troops at twenty-five hundred, of whom one-third were unarmed or only half armed. Weapons were blunderbusses, flint muskets and bows and arrows and the system of warfare was to surprise the enemy." "The Amazons were carefully trained and the king was in the habit of holding 'autumn maneuvers' for the benefit of foreigners. Many Europeans have witnessed a mimic assault, and agree in ascribing a marvelous power of endurance to the women. Lines of thorny acacia were piled up one behind the other to represent defenses, and at a given signal the Amazons, barefooted and without any special protection, charged and disappeared from sight. Presently, they emerged within the lines, torn and bleeding but apparently insensible to pain, and the parade closed with a march past, each warrior leading a pretended captive." . . .

The Kingdom of Abyssinia was, for many years wisely governed by King Menelik, who called himself, among other things, "the King of Kings and the Lion of the Tribe of Judah." Because the King had been in ill health for some time, Prince Lidj Jeassu was, in May, 1909, at the age of thirteen, proclaimed heir to the Abyssinian throne, and Ras Hessama was appointed to act as guardian of the little heir and to govern in his stead. In May, 1911, Prince Lidj Jeassu was proclaimed Emperor.

The inhabitants are justly proud of their centuries-old history and prefer to be known by their ancient name of Ethiopians. As a whole they are an extremely intelligent people, grave of countenance, elaborately courteous and it is said that with training and experience they will be fully "capable of meeting the competition of the Western world." Their dress is the toga such as was worn by the Greeks and Romans. Menelik is described as "tall and straight, with a face full of intelligence and the manners of a gentleman as well as a king." As a part of their literature, handed down for centuries, the Abyssians prize extracts from the Old Testament, in the Gheze language, the Sabbatical laws, commandments given to Moses by God and a translation of Josephus.

It is said that on the plains and lower lands the soil of Abyssinia is very fertile and produces sometimes three crops per year; nearly every grain that will grow anywhere, can be grown in Abyssinia. The inhabitants also engage in raising sheep and goats and a certain amount of commerce is carried on. "By methods as old as Moses, gold to the average amount of five hundred thousand dollars is annually produced."

Recently a commission was appointed by the President of the United States to visit Abyssinia and to endeavor to establish friendly relations between the two countries. The commissioners were received with great pomp and assured of the interest and friendship of Menelik. Modern Abyssinia is said to be one of the few remaining lands of romance and adventure.

You have already heard of the Congo Free or Independent State. It was so called because in 1885, representatives from fourteen countries, the United States included, met and agreed that in that part of Africa, at least, trade should be free to all, the navigation of the Congo river should be free and the natives should not be oppressed, but encouraged to make the most of themselves. King Leopold of Belgium was one of those who consented to this and he succeeded in having himself appointed a kind of guardian to see that the agreement was carried out; but he was a wicked, cruel king, sly and crafty and by degrees he obtained absolute power over every soul in the Congo. He claimed that the Congoland and everything in its was his and that the natives were simply his tenants and, strange to say, the thirteen other countries allowed him to do so.

The Congo is a vast region and has been described as being as large as the whole of Europe, omitting Spain and Russia. Leopold placed over every village in the Congo, men as heartless and cruel as himself, and if the natives of a village failed to bring out of the forest as much ivory and rubber as the overseers thought they should, these wicked men would send after them cannibal soldiers who would burn the huts and kill and eat the natives. The terrible things that were reported from the Congo, horrified the civilized world, and more than once Leopold pretended to stop them, but recently accounts of awful conditions have been published. It is said that in seven years, driven by their cruel taskmasters, the natives gathered fifty-five millions of dollars' worth of rubber for which they received barely enough to keep them alive.

Dr. W. H. Sheppard, himself a colored man and a citizen of the United States, took up missionary work in Africa in 1893. In 1911 he returned to America from the Congo region and tells many interesting things of the tribes with which he came into contact. Among them there was a tribe which he was the first civilized man to visit. The king of this tribe had heard of foreigners and their cruelties to the natives, and as he thought they were all alike, he issued an edict that no foreigner should enter his kingdom. But Dr. Sheppard had won the love of the tribes around Stanley Pool, and accompanied by some of them, he finally made his way into the forbidden land. He found the natives weaving their own cloth, making their own farming and domestic implements, and living very contentedly. He also came into contact with a tribe of cannibals, whose lives were, as a matter of course, on a much lower plane. He preached to them the Gospel, and after many years has the happiness to know that he and his helpers have been the means of bringing many to Christianity and civilization.

There are still in Central Africa, regions which are unknown to the civilized world, but in some places of which until recently little has been heard, the natives have reached a high state of development. As you know, the Arabs who believe in the Mohammedan religion have for centuries been traveling through Africa, and in many places have erected villages for permanent homes and intermarried with the natives. This is true of Nigeria where the natives show their contact with the Arabs in many ways...

Uganda, where good King Mtesa reigned in Stanley's time, is now a British protectorate; but there is still a native king. It is said that one hundred thousand of the natives are Christians and twice as many of them can read and write. Beside the king there is a court and a parliament, nobles, ministers and a code of laws. The people are industrious, cultured and peaceable. "The white man cannot live here long at a time, for in his flesh every cut or scratch festers, small wounds become running sores and malaria turns to the fatal black-water fever."

South Africa is rich in gold and diamonds and for many years was governed by people called Boers, who are of Dutch descent. Recently the Boers and England went to war and England conquered the country and added it to her other possessions. It was to this country that Livingstone, the explorer, went, taught and preached to the people and converted many to Christianity. But the Boers were not kind to the natives and oppressed them in many ways.

Spreading all over South Africa is a great tribe of natives called Kaffirs and of these the Zulus are said to be the best type. They are noted for their hospitality and though partly nomadic, they are lovers of home and children.

Those Kaffirs who have not been tainted by the vices of the Boers are described as the "most intellectual of all savage races, with lofty, thoughtful foreheads." In complexion they are dark with a tinge of red, the skin is thin and fine grained and the hair crisp and curly. They are very proud of their appearance and if asked what complexion they prefer will say, "black like mine, with a little red." The blacker a person is the more beautiful the Kaffirs consider him and though Albinos are sometimes found among them they are pitied rather than admired. In recent years several Negro missionaries have gone to South Africa as well as to other sections and the natives are joining the churches, educating their children and learning many of the arts of civilization.

Of the West Coast of Africa a writer has recently said that "to partition finally among the powers this strip of death and disease, of unaccountable wealth, of unnamed horrors and cruelties, has taken many hundreds of years, has brought to the black man every misery that can be inflicted upon a human being and to thousands of white men, death and degradation or great wealth." It was from this part of Africa that the majority of slaves were brought to America.

Sierra Leone was founded on the West Coast by English philanthropists as a home for freedmen, and later American friends of humanity established a colony adjoining Sierra Leone for the same purpose, and this colony was finally called the Republic of Liberia.

The native tribes which live in Sierra Leone and Liberia and in that part of the adjoining country which reaches toward central Africa and which is called the hinterland, are a very interesting people. The most progressive of them are the Mandingoes (whose language Mungo Park learned) and the Vai. Of these the men are, as a rule, stalwart and handsome and many of the women are beautiful. Other tribes are the Gora, the Sunu, and the Kru, to which belong the Grebe, the De, the Basa and the Gibi. The Krumen are the workingmen of the West Coast. They are heavily built and muscular and neither the women nor the men are especially attractive in appearance; but they are very industrious and much of coast traffic depends on their labor.

The natives of this section manufacture a kind of pottery which is very artistic and not unlike that made by the Indians in this country. They also weave a cloth which is called "country cloth," and rude musical instruments, swords, wooden plates, drums and similar articles are made.

Throughout Africa there exist secret societies known by different names in different places. The societies for men and women are separate and distinct and they are not allowed to hold sessions at the same time. In the vicinity of Sierra Leone the women's society is called the Bandu and the men's, the Poro.

When the older women of the tribe decide to hold a meeting, a space is cleared in the forest or bush and thus the session has been named the Bandu Bush. The chief officers are called "dibbles," "boogies," or "devils," and they dress in a very fantastic manner. Over the head and face is worn a hideous mask from which hangs a covering of palm fiber so adjusted as to completely hide the figure and disguise the individual. They pretend to be supernatural and only the highest officials know who they really are.

Into the Bush the girls from about twelve to sixteen are taken to be initiated. The girls who do not go are looked upon with contempt and are called "silly" and "idiots." The initiates remain in the Bush for months and the women teach them many useful things; among others, to be obedient and respectful to their elders and to be good wives and mothers. After they have been sufficiently instructed, they are "medicine washed" and a public feast takes place in their honor, something like a debut party in civilized countries. When the boys go into the Poro bush they are told the laws and legends of their tribe and commanded to respect them, they are taught to hunt and fish and are also made to understand their duties and responsibilities as future husbands and fathers.

Of the natives of western Africa a missionary has said: "Whatever other estimate we may form of the African, we may not doubt his love for his mother. Her name, whether she be dead or alive, is always on his lips and in his heart. She is the first thing he thinks of when awakening from his slumbers and the last thing he remembers when he closes his eyes in sleep; to her he confides secrets which he would reveal to no other human being on the face of the earth. He cares for no one else in time of sickness, she alone must prepare his food, administer his medicine, perform his ablutions and spread his mat for him. He flies to her in the hour of his distress, for he well knows if all the rest of the world turn against him, she will be steadfast in her love, whether he be right or wrong." How wonderful must be the women who can inspire and keep such deep and constant love and devotion in the hearts of their children!

All lovers of humanity earnestly desire the civilization and redemption of the entire continent of Africa, and many plans to that end have been suggested. Speaking of these, Didwho Twe, a native African, and a man of great culture and discernment, has said: "A new form of Christianity for the African race will develop from the present commercialism. The initiative of this great change will come from men of pure African blood—Africans in appearance, Africans in body, Africans in spirit, Africans in pride, Africans in thought."

SEVENTEEN

Olivia Ward Bush-Banks
(1869–1944)

OLIVIA WARD BUSH-BANKS WAS BORN to parents of African and Montauk Indian descent in Sag Harbor, New York. Her father, Abraham Ward, was an African-American Mormon, and her mother, Eliza, died when she was nine months old. Her father then sent Olivia to live with her aunt, Maria. Upon completing Providence High School, Olivia prepared for a career as a nurse. She married instead, and bore two daughters to Frank Bush, who she divorced at some point between 1895 and 1910. Following her divorce, she went to live again with her aunt before moving her girls to Boston, where she took a job as the assistant dramatic director at the Robert Gould Shaw Community House. *Original Poems*, her first volume of poetry, was published in 1899. In that volume, she addressed religious life, women's work in reform efforts, and the falsifying images of blacks in American culture. In 1914 she completed a more substantial poetic effort. *Driftwood* included twenty-four poems and three prose pieces arranged in nine sections with seashore motifs. Writing of the poems in this volume, Paul Laurence Dunbar noted that he liked her book, that "there is a high spiritual tone about it that is bound to please.... Your book should be an inspiration to the women of our race."[1]

After marrying Anthony Banks in the early 1920s, Olivia moved to Chicago, where she opened the Bush-Banks School of Expression while

Source: Olivia Ward Bush-Banks, "Unchained, 1863" and "A Hero of San Juan Hill," *Driftwood* (Providence, R.I.: Atlantic Printing Co., 1914), 34–39.
[1] Bernice F. Guillaume, "Olivia Ward Bush: Factors Shaping the Social and Cultural Outlook of a Nineteenth-Century Writer," *Negro History Bulletin* 43:2 (April/June 1980), 34.

working as a drama instructor in the Chicago public school system. In the 1930s she returned east, wrote an arts column for the *Westchester Record-Courier*, offered drama coaching at the community center for Abyssinian Baptist Church (the first African-American Baptist church in the state of New York), and cultivated relationships with the leading lights of the Harlem Renaissance. Although she was never a leader in the New Negro movement, she was a friend to many, working as a theater manager and performance adviser, and importing from Chicago other sounds and motifs. Her poetry was distinctly picturesque, establishing concrete images of piety, courage, and primitive beauty. The first poem, "Unchained, 1863," celebrates the Emancipation Proclamation, the executive order issued by President Abraham Lincoln on January 1, 1863, that freed the slaves. The second commemorates the Battle of San Juan Hill, the bloodiest battle of the Spanish-American War, which took place the first days of July 1898. Both poems move from individual heroism to race-wide triumph, ennobling the pursuit of freedom at any cost.

Unchained, 1863 (1914)

O'er the land, a hush had fallen,
　Hearts Thrilled expectantly,
Till from twice two million voices,
　Rang the glad cry, "We are free!"
Then the whole world caught the echo,
　"We are free! Yes! We are free!"

What a dawning from the midnight!
　What a day of jubilee!
Twas the New Year's song of triumph,
　That they sang so joyously,
Till it echoed and re-echoed
　"We are free! Yes! We are free!"

From the voice of one brave woman,
　Who, in human sympathy,
With a pen of love and pity
　Wrote the wrongs of slavery,
Came the glad new cry of triumph,
　"They are free! Yes! They are free!"

And the freedmen, still rejoicing,
   Sang of John Brown's victory,
Sang of Lincoln's Proclamation,
   Saying, "These have made us free."
Sumner, Garrison, and Phillips,
   All too fought to make us free.

Then the joyous song grew louder,
   By that price of loyalty,
Paid by us with our best lifeblood,
   We attest that we are free!
On the battle-field with honor,
   Our own blood has made us free."

Free indeed, but free to struggle,
   Free to toil unceasingly,
Naught of wealth, naught of possession,
   Was their portion, e'en tho' free;
But they faltered not, they failed not,
   Saying ever, "We are free!"

For their rightful place contending,
   They foresaw their destiny,
And they pleaded, never ceasing,
   "Give us opportunity!"
"Give us justice, recognition,
   'Tis our right! for we are free!"

From the lips of Frederic Douglass,
   Came these words of loyalty,
"Judge not harshly these my people,
   This is but their infancy,
From the depths they have ascended,
   Give them rights, for they are free!"

After years of ceaseless striving,
   Struggling for the mastery,
Over self and ill conditions,
   Still they're singing, "We are free!"

By the virtue of our struggle,
   We shall reap our destiny.

Though we suffer, in our freedom,
   By the hand of cruelty,
In the lawlessness of Evil,
   God is just, and we are free;
Life and love, not woe or slaughter,
   Are the birthright of the free.

When by predjudice untrammeled,
   Rich in manly liberty,
We receive that recognition
   Rightly given to the free,
Then the whole world shall proclaim it,
   "Free indeed! Yes! Ye are free!"

A Hero of San Juan Hill (1914)

Among the sick and wounded ones,
   This stricken soldier boy lay
With glassy eye and shortened breath,
   His life seemed slipping fast away.

My heart grew faint to see him thus,
   His dark brown face so full of pain,
I wondered if the mother's eyes
   Were looking for her boy in vain.

I bent to catch his feeble words;
   "I am so ill, and far from home,
I feel so strange and lonely here,
   You seem a friend, I'm glad you've come."

"I want to tell you how our boys
   Went charging on the enemy,
'Twas when we climbed up San Juan's Hill
   And there we got the victory."

"The Spaniards poured a heavy fire,
    We met it with a right good-will,
We saw the 71st fall back,
    And then our boys went up the hill."

"Yes up the hill, and gained it too,
    Not one brave boy was seen to lag;
Old Glory o'er us floating free,
    We'd gladly died for that old flag."

His dim eye brightened as he spoke,
    He seemed unconscious of his pain,
In fancy on the battle-field,
    He lived that victory o'er again.

And I, I seemed to grasp it too,
    The stalwart form, the dusky face,
Of each black hero climbing up,
    To win fair glory for their race.

The Spaniards said, "That phalanx seemed
    To move like one black solid wall."
They flung defiance back at death,
    To answer to their country's call.

They fought for Cuban liberty,
    Up San Juan Hill they fought their way,
Until their life-blood freely spent,
    Marked how these heroes won the day.

March on dark sons of Afric's race,
    Naught can be gained by standing still,
Retreat not, quit yourselves like men,
    And like these heroes, climb the hill.

Till pride and predjuice shall cease,
    Till racial barriers are unknown,
Attain the heights, and thou shalt find,
    Equality upon the Throne.

EIGHTEEN | Drusilla Dunjee Houston
(1876–1941)

DRUSILLA DUNJEE HOUSTON WAS THE first African-American woman
to write a comprehensive history of Africans in the ancient world. One of
ten children of the Rev. John William Dungy, a former slave, and Lydia Ann
Taylor Dunjee, Drusilla was born in Harper's Ferry, West Virginia. Her father
was a part-time journalist and "race man," and was known for his extensive
library of books celebrating black history and achievement.[1] Both parents were
members of the American Baptist Home Missionary Society, and they spent the
early years of Drusilla's life moving the large family from one town to another,
establishing churches in New England, Minnesota, and the South. They finally
settled in Oklahoma, where Houston would remain for most of her adult life.

In 1898, at twenty-two, Drusilla eloped with Price Houston, a storekeeper
and member of a Latino/Anglo pioneer family, with whom she had a daughter.
Trained as a classical pianist, Drusilla instead decided to become a school
teacher. The family settled in McAlester, Oklahoma, where Drusilla established
McAlester Seminary, a school for girls. Drusilla also began to write for local
papers, and eventually had a regular column for the Oklahoma City *Black
Dispatch*, a weekly paper that she ran with her brother, Roscoe, beginning in

Source: Drusilla Dunjee Houston, *Wonderful Ethiopians of the Ancient Cushite Empire* (Oklahoma
City, OK: Universal Publishing Company, 1926), 1–26.

[1] The Reverend Dungy reportedly changed the spelling of his last name sometime after he began his
studies at Oberlin College, having been told that the "black" spelling of the name was "Dunjee," not
Dungy. See Peggy Brooks-Bertram, ed., *Origin of Civilization from the Cushites*, book 2 of Drusilla
Dunjee Houston, *Wonderful Ethiopians of the Ancient Cushite Empire* (Buffalo, NY: Peggy Bertram
Publishing, 2007), vii.

1914. From that platform she disseminated her ideas about racial uplift, domesticity, education, and African history. A believer in both race pride and the centrality of the Baptist Church in the black community, Houston became one of the most prominent advocates for African Americans in the state.

As early as 1906, Houston began work on a historical study of the African race. Houston felt an urgent need to correct the mistakes and omissions of Euro-American scholarship about the contributions of Africans to world history. Believing that whites systematically had conspired to cover up African achievements, Houston's study was part of a pedagogical and cultural vision intended to shape black identity from cradle to grave."[2] She worked with the Women's Baptist Convention of Oklahoma to found a training school for African-American women and girls, and in that capacity she insisted that the curriculum include works on the history of African peoples. Her books, she believed, would help to inculcate racial pride and success.

Houston wrote articles in the *Dispatch* about her book for many years before it appeared. She originally planned a multivolume work, one that would not only unveil the extent of early African attainments, but would also explore the contributions of other races to world history. Turned away from segregated libraries in Oklahoma and plagued by a lack of funding, Houston had to conduct her research in the inferior all-black libraries, which contained outdated books and discards from white facilities. When she could afford to, she traveled to California to use libraries that were not closed to blacks. After raising expectations in the *Dispatch* for several years about the volume, Houston self-published the first part of her history in 1926 with a run of 500 copies. It met with modest success, although through her own efforts Houston convinced the state of Oklahoma to place it on a list of recommended texts for black public schools.

Houston also sought validation from the black male academic establishment and was met with rejection. She sent a copy of her book to W. E. B. DuBois, with whom she was connected through her family. Houston requested his feedback and hoped that DuBois would review the book in the pages of *The Crisis*, an African-American journal that he edited. Instead, DuBois sent her back a curt reply in which he suggested she take a correspondence course in history. Similarly, when she applied for membership in the Association for the Study of Negro Life and History she was rejected.[3] Not surprisingly, Houston described her work as having been completed "in hermitage." She was never able to publish the other volumes in her lifetime.

[2] Ibid., xiv.
[3] Ibid., xxxii, xxxiv.

Nonetheless, the reader of Houston's text meets an author with a broad historical vision and a rich repository of scholarship at her command. In the preface and first chapter, reprinted here, Houston provides a sweeping tour of ancient cultures around the world, hinting at the many evidences of ancient Cushite (Ethiopian) arts and achievement that could be seen in other parts of the world, including the Americas. Houston, like other historians of the 1920s, saw in the legacy of the recent world war a judgment on contemporary Western Civilization. She believed that a return to the educational and democratic accomplishments of the first civilization in Africa provided the only hope of restoring "world balance." Citing H. G. Wells, whose 1920 *Outline of History* was a popular best-seller, Houston wrote, "Human History becomes more and more a race between education and catastrophe."[4] Like the works of other African-American female authors, Houston's writing reflects the simultaneous tasks of explaining racial history to a white world and explaining herself—as a black female intellectual—to the many audiences that denied her ability.

Wonderful Ethiopians of the Ancient Cushite Empire (1926)

PREFACE: THE ORIGIN OF CIVILIZATION

The minds of men today are stirred with eager questionings about the origin of civilization and about the part the different races of mankind played in its development from primitive ages. The remains that archaeologists are uncovering in Egypt, old Babylonia, and South America, reveal that there were significant factors in the first development of the arts and sciences that history has failed to make clear. Scientists are busy today studying the types of those old civilizations and comparing them with those of the present. Our modern systems do not function for the masses to give them development and happiness as did some of the ancient cultures. Books upon the early life of man are very hard to secure. Few have been written that are authentic, because it requires technical skill to assemble and condense such matter. Exhaustive research work is necessary to secure this kind of information, with only a line here and there in modern books to help the reader to reach definite conclusions. Only the trained mind holds the multitude of details and possesses the ability to impartially weigh and classify the facts, that prove the influence of the races upon the civilization of today.

---

[4] *Outline of History*, 3rd ed. (New York: Macmillan & Co., 1921), 1100.

The quest for the innumerable and startling facts of the succeeding volumes arose, much as did the motive of Schliemann to seek the buried ruins of Troy, from the oft repeated expression found by the author in research work, that "what the ancients said about the Ethiopians was fabulous." Curiosity was aroused to go back over the story of the ancients to agree or draw new conclusions. The finds were so astonishing that the vow was made to spend upon this study many years if necessary. Like the "Quest of the Holy Grail" the aim became sacred, for the trail led backward into the heart of all that the world holds most precious and to the primal roots from which all culture sprang. At first the reading of an afternoon in the average public library would hardly reveal a line to the credit of the Ethiopian. Sometimes a ten volume set of modern books might yield only a few paragraphs; but the vow and the richness of the finds, gleaming like diamonds, led the eager searcher on. The trail was followed into the dry dusty books of the ancients, where the path widened and truth was revealed that will answer some of the baffling problems of civilization today. Here were missing links of the chain of culture vainly sought for elsewhere.

Our story will deal with the ancient Cushite empire of Ethiopians, that covered three continents and held unbroken sway for three thousand years. We will visit old Ethiopia, where as Herodotus said, "the gods delighted to banquet with the pious inhabitants." We will study the land and the ancient race. The "Old Race," will next win our attention, that Petrie found in Egypt of distinct and unique culture, who were the people of the earlier and superior civilization of the first dynasties. Down through this prehistoric vista we see "Happy Araby" with her brilliant primitive culture and her unrivalled literature of later days. On the screen flashes the rich and surpassing culture of old Chaldea, which belonged to the ancient Cushite empire of Ethiopians. Next comes veiled and mysterious India, the scene of charming story and magic fable, with her subtle mysticism and philosophy. Tarrying a while with the conquest and life of the ancient Medes and Persians, the trail runs far afield into the dominions of Western Europe and the striking questions array themselves demanding to be answered. Who were the Celts? Who were the Teutons? and what was the origin of the so-called Aryan race? The author was as much astounded as will be the reader, as to what this study reveals. It leaves us wondering if there is any Aryan race.

We learn in the study of the races of Western Europe, to understand the hatreds of Europe that underlaid the world war. We learn that when the Celt and Teuton call the Ethiopians of the new world "Uncle" and "Auntie," they are using titles that are scientifically true. Our story passes on to another remnant of the ancient Cushite empire, that baffling race, the Iberians, now represented by the Basques; then to the Berbers of North Africa, another branch of the Cushite race. Some scientists have called them the descendants of the "People of Atlantis." Next succeed the singular facts about the life of the mysterious Etruscans of old Italy, who were the teachers of the Romans; then we follow the life and tragedy of the fleeting Pelasgians, who were the fountain out of which later Greek culture welled. They were the people of the legends of Greek mythology. It is almost impossible to find anything but scanty fragments in the world's literature about any of these people of pre-historic days, but our text has compiled these fragments, so many of them, as to form fascinating chapters. Today all of these subjects remain unexplained mysteries in the average book. We dwell for a while on the marvels of the lost civilization of the Ægean and stop to study the Greece of Homer and the meaning of the Greek legends. All having direct relation to the ancient Cushites.

Historic Greece in all her glory, but viewed from new angles, passes before us with the older and superior civilization of Asia Minor, which has been almost entirely overlooked in modern literature. Next we come to the fact that the Phoenicians called themselves Ethiopians and that the Hebrew writers gave them the same name; then we reflect upon the strange relationship of the family of Cushite tongues to the so-called Indo-European group of languages. The trail leads us high up to where we get a breathless view of the astounding Ethiopian religion, which gives us the answer to many strange and incomprehensible traits in the Ethiopian of today. Next follows the chapter on the "Wonderful Ethiopians," who produced fadeless colors that have held their hues for thousands of years, who drilled through solid rock and were masters of many other lost arts, and who many scientists believe must have understood electricity, who made metal figures that could move and speak and may have invented flying machines, for the "flying horse Pegasus" and the "ram of the golden fleece" may not have been mere fairy tales. Next out of the forgotten wastes of the dark continent rise before us ancient African empires, representing other lost civilizations of the time of the Cretan age. Then across the screen comes flashing the "Ancient Cushite Trade Routes," which contrary to our notion were the medium by which rich and varied products were interchanged.

In the chapter on "Ancient Cushite Commerce," we follow the ships of these early, daring and skillful seamen, who before the dawn of history had blazed out the ocean trails that the Phoenicians later followed. We find irrefutable evidence of the presence of these daring conquerors in the primitive legends, religion, customs and institutions of America. Next out of the dim haze of far antiquity, rise the indistinct lines of "Atlantis of Old," the race that gave civilization to the world, the race that tamed the animals and gave us the domestication of plants. The gods of the ancient world were the kings and queens of mystic "Atlantis." The chapter the "Gods of Old" makes plain that the deity of Greece and Rome were also the kings and queens of the ancient Cushite empire of Ethiopians, which was either the successor or the most famous branch of the Atlantic race. It was about these princes and heroes that all the wonderful mythology of the ancients was woven. They were the deity that were worshipped in India, Chaldea, Egypt, and in Greece and Rome, which nations themselves must have been related to the race of Atlantis, that tradition said had been overwhelmed by the sea. Atlantis could not have been mythical, for her rulers were the subjects of the art and literature of all the primitive nations until the fall of Paganism long after the birth of Christ.

Another division of Atlantis was trans-Atlantic America. There the mysterious Mound Builders represent the ancient Cushite race. We study the peculiar culture and genius of the fierce Aztec, who acknowledged that he received the germs of civilization from the earlier Cushite inhabitants. We pass southward and examine the higher development of the wonderful Mayas of North America, whose ruins are attracting special study today, and we find there transplanted the Cushite arts of the ancient world. Next flash the pictures of the marvelous culture and arts of the Incas, superior to those of Western Europe in 1492. From America the story turns to the "Bronze and Iron Ages," we seek the origin of the mysterious bronze implements of Western Europe found in the hands of seemingly barbarous people. We seek for the place and the race that could have given the world the art of welding iron. The trail reveals that the land of the "Golden Fleece" and the garden of the "Golden Apples of Hesperides" were but centers of the ancient race, that as Cushite Ethiopians had extended themselves over the world. These are subjects that have attracted the study of world scholarship. They represent not mere myths but are all that vast ages have left to us of events of primitive race history. "Cushite Art" and "The Heart of the African" answer many questionings of our hearts about Ethiopians. The series closes with a comparison of ancient culture with modern forms. The intelligence of the Cushite, his original genius is held up beside the decadence of true ideals in the art and literature of the present. The "Revolt of Civilization" and "Dawn of a new World" voice the concern of the thoughtful over the present decay of culture.

We are sending forth this information because so few men today understand the primitive forces that are the root of modern culture. So superficial and prejudiced has been most modern research, that many important and accepted theories of universal history have no actual basis in fact. The average modern historical book contradicts what the ancients said about the nations that preceeded them. We cannot solve the stupendous problems that the world faces until we can read aright the riddle of the evolution of the races. Uninformed men make unsafe leaders, that is the primal cause for so many errors of judgment in state and national councils. We look upon them not as statesmen but as promoters of petty politics, for out of their deliberations spring no alleviation of the woes of the world. It is from this lack of understanding in leadership that the world suffers most today. We could discriminate between the true and false in our civilization, if we knew more about primitive culture. The way by which the first man climbed must ever be the human way. Racial prejudices are the greatest menace to world progress. Classes clash because the wealth of the world concentrates more and more in the hands of a few. The tragedy of human misery increases, the increase of defectives, the growing artificiality of modern living, compels us to seek and blazen forth the knowledge of the true origin of culture and the fundamental principles that through the ages have been the basis of true progress. Only by this wisdom shall we know how to lift human life today.

In most modern books there seems to be preconcerted understanding to calumniate and disgust the world with abominable pictures of the ruined Ethiopian, ruined by the African slave trade of four hundred years. There seems to be a world wide conspiracy in literature to conceal the facts that this book unfolds. Because of this suppression of truth, world crimes have been easily made possible against the Ethiopian. These people are held in low estimation because truth is hidden which proves that today though more favored races are at the apex of human accomplishment; yet in the earlier ages the wheel of destiny carried upward those, who now seem hopelessly under. To wipe away the black stain of the slave trade, modern literature has represented the slave trader as having trafficked in depraved human beings. Today the lower types of the Aryan race look upon them as creatures only fit for political and economic spoilation, to fill the coffers of the colonial renegade, who could not succeed at home. This type of the world finds it easy to stifle the life of ruined and defenceless races. This spoilation of the weak, returned in a counter stroke from which it was impossible to escape in the world war. Belgium reaped in identical measure and kind, what this type had meted out to the defenceless people of the Congo. Nations must reap what they sow.

This is not the nature or intention of the better men of the civilized nations but we are uninformed about alien peoples. We are narrow and provincial in our views. The hatred of the races springs out of misunderstanding. The men of the world who have traveled, and read, and thought, upon ethnological problems are the men who have the cultivated instincts of human brotherhood. Shall England, France, Germany, America, suffer further because we have not taught the uninformed of the nations that we must pay a still heavier toll for a continued measure of injustice to weaker peoples? Innocent must suffer with the guilty, for it is in our power to inform and curb the power of the selfish. The question looms large in the minds of thinking men today, whether Ethiopians are worthy of equal opportunity. Let us settle forever out of time's irrefutable evidence, whether if we gave him the chance, the Ethiopian would treat us as we have treated him. There need be no conjecturing; for the archives of the past hold the facts. The history of the Cushite Ethiopians down through the ages is one of the most thrilling as well as tragic of all time's age old stories. It is almost incredible that its rich treasure for developing our understanding has so long remained veiled.

The Ethiopian is a great race, probably the oldest. It is a race that does not die out under adversity. When other races are sullen, or despairing and turn to self destruction, these people cheerfully press on. When they think the way is blocked they turn aside to pick flowers along the pathway of pleasure. We hear their happy voices in the cotton field, they can be the life of the carnival, their zealous fervor in camp meeting and the swing song of the marching black regiments of the world war and the stevedore regiments in peace, show these people as they employ themselves, patiently waiting for bars to progress to rot down, if nothing else will remove them. Then again they take up the steady march onward, that has been the wonderful element of their history on down through the ages. We need our eyes opened, this type that we in ignorance despise, built the eternal pyramids of Egypt and laid the foundation of the civilization of the historic ages. Because the slave trade broke the threads of remembrance, they walk among us with bowed heads, themselves ignorant of the facts that this story unfolds.

Lift up your heads, discouraged and downtrodden Ethiopians. Listen to this marvelous story told of your ancestors, who wrought mightily for mankind and built the foundations of civilization true and square in the days of old. Awake ye sleeping Aryans, become aware of the acute need of the world today of this enchained energy and ability. The absence of this power is the cause of many a breakdown in modern civilization. Out of our own accepted sciences, the chapters of this book, prove the Cushite race to have been the fountainhead of civilization. If you desire truth, if you desire to be fair minded, to be educated in vital knowledge not possessed by the average college student, if you desire to be an authority upon the life of the ancients, go down with me as archaeology, ethnology, geology and philology disclose; not in a dry and tedious way, but through the unfolding of this the most intensely interesting and startling drama of the ages. The Cushite race, its institutions, customs, laws and ideals were the foundation upon which our modern culture was laid. Let this not stir the pride of the modern Cushite, but rather inspire him to a greater consecration to the high idealism that made the masteries of olden days.

Knowledge of the primal strength and weaknesses of each world group must be possessed by world leadership or we shall still further go astray. Without this knowledge international councils cannot intelligently assign each race to its rightful place in the consummation of God's plan of the Ages. Without this truth the nations cannot put over their programs. The world war proved that we have no international stability. The world's securities and diplomatic relations are propped. Because the real history of mankind is not a part of our general knowledge, we are discounting factors most needed to secure world balance. There can be no more needed contribution to civilization, than to gather from the archives of the past and present day science all the truth about the origin of culture. Only thus will we know how to develop better men today. If we knew just what contribution each race has made to art, science and religion, we would know what would be its fitness to take part in world government and control. Has the influence of a race been creative or destructive throughout the ages? That should point plainly to the part they would be likely to play today.

Because we are without this knowledge, we cannot read aright the past or present history of civilization. Modern crimes of injustice toward weaker peoples have been made easy by this suppression of truth. It has been popular and remunerative to write and speak on the side of prejudice. A better spirit is rising in the world. Men are eager for information, for the truth. Through the teaching of sociology, the most popular and crowded classes of our great universities, in a scientific way, man is beginning to see the need of a realization of our common brotherhood and to reach out to solve unmastered problems and unfulfilled duties. Many problems are an international consternation because they are too gigantic for the handling of any one world group. Civilization was appalled at its helplessness in the world war. The leading nations faced annihilation, yet were unable to walk out of the trap until the flower of European manhood had perished. The noblest offered themselves for sacrifice, the more selfish remained at home. The world may never be capable of calculating its artistic and moral loss. We see the difference in the crime and debauchery breaking down the culture of today. Unless we can rouse men to truth and united effort, there is no hope for our civilization which is tottering and must fall.

In justice to that Divine Leading that piloted this search of a decade over trails, that otherwise might not have been found in a lifetime, in tribute to the pluck and consecration to a purpose—to add to the light of truth, that has gathered such an avalanche of testimony from authoritative sources, we speak of this work which has taken all those spare moments, that are our right to spend in leisure, that a frail unflagging spirit might make possible this marvelous story, as strange as any olden fairy tale; yet by the light of our accepted sciences true. We lift the veil lightly lest the careless skim over these pages carelessly, little recking what they have cost. Often when limbs and weary brain cried out in protest, the searcher pressed on, seeing fully the power in this truth if patiently, carefully gathered, to lift the men of all races to a clearer comprehension of the contribution of each race to all that we prize in civilization, and to stir within us the determination to lift and bear aloft the "torch" lit in primitive ages by a race today despised and misunderstood. The average book has its dozen helpers and advisors, this work has been done in hermitage. The hermitage of a life submerged in service. Humbly, reverently, this truth is offered in love to all races. Ten years more may be devoted to its final setting but the facts imbedded in these pages are too important to be longer withheld.

CHAPTER I: THE EMPIRE'S AGE AND SCOPE

The excavations of Petrie revealed in Egypt the remains of a distinct race that preceeded the historic Egyptians. The earliest civilization was higher than that of the later dynasties. Its purer art represents an "Old Race" that fills all the background of the pre-historic ages. It colonized the first civilized centers of the primitive world. The ancients called this pioneer race, which lit the torch of art and science, Cushite Ethiopians, the founders of primeval cities and civilized life. The wonders of India, to which Europe sought a passage in the age of Columbus, the costly products and coveted merchandise of Babylon, and the amazing prehistoric civilization of Asia Minor, sprang from this little recognized source. The achievements of this race in early ages were the result of co-operation. Cushites reached the true zenith of democracy. Their skillful hands raised Cyclopean walls, dug out mighty lakes and laid imperishable roads that have endured throughout the ages. This was the uniform testimony of ancient records. Modern writers seem of superficial research, either being unaware of these facts, or knowing, purposely ignore them. Archaeologists dig up the proofs, ethnologists announce their origin, but history refuses to change its antiquated and exploded theories.

General history informs us that when the curtain of history was lifted, the civilization of Egypt was hoary with age. It was a culture that must have developed from thousands of years of growth. Why is the scholarship of the world so silent as to what lay behind historic Egypt? No nation throughout the ages has "as Athene sprung full fledged into knowledge of all the arts and sciences." The story of what lay behind Egypt fascinated the whole ancient world. The culture of Egypt did not originate upon the Lower Nile. Who then was her teacher? It was the ancient Cushite empire of Ethiopians, which weighty authorities tell us ruled over three continents for thousands of years. Should the world wait longer to test the truth of these ancient witnesses? Beside these gigantic achievements, the petty conquests of Alexander the Great, Julius Caesar, and of Napoleon Bonaparte, fade into insignificance. There seems to be fear to tell about these ancients, who built mighty cities, the ruins of which extend in uninterrupted succession around the shores of the Mediterranean Sea. Traces of this hoary empire, works appearing to have been wrought by giants, bearing marks of Cushite genius, have been found by scientists all over the primitive world.

We marvel at the wonders recently unearthed in Egypt. Let us look behind her through the glasses of science at the "Old Race" of which she was in her beginning, only a colony. Ethiopia was the source of all that Egypt knew and transmitted to Greece and Rome. We are accustomed to think of Ethiopia as a restricted country in Africa but this was not true. The study of ancient maps and the descriptions of the geographers of old, reveals that the ancient Land of Cush was a very widespread and powerful empire. Rosenmuller shows us that the Hebrew scholars called Cush, all the countries of the torrid zone. It was the race that Huxley saw akin to the Dravidians of India, stretching in an empire from India to Spain. The Greeks described Ethiopia as the country around the Indus and Ganges. (*Rosenmuller's Biblical Geography*, Bk. III, p. 154.)

H. G. Wells says that the Hamitic tongue was a much wider and more varied language than the Semitic or Aryan in ancient days. It was the language of the Neolithic peoples who occupied most of western and southern Asia, who may have been related to the Dravidians of India and the people of George Elliot's Heliolithic culture. Sir H. H. Johnson says that this lost Hamitic language was represented by the scattered branches of Crete, Lydia, the Basques, the Caucasian-Dravidian group, the ancient Sumerian and the Elamite. The peoples of this race were the first to give the world ideas of government. Stephanus of Byzantium, voicing the universal testimony of antiquity wrote, "Ethiopia was the first established country on earth and the Ethiopians were the first to set up the worship of the gods and to establish laws." The later ages gained from this ancient empire, the fundamental principles upon which republican governments are founded. The basic stones of that wonderful dominion were equality, temperance, industry, intelligence and justice.

The average historical book ignores this testimony and disputes in its theories the records and monuments of Egypt and Chaldea. They group the races in utter contradiction to the records of the Greeks and Hebrews. In the light of reason, who would know about the ethnic relations of the ancients, the scholars and historians of Egypt, Chaldea and Greece, who are more and more corroborated by the findings of science, or the theories of the men of today? The modern writer whose research has been superficial does not know that before the days of Grecian and Roman ascendency, the entire circle of the Mediterranean and her islands was dotted with the magic cities and the world-wide trade of Ethiopians. The gods and goddesses of the Greeks and Romans were but the borrowed kings and queens of this Cushite empire of Ethiopians. So marvelous had been their achievements in primitive ages, that in later days, they were worshipped as immortals by the people of India, Egypt, old Ethiopia, Asia Minor and the Mediterranean world.

Rawlinson, after his exhaustive research into the life of ancient nations, says, "For the last three thousand years the world has been mainly indebted to the Semitic and Indo-European races for its advancement, but it was otherwise in the first ages. Egypt and Babylon, Mizraim and Nimrod, both descendants of Ham, led the way and acted as the pioneers of mankind in the various untrodden fields of art, science and literature. Alphabetical writings, astronomy, history, chronology, architecture, plastic art, sculpture, navigation, agriculture and textile industries seem to have had their origin in one or the other of these countries." (*Rawlinson's Ancient Monarchies*, Vol. 1.) The taming of the animals was the gift to us of these prehistoric men. By skill and perseverence they developed from wild plants the wheat, oats and rye that are the foundation of our agriculture. This work was done so many ages ago, that their wild origin has disappeared. The average man little realizes the gifts of the prehistoric ages, or how helpless we would be without them today.

Rawlinson continues, "The first inventors of any art are among the greatest benefactors of mankind and the bold steps they take from the known to the unknown, from blank ignorance to discovery, are equal to many subsequent steps of progress." Bunsen says in his *Philosophy of Ancient History*, "The Hamitic family as Rawlinson proves must be given the credit for being the fountainhead of civilization. This family comprised the ancient Ethiopians, the Egyptians, the original Canaanites and the old Chaldeans. The inscriptions of the Chaldean monuments prove their race affinity. The Bible proves their relationship. It names the sons of Ham as Cush, Mizraim, Phut and the race of Canaan. Mizraim peopled Egypt and Canaan the land later possessed by the Hebrews. Phut located in Africa and Cush extended his colonies over a wide domain." (*Philosophy of Ancient History*, Bunsen, p. 52.)

Bunsen concludes by saying, "Cushite colonies were all along the southern shores of Asia and Africa and by the archaeological remains, along the southern and eastern coasts of Arabia. The name Cush was given to four great areas, Media, Persia, Susiana and Aria, or the whole territory between the Indus and Tigris in prehistoric times. In Africa the Ethiopians, the Egyptians, the Libyans, the Canaanites and Phoenicians were all descendants of Ham. They were a black or dark colored race and the pioneers of our civilization. They were emphatically the monument builders on the plains of Shinar and the valley of the Nile from Meroe to Memphis. In southern Arabia they erected wonderful edifices. They were responsible for the monuments that dot southern Siberia and in America along the valley of the Mississippi down to Mexico and in Peru their images and monuments stand as voiceless witnesses." This was the ancient Cushite Empire of Ethiopians that covered three worlds. Some of our later books recognizing their indisputable influence in primitive culture, speak of them as a brunet brown race representing a mysterious Heliolithic culture.

Wells testifying from researches of Eliot Smith admits that this culture may have been oozing round the world from 1500 B.C. to 1000 B.C. He calls it the highest early culture of the world. It sustained the largest and most highly developed communities, but as in other modern books there is failure to give us clearer light upon this ancient culture and its origin. Baldwin speaking more frankly affirms that Hebrew writers describe these first inhabitants of cities and civilized life as Cushites. "The foundations of ancient religions, mythology, institutions and customs all had the same source. He considered the Egyptian and Chaldean civilizations as very old but the culture and political organization of Ethiopia was much older. They belonged to what Egyptians and Chaldeans regarded as real antiquity, ages shrouded in doubt because they were so remote. The oldest nations mentioned in history did not originate civilization, the traditions of Asia bring civilization from the south, connecting it with the Erythraean Sea. These traditions are confirmed by the inscriptions found upon the old ruins of Chaldea." (*Prehistoric Nations*, Baldwin.)

Wilford, that eminent student of the literature of India, found that Ethiopia was often mentioned in the Sanskrit writings of the people of India. The world according to the Puranas, ancient historical books, was divided into seven dwipas or divisions. Ethiopia was Cusha-Dwipa which included Arabia, Asia Minor, Syria, Nubia, Armenia, Mesopotamia, and an extended region in Africa. These Sanskrit writings prove that in remote ages these regions were the most powerful richest and most enlightened part of the world. From these authoritative records and the conclusions drawn by historians of deeper research we would decide that many ancient peoples, who have been assigned to other races in the average historical book of modern times, were in reality Ethiopians. There were nations that called themselves Cushites who never knew themselves under the titles and classifications that superficial students have given them. The Phoenicians in the days of Christ called themselves Ethiopians. The Scriptures and ancient records called the Samaritans Cushites. To create a true story of the ages the entire fabric of the ethnological relationship of the races will have to be torn down to be more honestly laid.

This Ethiopia, which existed for long ages before its wonderful power was broken, cannot be limited to the short chronological period of history, that, the facts of geology prove to be in error. The Bible gives no figures for the epochs of time. It speaks of Creation and its after periods in God cycles that we cannot resolve into figures. We read in *Prehistoric Nations*, "In the oldest recorded traditions, Cushite colonies were established in the valley of the Nile, Barabra and Chaldea. This beginning must have been not later than 7000 or 8000 B.C. or perhaps earlier. They brought to development astronomy and the other sciences, which have come down to us. The vast commercial system by which they joined together the "ends of the earth" was created and manufacturing skill established. The great period of Cushite control had closed many ages prior to Homer, although separate communities remained not only in Egypt but in southern Arabia, Phoenicia and elsewhere." (*Prehistoric Nations*, pp. 95, 96.)

Baldwin continues, "5000 B.C. Egypt and Chaldea became separate. The Cushites were still unrivalled. 3500 to 3000 B.C. the kingdom divided again. We do not know what caused the breaking up of the old empire, which for thousands of years had held imperial sway." It may have been that the first cities and civilization extended beyond the "Deluge." The Sabaeans, Himyarites, and Ethiopians maintained supremacy almost to modern times; but the ancient glory had departed previous to the rise of Assyria 1300 B.C. Not long before the Arabian peninsula had been overrun by Semites, chiefly nomads, who became the permanent inhabitants. The previous conquests of the ancient world denominated by modern books as Semitic were Cushite Arabian and not of the later Semitic Arabian race. Through this error many ancient branches of the Hamitic race are lined up as Semitic. After the rise of Assyria, the Ethiopians above Egypt became the central representatives of that power that had exercised world empire for thousands of years. What kind of race could this have been that could throw such giant shadows upon time's dawn?

The stories of the *"Arabian Nights,"* which so enthralled us in childhood and to which the childhood of the world clings as though they were true has this historic basis. They picture the activities and world wide scope of Cushite civilization in the declining days of Ethiopian glory. Its scenes represent India, Persia, Arabia and Chaldea, which were primitively Cushite, in the decline of the Gold and Silver Ages of ancient tradition. Archaeological research and findings are proving that there were such ages. The tales of the Arabian Nights, so marvelous and gripping in interest, did not spring from mere fancy alone, and because of this have for mankind an alluring and undying fascination. These tales minus their genii and fairies form an imperishable book picturing a far distant but powerful civilization. In the land of the ancient Chaldean, in Egypt, in happy "Araby the Blest," and along the shores of the Mediterranean, the evidences of this prehistoric civilization are being dug up in wonder by the archaeologists of the civilized nations today. Relics in their way as wonderful as the gems called up by Aladdin's Lamp, hidden just as were his finds in chambers of the earth.

Heeren, whose researches furnish invaluable information to the later historians says, "From the remotest times to the present, the Ethiopians have been the most celebrated and yet the most mysterious of nations. In the earliest traditions of the more civilized nations of antiquity, the name of this most distant people is found. The annals of the Egyptian priests were full of them; and the nations of inner Asia on the Euphrates and the Tigris have woven the fictions of the Ethiopians with their own traditions of the wars and conquests of their heroes; and at a period equally remote they glimmer in Greek mythology." Dionysus, Hercules, Saturn, Osiris, Zeus and Apollo were Cushite kings of the prehistoric ages. Around these and other Ethiopian deities the people of the Mediterranean and the Orient wove their mythologies. Prejudice and ignorance may have marked their deeds as fabulous but the imperishable monuments that they left are not imaginary. They are the realistic reminders of a people who deeply impressed and colored the life, art and literature of the ancient world.

The prehistoric achievements of Cushite heroes were the theme of ancient sculpture, painting and drama. They were the object of worship of all the nations that appear civilized at the dawn of history. The literature and music of Greece and Rome was permeated by this deep Ethiopian strain. These classic forms and ideals maintain supremacy in the art of modern times. Heeren continues, "When the Greeks scarcely knew Italy and Sicily by name, the Ethiopians were celebrated in the poems of their bards. They were the remotest nation, the most just of men, the favorites of the gods. The lofty inhabitants of Olympus journey to them and take part in their feasts. Their sacrifices are the most agreeable that mortals can offer and when the faint beams of tradition give way to the clear light of history, the luster of the Ethiopians is not diminished. They still continue to be objects of curiosity and admiration; and the pens of cautious and clear sighted historians often place them in the highest rank of knowledge and civilization."

NINETEEN

Hallie Quinn Brown
(1845–1949)

H ALLIE QUINN BROWN WAS BORN in Pittsburgh to former slaves who
were active members of the African Methodist Episcopal (AME) Church
and participants in the Underground Railroad, a legacy that Brown never
forgot. Her father, a riverboat steward, and her mother, a student advisor at
Wilberforce University in Ohio, had both been freed before the war. Around
1864 the family moved to Chatham, Ontario. They then returned to
Wilberforce in 1870, where Hallie enrolled at the AME-run college as a student. After graduation she worked as an educator while also continuing her
training in public speaking and elocution. For the next twenty years she
labored in the south, teaching freed adults and children and serving as a school
administrator at Booker T. Washington's Tuskegee Normal and Industrial
Institute in Alabama as the dean of women. In 1893 Wilberforce hired her to
teach elocution, a position that Brown held for the rest of her life.

Relying upon her grounding in the AME community at Wilberforce, she
gained fame internationally as a speaker. She lectured extensively in Europe,
speaking about women's rights, temperance, segregation, and lynching. She
spoke to the International Congress of Women in London in 1899, lectured
before Queen Victoria, and was named a member of the Royal Geographical
Society in Edinburgh. She authored several technical studies of recitation and
elocution (*Bits and Odds*, 1886; and *Elocution and Physical Culture*, 1910), both
of which addressed issues specific to African-American orators. A pioneer in

Sources: "Harriet—The Moses," in *Homespun Heroines and Other Women of Distinction* (Xenia, OH: Aidine Pub. Co., 1926), 55–60.

the black women's club movement, Brown served as president of the Ohio State Federation of Colored Women's Clubs between 1905 and 1912, and the National Association of Colored Women from 1920 to 1924.[1]

Brown's most popular work, published in 1926, did not celebrate her many accomplishments. Instead, *Homespun Heroines and Other Women of Distinction* lauded the heroism and labor of dozens of other African-American women, some of them little known beyond their own local communities, who had contributed to the history of the race. Dedicating her work to the memory of "the many mothers who were loyal in tense and trying times" as well as to the National Association of Colored Women, Brown hoped to show that women were capable of making history, and to pass along that knowledge to children.

Sandwiched between slave grandmothers, the mothers of AME Church leaders, and a host of activist great aunts, Harriet Tubman was one of those "homespun heroines" who achieved epic status in Brown's interpretive hands. Tubman, a conductor on the Underground Railroad, must have reminded Brown of the labors of her own parents during her youth. She began by likening Tubman to Joan of Arc and Moses, rendering her as a mixture of "practical shrewdness" and "visionary enthusiasm." Amazonian in physical endurance and strength, Tubman here emerged as a heroic crusader who had changed the course of history by assisting John Brown in his planning of the attack on Harper's Ferry. At the same time, Brown presented an intimate portrait of Tubman's rescue of a slave named Joe, a tale that emphasizes the personal relationships that lie at the heart of black collective life. History, for Brown, could only be understood as a thicket of efforts to reach out from challenges of social circumstances in the uplift of the individual. Her job, as she saw it, was to ensure that the courageous actions of generations of African-American women were included in the accounting.

<hr>

Harriet—The Moses (1926)

1821–MARCH 10, 1913

When America writes her history without hatred and prejudice she will place high in the galaxy of fame the name of a woman as remarkable as the French

[1] J. F. Duchan and Y. D. Hyter, "Elocutionist Hallie Quinn Brown," *The ASHA Leader*, 13(2), 20–21; Hazel V. Carby, *Reconstructing Womanhood: The Emergence of the Afro-American Woman Novelist* (New York: Oxford University Press, 1987), ch. 1.

heroine, Joan of Arc, a woman who had not even the poor advantages of the peasant maid of Domremy, but was born under the galling yoke of slavery with a long score of cruelty.

Her service to her race and country are without parallel in like achievements by any member of her sex in the history of the world.

Harriet Tubman may be justly styled a Homespun Heroine.

This historic character is in a class to herself. She had the skill and boldness of a commander,—the courage and strategy of a general. A picturesque figure standing boldly against the commonplace, dark background of a generation in which her lot was cast.

Stranger than fiction have been her escapes and exploits in slavery.

She was called "Moses" because of her success in guiding her brethren out of their land of Egypt.

She was also called "General Moses"—an Amazon in strength and endurance and is described as a woman of no pretensions, a most ordinary specimen of humanity. Yet in point of courage, shrewdness and disinterested exertions to rescue her fellow men she had no equal.

Harriet appears to have been a strange compound of practical shrewdness and of a visionary enthusiasm. She believed in dreams and omens warning and instructing her in her enterprises. At times she would break forth into wild and strange rhapsodies which to her ignorant hearers seemed the work of inspiration, to others a power of insight beyond what is called natural, to excel in the difficult work she had chosen for herself. The first twenty-five years of her life were spent as a slave on a Maryland plantation.

She worked beside oxen and horses as a field hand and developed a strong muscular body and at the same time an unconquerable spiritual force which was regarded as dogged stubbornness in not submitting to the lords of the lash. One fair morning Harriet left for freedom. She managed it so easily that she began planning to help others. She worked in Northern hotels till she saved enough money to pay the expenses of a trip to her old neighborhood.

The first to be rescued were her own family at different times. Her three brothers left under her direction hiding for days in their father's corn crib, among the ears of corn. The father was in the secret but they feared to trust their mother's excitable nature lest it betray them.

The boys could see their mother come out shading her eyes and gazing down the long road, in the fond hope of seeing her boys coming home to spend the Christmas with her.

The father pushed food through the chinks but took care not to set eyes on them, that he might be able to swear when the time came for questions. At night they started looking through the cabin window at the poor old mother crooning over the fire, pipe in her mouth, rocking her head on her hand mourning that the boys did not come.

The father went some miles blindfolded, the sons holding his arms and when they took leave of each other he could still say he had not seen them.

Notwithstanding all this precaution the old man came under suspicion and was to be tried for helping fugitive slaves. At this juncture Harriet came to settle the matter by "removing the case to a higher court." In an old broken down sort of a wagon she quietly drove off with her parents and seemed to have met no trouble in reaching free soil.

For two decades, prior to the Civil war, Harriet made many journeys to the South and brought four hundred slaves to the North and Canada not one of whom was caught nor did she ever fall into the hands of the enemy, though at one time twelve thousand dollars reward was offered for this mysterious "black ghost." Along the route this modern Joan of Arc marched without an army or panoply of war; with neither shield nor spear, but many lurking foes and hidden perils to be met and overcome.

Swamps and tangled brush their bed at night, preferring the company of the wild things of the forest, even venomous reptiles to the infuriated slave catcher. Foot sore and weary with her scared and hunted followers, she forged ahead with an unconquerable spirit truly heroic in her sacrifice for her fellow creatures.

Harriet was employed in the Underground Rail Road service. William Still in his records regards her as a highly trusted ally. On this work in the late forties she would be absent for weeks at a time dropping completely out of sight, running daily risks making preparations for herself and passengers, but she seemed wholly devoid of personal fear, and seemed proof against all adversaries. While she manifested such utter personal indifference she was most watchful with regard to those she was piloting.

Half of her time she appeared to be asleep and would actually sit down by the roadside and go fast asleep, yet she would not suffer one of her party to whimper once about "givin' out and goin' back," however wearied they might be from hard travel. She had one short, pointed law of her own which implied death to any one who talked of "givin' out or goin' back." Her followers had full fatih (sic) in her and would back up any words she uttered. So, when she said to them that a live runaway could do a great harm by going back, but a dead one could tell no secrets, she was sure to have strict obedience.

She was the friend and counselor of John Brown, who spoke of her with enthusiasm as the "Most of a man," he had ever met with. In his hut at North Elba in the Adirondacks—"Today a worthier goal or pilgrimage than any medieval shrine"—they drew plans for his attack on Harpers Ferry.

During the Civil War, Harriet served with distinction as a scout for Governor Andrews with his Massachusetts troops and guided Colonel Montgomery of the Union forces in his memorable expedition in South Carolina. She had many narrow escapes but succeeded in out-witting the Confederates and avoided capture as well.

She was introduced to Boston's cultured audience by noted Abolitionists as "Our foster sister Moses."

Her courage and deeds of self-sacrifice should be a lasting inspiration to the youth of the race.

Harriet's proceedings and her peculiar methods of escape are not related in detail. Only one complete story of any length is presented.

THE STORY OF JOE

A slave named Joe fell into the hands of a new master whose first order to him was to strip and take a whipping as a reminder to better behave himself. Joe, seeing no present help submitted to the lash, but thought to himself, "This is the first time—and the last!" That night he went to the cabin of Harriet's father and said, "Next time Moses comes let me know." In a few weeks Harriet came, then as usual men, women and children began to disappear from the plantations. Joe, his brother and two others went with the party. Hunting and hiding,—separated and brought together again by roundabout ways, passed on through the aid of secret friends they got at last opposite Wilmington, Delaware. The pursuers were hot after them and large rewards offered for the arrest of each member of the party.

It was Harriet's method, we are told, to leave on a Saturday night, since no advertisements could be issued on Sunday, thus giving the fugitives a day's start of publicity. They found the bridge at Wilmington closely guarded by police officers on the lookout for them. It seemed impossible to cross in safety. But in that city lived Thomas Garrett a great lover of humanity through whose hands two thousand slaves are said to have passed on their way to liberty. His home was the North Star to many a fainting heart.

This century has grand scenes to show and boast of among its fellows. But few transcend that auction-block where the sheriff was selling all Garrett's goods for the crime (?) of giving a breakfast to a family of fugitive slaves. As the sale closed the officer turns to Garrett saying: "Thomas, I hope you'll never be caught at this again." "Friend," was the reply, "I haven't a dollar in the world, but if thee knows a fugitive who needs a breakfast, send him to me." Harriet had secret news sent to this good Quaker. He was equal to the emergency. He engaged two wagons and filled them with brick-layers,

Irishmen and Germans. They drove over the bridge, shouting and singing as if for a frolic in the country. The guards let them pass and naturally expected to see them return. As night fell the merry party came back making as much noise as before and again passed without suspicion, but this time the runaways were concealed at the bottom of the wagons and soon hidden away in the home of Mr. Garrett. So far so good, but Joe could not feel at ease until he was safe in Canada.

As the train in which they were approached the suspension bridge below Niagara Falls, the rest of the excited party burst into singing even before they were out of danger, but Joe was too oppressed to join in their joy.

When the cars began to cross the bridge Harriet anxious to have her companions see the Falls, called eagerly for them to look at the wonderful sight, but still Joe sat with his head upon his hand.

"Joe, look at de Falls!" "Joe, you fool you—come see de Falls! It's your last chance." But Joe sat still and never raised his head. At length Harriet knew by the rise in the center of the bridge and the descent on the other side that they had crossed the line. She sprang across to Joe's seat, shook him with all her might and shouted, "Joe, you've shook de lion's paw." Joe did not know what she meant. "Joe, you are free."

Then the strong man who could stand under the master's whip without a groan, burst into a hysterical passion of weeping and singing, so that his fellow passengers thought he had gone crazy. But all rejoiced and gave him sympathy when they knew the cause of his emotions.

HARRIET TUBMAN

In 1441 Negro slaves were introduced into Portugal; in 1474, Seville, Spain, had Negroes in abundance and their welfare was the special care of the joint sovereigns. A letter is extant signed by Ferdinand and Isabella describing a certain Negro as of noble birth, investing him with the title of Mayoral of the Negroes and giving him credit for "sufficed ability and good disposition." This proves that all African slaves were not debased savages, that under human treatment they displayed the better phases of human nature, that not innate depravity but inhuman depression tended to lower them into a submerged stratum of sordid existence.

The entrance of the African into what is now the United States is at once a tale of glory and of shame. His presence remains a monument to the cupidity of those who abrogated to themselves inherent superiority. His survival and steady numerical increase despite oppression strongly confirms the facts of his innate power of endurance and of his power of recuperation. Generations of slavery failed to blot out entirely all vestiges of manliness from this maltreated African and his descendants. The stories of thousands of self-emancipated slaves are recitals of deeds of daring, determination, and decision that favorably compare with the far-famed exploits of universally acknowledged heroes. Again and again men and women voluntarily exposed themselves to the miseries of stealthy journeys involving hunger, thirst and fatigue with perils by land and by water. Sustained by a burning desire to be free they risked discovery which meant virtual death by torture. Nor have the qualities which proved their manhood in days of bondage lessened in either force or character during the days of nominal freedom that have followed formal emancipation. Despite a pernicious "custom of the country," the contingent of American citizens of African descent is steadily forging ahead with a growing consciousness of both the duties and prerogatives attached to unshackled manhood. Our country's history is replete with instances of Negro patriotism. Unlike the Indian, the American Negro will continue to live. His future is inextricably bound up with the fate of the land where his loyalty has been repeatedly tested and never found wanting.

In the Negro are fundamental traits which have insured his practical salvation. Negro faith, fidelity, patience, patriotism, have passed into proverbs. Negro imagination, optimism, appreciation of the artistic sense of humor, are the occasional stars illumining the habitual gloom of surrounding mists of insensate race prejudice. Therefore there is a broader than individual application implied in the forceful tribute written many years ago by Miss Pauline Hopkins in honor of Harriet Tubman. Of this grand woman she speaks with rare delicacy, accuracy and appreciation: "Harriet Tubman, though one of earth's lowliest ones, displayed an amount of heroism in her character rarely possessed by those of any station of life. Her name deserves to be handed down to posterity side by side with those of Grace Darling, Joan of Arc, and Florence Nightingale; no one of them has showed more courage and power of endurance in facing danger and death to relieve human suffering than did this woman in her successful and heroic endeavors to reach and to save all whom she might of her oppressed people."

Harriet was born a slave; at the immature age of six years hired out by a cruel master and mistress who surpassed him in fiendish ingenuity, she had literally no childhood. In her early teens she was put to work in the fields. There she followed the oxen, loaded and carried wood, for the work of a full grown man was expected of her. The hard work she performed and the heavy burdens she carried developed her physically until her feats of strength and muscular agility made her a wonder. Yet she suffered under the strokes of the lash as if she were one of the least willing or efficient. Till the day of her death her scarred shoulders and bruised back bore mute though eloquent testimony to the inhumanity of the customary plantation discipline. A blow on the head with a weight from the scales inflicted permanent injury. She had in consequence irregular fits of apparent insensibility. Her lucid moments were nevertheless frequent enough and lasted long enough for her to do some thinking and to the purpose. She at last decided she could no longer exist in the miasmatic atmosphere of thraldom; the prospect of being sold brought the matter to a crisis. Late one afternoon she set off singing, but with painful step and slow. Though her body was weak from deprivation, her spirit was brave and steadfast. She thought "there's two things I've got a right to—'Death or Liberty'— one or t'other I mean to have." That such a woman inspired by such a resolve should succeed is more a matter of admiration than of astonishment; that such a woman could be satisfied to become free while so many dear to her were still in bondage would have been indeed a surprise. A person of her broad sympathies could find permanent happiness only in concentrating her energies outside and beyond herself upon finding there was now but little comparatively speaking to call for strenuous action on her own behalf. Not only did this intrepid woman essay but she succeeded in leading ten of her immediate family and many friends to attain the boon she had so assiduously sought. Nineteen times she essayed the hazardous journeys covering and recovering the trackless waste stretching between the desert of bondage and the promising fields of freedom. She began this crucial traverse of a "via dolorosa" in her prime and continued it through her mature years until the need for such sacrifice no longer existed. Not once did she fail in her attempts to discharge what she considered her duty; during the interim she was never one hour free from the handicap of broken health. A reward of forty thousand dollars was at one time offered for the head of this woman whose only crime was that she loved liberty more than life. She traveled where posters advertising her were read by others in her hearing—"being unable to read herself, she went on trusting in the Lord." By her people she was known as "Moses" and they too believed: "De Lord he gave Moses the power." In underground circles she was called "Moll Pitcher" because of her energy and determination.

The struggles of the pioneer mothers of this great republic supply themes for many an absorbing romance, many a glowing verse of poetry; the equally unique tales of the self-abnegation of the black woman of the South are largely as yet traditional. Some day they will be enshrined in permanent form and the world will learn in detail what they effected by their exercise of indomitable will, enduring fidelity and unsullied faith. In no other way can the need of simple justice be accorded a host of noble souls of whom Harriet Tubman was a distinguished representative.

When in the march of affairs Harriet found no further need for continuing her mission of mercy she transferred her activities from her people to her country. During the earlier stages of the Civil War, "Moses" hung upon the skirts of the Union Army, helping the "contrabands" who sought refuge within its lines. When the freedmen became soldiers she went from camp to camp nursing the sick and succoring the wounded. To the ordinary pursuits she added another, one none the less important because carried on in secret; she became virtually a volunteer spy and penetrating the lines of the enemy, gained valuable information as to the strength of armies and batteries. Illiterate as she was her mental alertness and spiritual development were extraordinary. Shrewd, loyal, God fearing, "Moses" was in her glory while she still found she could be of service. To do for others was more than a principle with her, it was a passion.

In personal appearance Harriet was ordinary almost to repulsiveness; at most times she had a half vacant stare, and rarely when quiet seemed more than half awake. Yet her lack of education did not prevent the most cultured persons from listening absorbed to her strange eventful tales, told with the pathos and simplicity that bore conviction with their recital. She knew all the leaders in the abolition movement and had in her possession letters sent to her by patriots like Gov. Andrews of Massachusetts, William H. Seward, and other prominent persons. At Concord, a welcome was always in waiting for her, for Lowell, Emerson, Alcott, and Mrs. Horace Mann all respected, admired and placed implicit confidence in and reliance upon her truthfulness. She was practically purely true African, but her patience, foresight, devotion and sagacity put her apart and above the rank and file of those who have passed meritorious careers under ordinary conditions, and elevated her to that high citizenship in the realm of genius where race nor sex, extraneous circumstances nor color are given even passing consideration.

When the "cruel war" was over, on the way to a northern home with a soul overflowing with rejoicing, an unfeeling conductor forcibly ejected her from a car. From the injury resulting she was a life long victim.

Through the good offices of Hon. William H. Seward, Harriet was enabled to procure a tract of land in Auburn, N.Y. Upon this she built a cabin and there placed her parents whom she had rescued during her last journey south. She also erected a home for aged and indigent colored people upon the same tract. Compelled later to relinquish the charge of this, she surrendered all her interest in the same to a religious organization. Constantly soliciting from others for others, for a long time she helped to support two schools for freedmen.

At length the combined disabilities of permanent ill health and advancing age overcame her and she was found to be in an enfeebled, destitute condition. A philanthropic woman, Mrs. Sarah H. Bradford of Geneva, wrote her story; a generous citizen of Auburn gave it to the world, having had it published by subscription, so that the gross receipts could be devoted to her needs, and the Empire State Federation sent its president, Mrs. Mary B. Talbert of Buffalo to pay her an official visit. From thenceforth the comfort of this veteran was assured. The thoughtful ministration of the Federation did not cease with her life, but continued until her final resting place was fittingly marked with a simple, but appropriate shaft of stone. Harriet deeply appreciated the practical sympathy of those good women, her sisters by ties of lineage and race extraction. The last message she sent was this: "Tell the women to stick together. God is fighting for them and all will be well!"

Upon her decease the city of Auburn erected a tablet to her memory. This adorns one of the public buildings and upon it is inscribed the outlines of the life story of this woman whose charity was unbounded, whose wisdom, integrity, and patriotism enabled her to perform wonders in the cause of freedom

"Harriet Tubman" uplift and betterment clubs are maintained by our women in Boston, Philadelphia and Greater New York. These are devoted to the laudable intention of keeping alive the influence of her persevering endeavor to incite to noble action, the friends of liberty, humanity and justice.